→ WHAT WOULD YOU DO IF YOU
HAD THE STANLEY CUP FOR A DAY?
During his day with the Stanley Cup, Los
Angeles Kings defenseman Willie Mitchell
proudly hoists it atop Mount Benedict,
close to his home in Port McNeill, B.C.

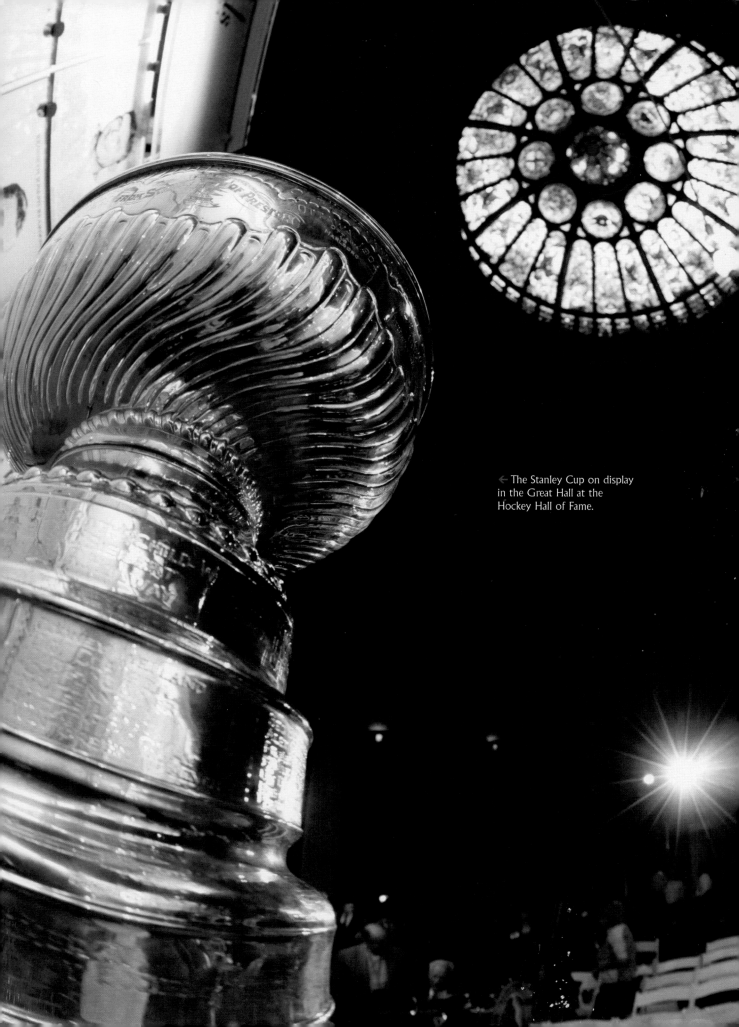

← The Stanley Cup on display
in the Great Hall at the
Hockey Hall of Fame.

THE ILLUSTRATED HISTORY OF
HOCKEY
THE NHL YEARS: COLLECTOR'S EDITION

Stories from
The Hockey News

QUARRY
HERITAGE

BOOKS

← **CAPTAINS OF THE SHIP**
Sidney Crosby and Alex Ovechkin each became captains of their teams and international stars in the mold of Wayne Gretzky and Mario Lemieux.

OUR BURIED TREASURES

WE DIDN'T HAVE TO DIG TOO DEEPLY IN THE THN ARCHIVES TO UNEARTH A BOUNTY OF AMAZING STORIES

WITH JASON KAY

With apologies to author Neil Pasricha, *The Hockey News* has its own Book of Awesome. And it dates back decades.

Tucked in our de facto attic, in a makeshift closet that contains some bric-a-brac, a clothing rack and a couple of Ikea bookshelves, lies 65-plus years of history. Each and every issue since Ken McKenzie and Will Cote launched THN in 1947 has been stored and bound in large volumes, by year. The sometimes yellowed and tattered contents of those red and blue tomes are pure gold. Every time we get the opportunity to scour stories from our past, we find another rich deposit. And to give this publication some texture beyond the cool artifacts we've displayed, we decided to include a small sampling of those "forgotten" tales.

We've reproduced some of the heavyweights, such as the Richard Riot, the pioneering efforts of Willie O'Ree and Herb Carnegie, and Bobby Clarke's inspirational NHL journey. Mostly, however, we've shone the spotlight on the obscure, wacky, compelling and curious. Remember Bill Stewart, the major junior coach who smuggled a Russian player across the Canada-U.S. border in the baggage compartment of a bus? Or the dude who crashed the Penguins' Stanley Cup party in 2009 without getting busted?

You may be less familiar with Jack Gelineau, a Calder Trophy winner who decided to pursue a career in insurance sales instead of the Boston crease. And it may tickle your funny bone to read why so many of the 1950-51 Detroit Red Wings were unmarried. Or that it was even a story. It made us guffaw when we discovered 'Ace' Bailey, the old Leafs star who was seriously injured by Eddie Shore in 1933, was erroneously reported to have died — twice. The first time came the day after the incident, the second 30 years later when he was the penalty time keeper at Maple Leaf Gardens.

Heck, the material is so deep, we could probably do an entire book on the things people have thrown on the ice over the years. We all know about the sea life that gets hurled in Detroit, but that's just the tip of the ice surface. While still in his skates, Camille Henry chased and caught a fan on the streets after having trash tossed at him. Boston goalie Don Simmons got a penalty for throwing the puck to a teammate — twice. Usually placid Glenn Hall went ballistic when a fan hit him in the head with a light bulb.

This book began as a special issue of *The Hockey News* and grew into something more as the publisher added a section on the history of the Stanley Cup. We realize we're throwing a lot at you in this publication, but we hope you agree it's pretty awesome. Besides, with so much treasure at our disposal, it's only right for us to start sharing the wealth.

Jason

↑ STITCHIN' PADS, STOPPIN' PUCKS
Can you guess which legendary goaltender strapped on these pads, winning multiple Stanley Cups and Vezina Trophies over a Hall of Fame career?

Text and images copyright © Transcontinental Media G.P. and Quarry Press Inc, 2014.

PUBLISHER:
Bob Hilderley
ART DIRECTION & DESIGN:
Erika Vanderveer, Anthony Smith & Susan Hannah

Special thanks to the team members of THN for their assistance in producing *The Illustrated History of Hockey*.

Printed and bound in Canada by Transcontinental Media G.P. Published by Quarry Heritage Books, an imprint of Quarry Press Inc, PO Box 1061, Kingston, Ontario K7L 4Y5 www.quarrypress.com

To purchase bulk copies of this book, contact the publisher at www.quarrypress.com. To subscribe to *The Hockey News*, contact www.myaccount.thehockeynews.com.

Table of Contents

↑ OH THE THRILL OF WINNING THE STANLEY CUP
Hands of the New York Islanders hoist the Cup in victory. If only the Cup could speak.

NHL Era Essays

SKATING DOWN MEMORY LANE

THE HALL OF FAME'S VAST ARRAY OF ARTIFACTS INSPIRED US TO TELL PRO HOCKEY'S TALE FROM COVER TO COVER

BY BRIAN COSTELLO

The genesis for this publication came a few years ago when former THN art director Jamie Hodgson and I were going through the cramped resource center at the Hockey Hall of Fame prior to its expansion and relocation to Etobicoke, Ont. We were there researching and photographing a variety of hockey sweaters for the best-seller 2009 special, Greatest Jerseys of All-Time.

Craig Campbell, manager of the HHOF resource center and archives, was in the midst of packing up thousands of artifacts and moving them 10 miles west. It was a daunting task made more difficult by our lumbering bodies in the way, sniffing out treasures and asking a million questions.

"Look at this, a Gordie Howe wooden hockey stick," said Hodgson, lifting it up gingerly. "I wonder if he left any goals in here…I wonder if they'd let me borrow it."

The Howe stick is, thankfully, still in safe-keeping, far away from the confines of beer-league dressing rooms. So too are the likes of Wayne Gretzky's bag of equipment, Allan Stanley's elbow pads and Aurel Joliat's knitted playing cap. We came across such a treasure trove of hockey memorabilia, the idea became a natural. Why not put together a history of the NHL and tie it in with a museum's worth of artifacts, generously made available to us by the fine folks at the Hall of Fame? And so we selected one — sometimes two — artifacts from each season since 1917-18. Some of these archives you'll see on display from time to time at Toronto's downtown Hall location. Others have been in secure storage for decades, waiting for someone to open like a genie bottle. (The Hall of Fame, by the way, would love to hear from you if you're in possession of interesting hockey artifacts, hidden away in storage.)

We've packaged each NHL season on one page with the top three stories or newsmakers (previously presented in our 1999 issue Century of Hockey). Other facts and stats we've included are each season's Cup winner, leading scorers, major rule changes, significant records, franchise news,

60 moments that changed the game (taken from the 2007 special by the same name), first draft pick (starting in 1963), Hall of Fame inductees and caricatures (starting in 1945), and nickname of the year.

These pages are separated by a series of six essays on the six distinct eras of the NHL. Long-time NHL writers such as Bob Duff, Stan Fischler and our own Ken Campbell and Adam Proteau examine the defining moments of each era and provide a flavor of that time. Fischler, for example, authored our 1942-1967 Original Six Era essay. He watched his first pro game at Madison Square Garden in 1939, has been writing professionally since 1954 and his report includes many first-hand anecdotes. Duff is a noted hockey historian and the author of many books on the game. You'd be hard-pressed to find anyone who has a better working knowledge of the 1917-1942 years, the Creation of the NHL.

Campbell tackles the Grand Expansion era (1967-1979) while Proteau writes about the go-go Live Puck Era (1979-1993). And don't overlook the two most recent eras, packaged with aplomb by two talented young THN staffers, Ronnie Shuker and Matt Larkin. They write about the Dead Puck Era (1993-2004) and the Post-Lockout Era (2005-present).

Finally, now that *The Hockey News* is enjoying life as a senior citizen — we turned 65 last year — we thought we'd dig into our archives to pull out some neat, perhaps forgotten tales from the past. In selected seasons since our birth in 1947, we present "Forgotten Tales From The Hockey News Crypt." Some of these stories are about impact moments in the game's history — like acclaimed writer Elmer Ferguson's first person report of the Richard Riot — while most are interesting tidbits you'd never heard before or had forgotten over the years. We tried to keep the stories and their headlines intact, as much as possible, to give you the flavor of the times.

For publication in this book we have included an extended story of the life and times of the Stanley Cup. Bruised but beloved, the Cup has more than one fascinating and amusing tale to tell.

Legendary Sticks

The Hockey Hall of Fame houses an impressive collection of historic hockey sticks from the NHL and the minor leagues (R-L):

1. Boston Bruin's star John Bucyk scored his 500th NHL goal with this stick in 1975.

2. While playing for the Ottawa Senators in 2005, Dany Heatly won the first shoot-out in NHL history using this stick.

3. During the 1997 World Championship, Michael Nylander scored 11 points in 11 games with this stick.

4. With this stick, Jean Ratelle scored his 250th NHL goal in 1973.

5. While playing for the Detroit Red Wings near the end of his NHL career, Brad Park used the first aluminum-shafted stick.

6. With this stick, scoring star Mike Bossy potted his 300th NHL goal, the youngest player to reach that goal.

7. While playing for the Quad City Mallards in 2007, Don Parsons scored his 623rd goal, making him the highest scoring American in professional hockey.

8. With this stick Andy Bathgate, while playing for the New York Rangers, scored his 200th NHL goal in 1961-62.

9. While playing with the Flint Generals, Kevin Kerr used this composite stick to score 664 professional goals, which was a world record.

10. While playing for the Chicago Wolves of the AHL, Darren Haydon scored his 52nd career playoff goal and 120th career playoff point with this stick during Game 2 of the Calder Cup final in 2008.

11. In the National Women's Hockey League final in 2004, Kelly Bechard of Calgary's Oval X-treme used this stick to score the championship goal against the Brampton Thunder.

12. Buffalo Sabre fan favorite Don Luce scored his 33rd goal in 1974-75 with this stick, joining five other teammates in scoring more than 30 games that season, which was an NHL record.

13. Skating sensation Glen Anderson played with this stick at the 1989 World Championship.

14. In a 1976 Russian star Valeri Kharamov was using this stick when his Red Army team protested against the violent tactics of the Philadelphia Flyers by leaving the ice.

15. While playing for the Vernon Vipers in 2009, Braden Pimm scored the championship-winning goal of the RBC Cup with this stick.

—1917-1942—

CREATION OF THE NHL

OVERCOMING WAR AND THE GREAT DEPRESSION, THE NHL FOUGHT TOOTH AND NAIL TO SURVIVE AND GROW THE SPORT IN ITS EARLY DAYS

In November 1917, when the board of governors of the National Hockey Association met in Montreal, the professional game was in a state of disarray. With the Great War ongoing in Europe, the majority of the game's best players had enlisted and shipped overseas, leaving the old and the infirm to contest games at what was supposed to be hockey's highest level and fan interest was waning. "Futile attempts have been made to get amateur stars to become professionals to replace the worn-out oldtimers who have been playing on NHA teams for years," reported the Toronto *Globe.* "Fast, young amateur stars have stolen the patronage from the pros."

On Nov. 10, 1917, the NHA announced it was disbanding for the 1917-18 season. But shortly after the conclusion of that meeting, owners of the Ottawa and Quebec franchises, as well as the operators of the Montreal Canadiens and Montreal Wanderers, met to form a new league. On Nov. 26, organization of the NHL was officially unveiled, consisting of the aforementioned four teams and a new franchise in Toronto.

Today's NHL fans wouldn't recognize the game of the league's infancy. Forward passing was prohibited. There were no zones on the ice and immediate substitution was permitted for penalized players. Goaltenders served their own penalty and since there was no backup goalie, a forward or defenseman took over between the pipes. At the end of the season, the NHL champs played off against the winners of the Pacific Coast and later the Western Canada League for the Stanley Cup.

In this era, whistles generally only blew following goals, the puck going out of play or after penalty. When a whistle sounded during a 1918 Canadiens-Ottawa game, Montreal defenseman 'Bad' Joe Hall, so nicknamed due to his frequent violations of the rules, immediately jumped into the penalty box. After Canadiens captain Newsy Lalonde ascertained from officials that Hall had committed no foul, he told his sheepish teammate to resume his position on the ice. "Sorry about that, Newsy," Hall said. "Force of habit, I guess."

Slick skaters and stickhandlers were the stars of the early NHL. Joe Malone of the Montreal Canadiens led the NHL with 44 goals in 1917-18,

but was absent most of the 1918-19 campaign because he simply couldn't afford to be an NHLer. "I had hooked on to a good job in Quebec City, which promised a secure future, something hockey in those days couldn't," Malone once explained to author Andy O'Brien. Top players earned less than $1,000 (the equivalent of around $15,000 today) in the early days of the NHL. After leading the NHL in scoring in 1922-23, Toronto's Babe Dye briefly quit hockey to pursue a career in pro baseball, which paid better.

The fabric of the game was definitely different. There were no official scorers, generally just a local reporter who kept track of goals and assists, which led to a curious altercation between Montreal *Herald* reporter Elmer Ferguson and Canadiens star Aurel Joliat during a 1924 game. Joliat stopped during play to berate Ferguson for not awarding him an assist on a goal earlier in the game. Angered when he lost his argument, Joliat grabbed the puck, tore in on the Ottawa goal and scored, swooping past Ferguson's rinkside spot to ensure he got that one down right.

By the mid-1920s, charismatic stars who would carry the league to prominence began emerging, the most exciting and glamorous of these being Canadiens center Howie Morenz and Boston Bruins defenseman Eddie Shore.

Morenz was fondly nicknamed 'The Stratford Streak.' His blazing speed and reckless rushes made him a fan favorite throughout the league. "He was colorful — supercolorful," Lester Patrick once said of Morenz. "He had a magnetic personality."

Many viewed Morenz as a superhero and he was at the very least a crimefighter. Returning from a family dinner in 1932, Morenz discovered an armed intruder in his mother-in-law's home. In fine hockey-fight fashion, Morenz jumped the burglar and pulled his overcoat up over his shoulders, forcing the criminal to flee.

Shore was immortalized in *Slap Shot* as one of the paragons of old-time hockey, though there were some in the game who would have easily classified him as part of hockey's criminal element. "I loved to hit," said Shore, who was as dashing as Morenz was modest and would take the ice

→ JERSEYED SHORE
Boston defensemean Eddie Shore
shakes the hand of Toronto great
Ace Bailey. Shore joined Howie Morenz
as one of hockey's first true stars.

for pre-game introductions wearing a matador's cape. When his ear was nearly severed by a skate and Shore was being attended to by doctors, he asked him not for anesthetic, but for a mirror, "to be sure you sew it on right."

The gleam from stars like these enabled the NHL to expand from a modest, Ontario-Quebec based operation into a major-league conglomerate with 10 teams by 1927, six of them America-based.

Salaries exploded with the league's growth. Lionel Conacher signed with the new Pittsburgh franchise in 1925 for $7,500. The league ultimately installed a $35,000 salary cap to control costs. That proved problematic for the Montreal Maroons when injuries decimated their roster late in the 1929-30 season. In need of a player but with no cash to spare, they signed Dinny Dinsmore for the final 10 games at a total salary of one dollar. At 10 cents per game, he's easily the lowest-paid player in NHL history.

As the league entered the 1930s, a new enemy was stalking hockey — the Great Depression. Steadily, teams slid by the wayside. Ottawa sold players to survive, eventually relocated to St. Louis and folded in 1935. Pittsburgh moved to Philadelphia, but ceased operations in 1931. By the end of the decade, the Maroons were also gone and the New York Americans were on their last legs.

As the outbreak of World War II loomed, the future of the NHL looked in jeopardy. THN

↑ ACE BAILEY

← HOWIE MORENZ
'The Stratford Streak' became the first NHL superstar.

↓ LITTLE GIANT
Montreal mighty mite Aurel Joliat wearing his signature black cap. Joliat and Morenz were a formidable scoring tandem.

↑ SPEEDBALL LINE
Howie Morenz's dressing room stall and Aurel Joliat. Joliat, Morenz and
Billy Boucher made up the Speedball line.

← THE BREAD LINE
Known as 'the Bread Line,' the Cook brothers, Bill (left) and Bun (right), were centered by Frank Boucher. They led the New York Rangers to two Stanley Cup victories.

FACTS & STATS
from 1917-18

Cup Winner
Toronto Arenas

Leading Scorers
1. Joe Malone, Mtl, 48 points
2. Cy Denneny, Ott, 46 points
3. Reg Noble, Tor, 40 points

Rule Changes
Goalies are permitted to fall to the ice to make saves. In past, netminders were penalized for dropping to the ice.

Franchise News
Montreal Canadiens, Montreal Wanderers, Ottawa Senators, Toronto Arenas, Quebec Bulldogs join National Hockey League, which replaces the National Hockey Association. Bulldogs fold before season starts.

Significant Records
Most goals by a player in his first NHL game: Joe Malone, Montreal Canadiens and Harry Hyland, Montreal Wanderers (5).

Nickname of the Year
Georges 'Chicoutimi Cucumber' Vezina

Worth Noting
The NHL season is divided into halves, with each team playing 14 games in the first half and eight in the second half...Assists are handed out at a premium in the early years of the league. Leading scorer Joe Malone has 44 goals and just four assists. The league leader in assists has just 10...Malone's 44 goals stand as the NHL single-season record until 1944-45...'Bad' Joe Hall leads the league in penalty minutes with 100 in just 21 games...There are only two shutouts this season, one each by Georges Vezina and Clint Benedict...Ottawa and Montreal complete a 20-minute period in just 21:52 of real time Feb. 16.

↑ WE HARDLY KNEW YE
The Montreal Wanderers last just six games (one win, five losses) in the NHL's first season before a fire and financial setbacks spell their demise.

← THE NHL'S FIRST CAP
Prior to joining the new NHL in 1917, the Wanderers had a successful run in various hockey leagues since 1903. Its red and white colors, depicted in this cap, are popular with Montreal's English-speaking community.

Newsmakers & Top Headlines

1 NHL starts first season with four teams
Two weeks after the National Hockey Association disbands, a new pro loop, the National Hockey League, is formed during a meeting Nov. 26, 1917 at Montreal's Windsor Hotel. Four NHA franchises — the Ottawa Senators, Quebec Bulldogs, Montreal Wanderers and Montreal Canadiens — survive with a fifth, the Toronto Arenas, being added. Quebec announces it is taking a leave of absence. Frank Calder is named president and the NHL's 22-game schedule commences Dec. 19.

2 Canadiens and Wanderers home burns down
A raging fire Jan. 2 destroys the 6,000-seat Westmount Arena, home to both of Montreal's NHL teams, the Canadiens and the Wanderers. Two days later, the Wanderers, citing losses of $30,000, withdraw from the league after six games. The Canadiens elect to continue, scrounging up new equipment from other teams and moving into the tiny, 3,250-seat Jubilee Rink.

3 Goalies allowed to drop to ice to make saves
The first major rule change in NHL history goes on the books Jan. 9 when the league removes the stipulation that assesses a minor penalty to any goalie who leaves his feet to stop the puck. Netminders — especially Ottawa's Clint Benedict — had become adept at making their sprawling saves look like accidents. "You could fake losing your balance and put the officials on the spot," Benedict admits. "Did I fall or did I intentionally go down?"

FACTS & STATS
from 1918-19

Cup Winner
None; series cancelled

Leading Scorers
1. Newsy Lalonde, Mtl, 32 pts
2. Odie Cleghorn, Mtl, 28 points
3. Frank Nighbor, Ott, 28 points
4. Cy Denneny, Mtl, 22 points
5. Didier Pitre, Mtl, 19 points
6. Alf Skinner, Tor, 16 points
7. Harry Cameron, Tor/Ott, 14 pts
8. Jack Darragh, Ott, 14 points
9. Ken Randall, Tor, 14 points
10. S. Cleghorn, Ott, 13 points

Franchise News
Toronto Arenas fold Feb. 20, leaving Montreal and Ottawa as NHL's only two teams.

Nickname of the Year
Joe 'Phantom' Malone

Worth Noting
Newsy Lalonde becomes first NHLer to win triple crown, leading the league in goals, assists and points…Lalonde scores 11 goals in five playoff games…Odie Cleghorn is the league's second-leading scorer after refereeing Game 4 of the previous season's Stanley Cup final…'Bad' Joe Hall leads the league in penalty minutes for second straight season with 135 in 16 games. Pro-rated to the modern 82-game schedule, he'd have 692 PIM…Hall dies from Spanish flu at 36 after declaring his body "good for at least 10 more years of hockey" at season's start…PCHA president Frank Patrick calls the cancelled 1919 Stanley Cup final "the most peculiar series in the history of the sport"…The Toronto Arenas record a .278 win percentage and allow five-plus goals per game…Goaltenders Clint Benedict and Georges Vezina play all 18 games for Ottawa and Montreal…Sprague Cleghorn, Odie's brother, plays three minutes in net to spell Clint Benedict, because penalized goalies have to leave the ice.

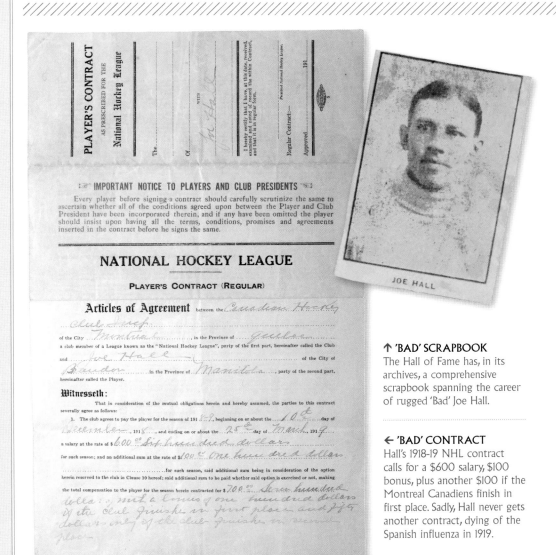

↑ 'BAD' SCRAPBOOK
The Hall of Fame has, in its archives, a comprehensive scrapbook spanning the career of rugged 'Bad' Joe Hall.

← 'BAD' CONTRACT
Hall's 1918-19 NHL contract calls for a $600 salary, $100 bonus, plus another $100 if the Montreal Canadiens finish in first place. Sadly, Hall never gets another contract, dying of the Spanish influenza in 1919.

Newsmakers & Top Headlines

1 Influenza epidemic wipes out Cup final
The Stanley Cup final is cancelled, April 1, with the Montreal Canadiens and the Pacific Coast Association's Seattle Metropolitans deadlocked at 2-2-1 in the series. Seattle declines to accept the title by default as six Canadiens — Joe Hall, 'Newsy' Lalonde, Louis Berlinquette, Billy Couture, Jack McDonald and manager George Kennedy — are hospitalized with the Spanish influenza virus, part of an epidemic that sweeps across the world. Hall dies five days later in a Seattle Sanitarium.

2 Toronto team folds, forcing end to regular season
The defending Stanley Cup-champion Toronto Arenas leave the NHL a two-team outfit when they withdraw from play Feb. 20. NHL officials halt the regular season and order Montreal and Ottawa to play a best-of-seven series for the league title. The dormant Toronto franchise is purchased Nov. 26, 1919, by a group headed by Fred Hambly. After originally calling their new team the Tecumsehs, the new owners switch the name to St. Patricks.

3 Malone misses most of season
As proof the NHL is still a major league in its infancy, Joe Malone, who led the NHL with 44 goals in 1917-18, plays just eight games for Montreal. "I had hooked on to a good job in Quebec City which promised a secure future, something hockey in those days couldn't," Malone says later. His 1917-18 salary was $1,000.

>1919-20 QUEBEC RIVALRY

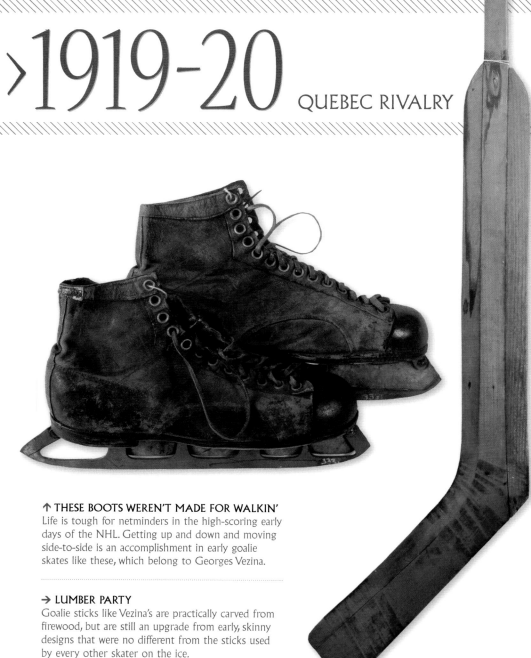

↑ THESE BOOTS WEREN'T MADE FOR WALKIN'
Life is tough for netminders in the high-scoring early days of the NHL. Getting up and down and moving side-to-side is an accomplishment in early goalie skates like these, which belong to Georges Vezina.

→ LUMBER PARTY
Goalie sticks like Vezina's are practically carved from firewood, but are still an upgrade from early, skinny designs that were no different from the sticks used by every other skater on the ice.

Newsmakers & Top Headlines

1 Quebec bullish in first NHL season
After a two-season sabbatical from pro hockey, Quebec enters the NHL. Although the team is called the Athletics, people still refer to it as the Bulldogs — Quebec's nickname in the old NHA. But even with the help of Joe Malone's league-leading 39 goals, Quebec sets NHL futility marks for the fewest wins (four) and highest goals-against average (7.38) and fails to win a game on the road. Quebec allows five or more goals 19 times in 24 games, allowing double-digits five times.

2 Canadiens fire 16 past Quebec
A 16-3 rout of the Athletics in Quebec City March 3 puts the Canadiens into the NHL record book for the most goals in one game. Filling the net is nothing

new for the Habs. Two months earlier, they celebrate the opening of the Mount Royal Arena Jan. 10 by outscoring Toronto 14-7. Newsy Lalonde's six goals and the combined total of both teams set an NHL record.

3 Wild man of the West shakes up NHL
One of the NHL's early bad boys, Cully Wilson leads the league in penalty minutes with 86 in 23 games in his first season. His presence is an indication of the frontier attitude that permeates the NHL; he is signed by the Toronto St. Patricks after being banned from the Pacific Coast Association when his cross-check shatters the jaw of Vancouver's Mickey MacKay. Wilson scores 20 goals and mellows in later seasons when he discovers horticulture.

Cup Winner
Ottawa Senators

Leading Scorers
1. Joe Malone, Que, 49 points
2. Newsy Lalonde, Mtl, 46 pts
3. Frank Nighbor, Ott, 41 points
4. Corb Denneny, Tor, 36 points
5. Jack Darragh, Ott, 36 points
6. Reg Noble, Tor, 33 points
7. Amos Arbour, Mtl, 26 points
8. Cully Wilson, Tor, 26 points
9. Didier Pitre, Mtl, 26 points
10. Punch Broadbent, Ott, 25 pts

Franchise News
Quebec Bulldogs rejoin league, boosting total to four teams. Toronto Arenas change name to Toronto St. Patricks.

Significant Records
Most goals, one game:
Joe Malone, Quebec (7)

Nickname of the Year
Bert 'Pig Iron' Corbeau

Worth Noting
Ottawa's Jack Darragh scores all three game-winning goals in the Senators' 3-2 Stanley Cup series win over Seattle. The final two games in that series are played in Toronto to take advantage of artificial ice during a warm March in Ottawa…Joe Malone's record seven goals in one game warm the hearts of everyone but himself. "The thing I recall most vividly is that it was bitterly cold," Malone says years later…Beleaguered Quebec goalie Frank Brophy allows a stunning 148 goals in 21 games for an eye-popping 7.11 goals-against average…Montreal's Harry Cameron scores four goals against Quebec, becoming the first defenseman to do that twice. He also did it two years earlier with Toronto against his future team…Ottawa's Clint Benedict records the only five shutouts of the entire league.

FACTS & STATS
from 1920-21

Cup Winner
Ottawa Senators

Leading Scorers
1. Newsy Lalonde, Mtl, 43 pts
2. Babe Dye, Ham/Tor, 40 pts
3. Cy Denneny, Ott, 39 points
4. Joe Malone, Ham, 37 points
5. Frank Nighbor, Ott, 29 points
6. Reg Noble, Tor, 27 points
7. Harry Cameron, Tor, 27 points
8. Goldie Prodgers, Ham, 27 pts
9. Corb Denneny, Tor, 26 points
10. Jack Darragh, Ott, 26 points

Franchise News
H.P. Thompson purchases Quebec franchise and league grants him permission to move it to Hamilton provided other NHL teams supply players to strengthen the team.

Nickname of the Year
Edouard 'Newsy' Lalonde

Worth Noting
Defeating the Vancouver Millionaires 3-2 in the championship series, the Ottawa Senators become the first team to win two Stanley Cups and the first to win back-to-back titles…The Toronto St. Patricks loan Babe Dye to the Hamilton Tigers to start the season and he scores two goals in his first game. Toronto immediately reclaims him and he goes on to lead the league with 35 goals…Dye also posts an 11-game goal-scoring streak…Dye is nicknamed 'Babe' because he plays professional baseball, too. His real name is Cecil…Hamilton becomes the first team to record a shutout victory in its debut. The 5-0 win over Montreal winds up the only shutout of Howard 'Holes' Lockhart's NHL career… Despite the shutout debut, Lockhart loses 18 of 24 starts and posts a 5.45 goals-against average…Newsy Lalonde wins his second and final scoring title at 32…Clint Benedict is the first goalie to 10 career shutouts.

MAGAZINE SECTION **The Seattle Sunday Times** JANUARY 30, 1921

STICKHANDLING the PUCK IN THE ARENA

← CREATIVE ART
One of the best artist renderings of the early NHL days is this clever drawing that appeared in the Seattle *Sunday Times*. It's multiple layers are deep, colorful and intense.

Newsmakers & Top Headlines

1 NHL tries to break up Ottawa juggernaut
Looking to balance competition in the league, NHL president Frank Calder awards the rights to Ottawa right winger Punch Broadbent and defenseman Sprague Cleghorn, both future Hall of Famers, to the fledgling Hamilton Tigers Dec. 30. The Senators protest vehemently and both players refuse to report to the Tigers, eventually finding their way back to Ottawa to help the Senators become the first NHL team to repeat as Stanley Cup champions.

2 Senators leave ice over officiating
Angered by what they feel is one-sided officiating by referee Cooper Smeaton, the Senators leave the ice with 5:13 to play in their Jan. 26 game against the Montreal Canadiens. With no opponent on the ice, Newsy Lalonde and Amos Arbour score uncontested goals and Smeaton awards the Habs a 5-3 victory. Smeaton resigns over the incident, but is convinced to return before the end of the season. NHL president Frank Calder fines the Senators $500 for their actions.

3 Aging Habs barred from driving automobiles
Alarmed by his club's lack of stamina, Montreal manager Leo Dandurand bars his players from driving their newfangled automobiles, believing it gives them cramps in their hands and legs. It's much more likely the physical ailments are a reflection of Montreal's average age — 30.9 years. The Habs are the oldest team in the league.

1921-22

PUNCH FRENZY

↑ STAR TREATMENT
Fitting that Punch Broadbent (left) and Cy Denneny (right), the leading scorers of '21-22, are featured in the front row of this Senators team photo.

← FOR WHOM THE BELL GOALS
The first stoppages in play and to signal a goal in the early years of the NHL come from the referee clanging a bell. It isn't long before whistles take over. A period ends with the bell or whistle from a referee until 1925, when the timekeeper assumes the responsibility and bangs a gong.

Cup Winner TORONTO ST PATS
Toronto St. Patricks

Leading Scorers
1. Punch Broadbent, Ott, 46 pts
2. Cy Denneny, Ott, 39 points
3. Babe Dye, Tor, 38 points
4. Harry Cameron, Tor, 35 pts
5. Joe Malone, Ham, 31 points
6. Corb Denneny, Tor, 28 points
7. Reg Noble, Tor, 28 points
8. S. Cleghorn, Mtl, 26 points
9. Georges Boucher, Ott, 25 pts
10. Odie Cleghorn, Mtl, 24 pts

Rule Changes
Goalies are allowed to pass the puck forward, up to their own blueline.

Significant Records
Longest consecutive goal-scoring streak: Punch Broadbent, Ottawa (16 games, 27 goals).

Nickname of the Year
Frank 'The Pembroke Peach' Nighbor

Worth Noting
Punch Broadbent excels on the ice, but he was also a battlefield hero during the First World War. He was awarded the Military Medal and recommended for a Commission For Bravery during three years in the trenches…The first player to sit out an entire season in a contract dispute is Toronto St. Patricks goalie Jake Forbes. Holding out for a $2,500 salary, he misses all of 1921-22 and Toronto goes with John Ross Roach instead. The dispute ends when Forbes is sold to Hamilton at the end of the season…Said referee Lou Marsh about Montreal's Cleghorn brothers: "They are a disgrace to the league and the game of hockey."…A Hamilton Tigers sweater from the 1920s is the Holy Grail of hockey artifacts. There's even a film about the quest to find one and take it to its rightful home.

Newsmakers & Top Headlines

1 Streaking Broadbent sets goal mark
Christmas Eve turns out to be special for Ottawa right winger Harry 'Punch' Broadbent. He scores once in a 10-0 rout of Montreal, beginning his NHL-record 16-game goal-scoring streak, a mark that still stands. Broadbent scores 27 goals during the streak and has nine multi-goal games. He goes on to lead the NHL in goals (32), assists (14) and points (46), netting at least one point in 21 of the Senators' 24 games.

2 St. Patricks and Senators record NHL's first tie
Following four NHL seasons with no tie games, the streak ends Feb. 11. After battling through 20 minutes of overtime, the Toronto St. Patricks and Ottawa Senators finish in a 4-4 deadlock — the first tie in NHL history. John Ross Roach makes 78 saves for Toronto, while the Senators' Clint Benedict stops 63 shots. St. Patricks defenseman Harry Cameron is credited with the first game-tying goal.

3 Two-man wrecking crew fined by league
Brothers Sprague and Odie Cleghorn, in their first NHL season together with the Habs, go on a rampage during a 4-2 loss in Ottawa Feb. 1. They put three Senators — Frank Nighbor (broken arm), Cy Denneny (leg injury) and Eddie Gerard (head injury) — out of the game. Both brothers are assessed major penalties and $30 fines and referee Lou Marsh tacks on a match penalty to Sprague's transgressions. The brothers lead the Habs in both scoring and PIM for the year.

FACTS & STATS
from 1922-23

Cup Winner
Ottawa Senators

Leading Scorers
1. Babe Dye, Tor, 37 points
2. Cy Denneny, Ott, 34 points
3. Billy Boucher, Mtl, 31 points
4. Jack Adams, Tor, 28 points
5. Mickey Roach, Ham, 27 pts
6. Odie Cleghorn, Mtl, 25 points
7. Georges Boucher, Ott, 23 pts
8. Reg Noble, Tor, 23 points
9. Cully Wilson, Ham, 21 points
10. Aurel Joliat, Mtl, 21 points

Nickname of the Year
Didier 'Cannonball' Pitre

Worth Noting
Teams agree no player can be traded or sold to other leagues without being offered to all other NHL clubs…Ottawa's **King Clancy** plays all six positions in a 1-0 victory over the Edmonton Eskimos during the Stanley Cup final. He even tends goal while Clint Benedict serves a penalty… Foster Hewitt on his first radio appearance: "If it had been left up to me, it would have been my first and last broadcast."…Babe Dye leads the NHL in goals for the second time, but the scoring title is his first…In his final season, Ottawa's Eddie Girard leads the NHL in assists for the first time…Clint Benedict's 2.18 goals-against average shatters his own NHL mark of 2.66…Didier Pitre's career ends in 1923. He goes by 'Cannonball' for his heavy wrist shot, which bursts through a net on a contested goal at one point in his career.

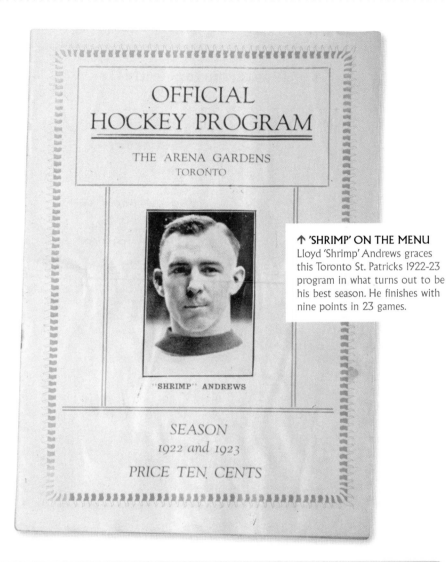

OFFICIAL HOCKEY PROGRAM

THE ARENA GARDENS
TORONTO

"SHRIMP" ANDREWS

SEASON
1922 and 1923

PRICE TEN CENTS

↑ 'SHRIMP' ON THE MENU
Lloyd 'Shrimp' Andrews graces this Toronto St. Patricks 1922-23 program in what turns out to be his best season. He finishes with nine points in 23 games.

Newsmakers & Top Headlines

1 Game aired over radio for first time
Pete Parker, not Foster Hewitt, performs hockey's first radio broadcast, describing an Edmonton-Regina playoff game in the Western Canada League March 14. Hewitt calls his first game eight days later using a telephone line linked to station CFCA from a cramped four-foot by four-foot broadcast booth. A reporter for the Toronto **Star**, Hewitt does play-by-play of an Ontario Hockey Association game at Toronto's Mutual Street Arena between Parkdale and Kitchener.

2 Canadiens trade legend Lalonde for unknown
Montreal Canadiens' manager Leo Dandurand stuns the hockey world when he trades captain and two-time NHL scoring champion Newsy Lalonde Sept. 18 to the Saskatoon Sheiks of the Western Canada League for $3,500 and the rights to an unproven amateur named Aurel Joliat. The move is panned — until Joliat finishes eighth in NHL scoring as a rookie, launching a Hall of Fame career which sees him play 16 seasons for the Bleu, Blanc et Rouge.

3 Dandurand suspends his best blueliners
Canadiens defensemen Sprague Cleghorn and Billy Coutu are suspended by Montreal manager Leo Dandurand after receiving match penalties for illegal hits against the Ottawa Senators during the first game of the playoffs. Minus their starting 'D' duo, the Habs lose the two-game, total-goals series 3-2 and Ottawa advances to its third Stanley Cup final in four seasons.

GOTTA HAVE HART

FACTS & STATS from 1923-24

Cup Winner
Montreal Canadiens

Leading Scorers
1. Cy Denneny, Ott, 24 points
2. Georges Boucher, Ott, 23 pts
3. Billy Boucher, Mtl, 22 points
4. Billy Burch, Ham, 22 points
5. Aurel Joliat, Mtl, 20 points
6. Babe Dye, Tor, 19 points
7. Jack Adams, Tor, 18 points
8. Reg Noble, Tor, 17 points
9. Frank Nighbor, Ott, 17 points
10. Howie Morenz, Mtl, 16 pts

Nickname of the Year
Harry 'Punch' Broadbent

Worth Noting
Future legend Howie Morenz debuts with the Canadiens, finishing in the top 10 in league scoring. The Habs go into Toronto's backyard to scout and sign him from the Stratford (Ont.) Indians. He later becomes known as 'The Stratford Streak' and teams with **Billy Boucher** and Aurel Joliat to form 'The Speedball Line,' the most dangerous offensive trio in the league...When Ottawa's train is snowbound on the tracks overnight en route to Montreal for a Jan. 19 game, Senator Cy Denneny leaves the train looking for something to eat and falls down a well. Fortunately, he's rescued by teammates and is uninjured... Gritty Hab Sprague Cleghorn finishes runner-up to Frank Nighbor in Hart Trophy voting... Harry 'Punch' Broadbent got his nickname because he could provide scoring punch and knockout punch as a top-notch fighter.

↑ ROARING IN THE '20S
Canadiens defenseman Sprague Cleghorn is among the decade's most feared players. He amasses 538 PIM in just 259 career games.

← HART AND SOUL
No major sport has a more iconic collection of trophies and one of the most coveted, the Hart, makes its debut in 1924. Frank Nighbor is the first man to grip the silver handles and hoist the Hart as league MVP.

Newsmakers & Top Headlines

1 Dye pursues field of dreams
Toronto sniper Cecil 'Babe' Dye, the NHL's leading scorer in 1922-23, shocks the team before the season when he announces he is retiring to pursue a career in baseball. Dye, who reaches the AAA level as a ballplayer, later changes his mind and returns to the St. Patricks lineup in December, which gives him enough time to produce 17 goals and finish fourth in the scoring race.

2 Denneny leading scorer in low-scoring season
Ottawa's Cy Denneny wins his only scoring title with the worst winning totals in NHL history. He finishes with 22 goals and two assists. Denneny is the only player to crack the 20-goal mark and average more than a point per game with 24 in 22 games. The league

goals-per-game average of 5.3 is nearly half what it was in 1917-18 (10.1). Following the season, the NHL implements the anti-defense rule, which prohibits teams from keeping more than one player (other than goalie) in the defensive zone when the puck is not there.

3 Nighbor first Hart Trophy winner
The NHL introduces its first individual award, the Hart Trophy, for "the player adjudged to be the most valuable to his team." Ottawa Senators playmaking center Frank Nighbor is the first winner. Nighbor and Toronto Maple Leaf Teeder Kennedy (1954-55) are the only forwards to win the Hart without finishing among the top 10 scorers. In 1924-25, Nighbor is named the first winner of the Lady Byng Trophy.

↑ SUCCESSFUL FOUNDATION
These bricks help build Detroit's Olympia Stadium in the 1920s. The NHL team there will one day be a triumphant group known as the Red Wings.

→ RISE OF THE FORUM
The Montreal Canadiens find a new home in the soon-to-be fabled Forum.

1924-25

MANIFEST DESTINY

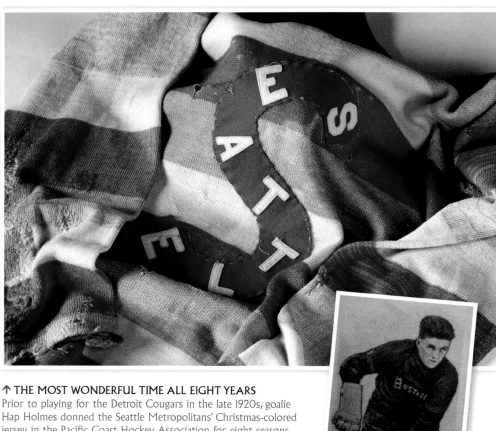

↑ THE MOST WONDERFUL TIME ALL EIGHT YEARS
Prior to playing for the Detroit Cougars in the late 1920s, goalie Hap Holmes donned the Seattle Metropolitans' Christmas-colored jersey in the Pacific Coast Hockey Association for eight seasons.

→ ONE AND DONE
Fern 'Curley' Headley plays just one playoff game in his only season in the NHL, but it's enough for him to win the Stanley Cup with the Canadiens in 1925. He starts the season with Boston, but is later loaned to Montreal.

F. ("CURLEY") HEADLEY

Newsmakers & Top Headlines

1 Hamilton players strike before NHL final
After finishing first and qualifying for the playoffs for the only time in franchise history, the Hamilton Tigers stun the hockey world by going on strike prior to the NHL final with the Montreal Canadiens. Players take issue with not receiving a pay increase when the NHL increases its schedule from 24-30 games. The players allege a $200 bonus had been promised, but Hamilton owner Percy Thompson denies it and NHL president Frank Calder suspends the team March 9, awarding the title to the Habs.

2 Bruins and Maroons join NHL
The NHL crosses the border when it awards its first American franchise Oct. 11 to Boston. The Bruins are selected along with a second team for Montreal: the Maroons. At the same time, it is announced Pittsburgh and New York have been granted franchises for 1925-26. Franchise fees are $15,000 and $11,000 of the Maroons' payment goes to the Canadiens for infringement on their territorial rights, the first such payment, but not the last, in league history.

3 Montreal Forum opens its doors
Billy Boucher opens the Canadiens' sparkling new $1-million Forum in style Nov. 26, firing a hat trick including the first goal of the game, as 9,000 fans watch the Habs beat Toronto 7-1. A month later, the largest crowd in NHL history — 11,000 fans — packs the building to see the Canadiens and Maroons play to a 1-1- tie.

FACTS & STATS
from 1924-25

Cup Winner
Victoria Cougars

Leading Scorers
1. Babe Dye, Tor, 46 points
2. Cy Denneny, Ott, 42 points
3. Aurel Joliat, Mtl, 41 points
4. Howie Morenz, Mtl, 39 points
5. Red Green, Ham, 34 points
6. Jack Adams, Tor, 31 points
7. Billy Boucher, Mtl, 30 points
8. Billy Burch, Ham, 27 points
9. Jimmy Herberts, Bos, 24 pts
10. Hooley Smith, Ott, 23 points

Franchise News
Boston Bruins and Montreal Maroons join the NHL, making it a six-team league.

Nickname of the Year
John Ross 'Little Napoleon' Roach

Worth Noting
Hamilton captain Shorty Green on the Tigers' strike: "The boys are unanimous in what they consider their just dues, hence the reason for the stand we have taken." Not only are the Tigers suspended, but Hamilton loses its team altogether. The roster is sold to the New York Americans for $75,000...Hamilton's Billy Burch is the second straight center to win the Hart Trophy... NHL regular season schedule increases from 24 to 30 games... The Lady Byng Trophy is donated to the league and awarded to the most gentlemanly player. Ottawa's Frank Nighbor is the first to win it...Toronto's Babe Dye leads the league in goals for the third and final time of his career...Alec Connell sets a single-season record with seven shutouts, as does Georges Vezina with a 1.81 goals-against average. Both are harbingers of the defensive era to come. Goalie John Ross Roach, who ties for the league lead with 19 wins, is nicknamed 'Little Napoleon' because he's just 5-foot-5 and 130 pounds.

FACTS & STATS
from 1925-26

Cup Winner

Montreal Maroons

Leading Scorers
1. Nels Stewart, Mar, 42 points
2. Cy Denneny, Ott, 36 points
3. Carson Cooper, Bos, 31 pts
4. Jimmy Herberts, Bos, 31 pts
5. Howie Morenz, Mtl, 26 points
6. Jack Adams, Tor, 26 points
7. Aurel Joliat, Mtl, 26 points
8. Billy Burch, NYA, 25 points
9. Hooley Smith, Ott, 25 points
10. Frank Nighbor, Ott, 25 points

Franchise News
Hamilton leaves NHL. Players are signed by new New York Americans franchise. Pittsburgh Pirates also added to make it a seven-team league.

Nickname of the Year
Howie 'The Stratford Streak' Morenz

Worth Noting
Pittsburgh coach Odie Cleghorn changes the way the game is played by rotating three set forward lines. Previously, teams iced a starting six and players came off only when in need of a rest. It isn't long before all teams employ sets of lines rather than one prime unit...Maroons center **Nels Stewart** joins the league as a 23-year-old rookie and goes on to lead the NHL in goals and points while winning the Hart Trophy. Stewart also finishes second in penalty minutes and the following season tops the charts with 133 PIM.

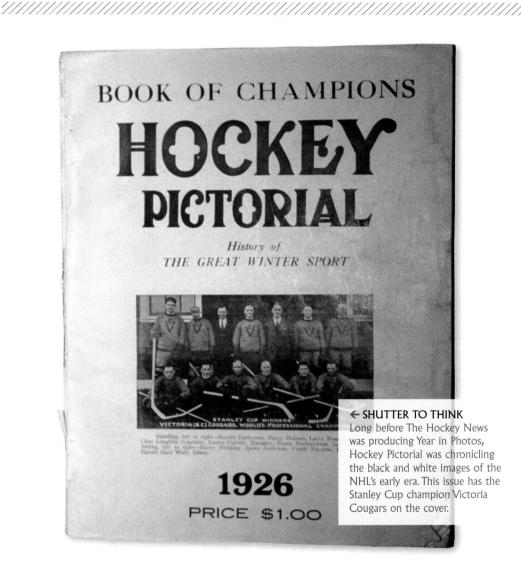

Newsmakers & Top Headlines

1 Americans open at Madison Square Garden
The NHL comes to the Big Apple and it's a huge success. An NHL-record crowd of 17,000 at Madison Square Garden Dec. 15 watches the Montreal Canadiens defeat the New York Americans 3-1. The boxing crowd at MSG quickly finds it is losing the promotional battle to hockey. "I can make bigger money with less worry and fewer risks out of hockey than I have been getting out of boxing," says Garden promoter Tex Rickard.

2 Salaries skyrocket league-wide
The growing popularity of hockey is evidenced in the rapid expansion of the NHL, going from four to seven teams in two seasons and in growing player salaries. A $35,000-per-team salary cap is introduced to slow the trend. Among the top earners are Pittsburgh's Lionel Conacher ($7,500), Montreal Maroon Dunc Munro ($7,500), New York Americans Billy Burch ($6,500) and Joe Simpson ($6,000), Toronto's Hap Day ($6,000) and Boston's Sprague Cleghorn ($5,000).

3 Vezina's longevity streak ends tragically
Montreal goalie Georges Vezina hasn't missed a game in 15 years when he appears for the season opener against Pittsburgh Nov. 28 despite a temperature of 102 Fahrenheit. He collapses in net during the opening period and backup Al Lacroix takes over. Vezina is diagnosed with tuberculosis and has to retire. He dies March 26. The Vezina Trophy, which goes to the NHL's best goalie, is named in his honor.

NO COMPETITION

Cup Winner
Ottawa Senators

Leading Scorers
1. Bill Cook, NYR, 37 points
2. Dick Irvin, Chi, 36 points
3. Howie Morenz, Mtl, 32 points
4. F. Fredrickson, Det/Bos, 31 pts
5. Babe Dye, Chi, 30 points
6. Ace Bailey, Tor, 28 points
7. Frank Boucher, NYR, 28 pts
8. Billy Burch, NYA, 27 points
9. Harry Oliver, Bos, 24 points
10. Duke Keats, Bos/Det, 24 pts

Franchise News
New York Rangers, Chicago Black Hawks and Detroit Cougars added to make it a 10-team league. Toronto St. Patricks sold, change name to Toronto Maple Leafs.

Nickname of the Year
Alec 'The Ottawa Fireman' Connell

Worth Noting
Herb Gardiner becomes the second – and with Nels Stewart and Wayne Gretzky one of just three players ever – to win the Hart Trophy as a rookie. After serving in the First World War, Gardiner lived and played for Calgary in the Western Canadian League while working as a railway surveyor in the off-season. When the WCHL folds in 1926, the Montreal Canadiens seek his services and, as a 35-year-old freshman, he plays 60 minutes a game on the blueline next to partner Sylvio Mantha. And though he registers just six goals and 12 points in 44 games, Gardiner's durability, leadership and overall defensive acumen win him the distinction of best player in the game. Ultimately, he plays just two more seasons…The expansion Detroit Cougars play all 22 of their home games across the border in Canada at Windsor's Border Cities Arena due to a lack of suitable facilities locally.

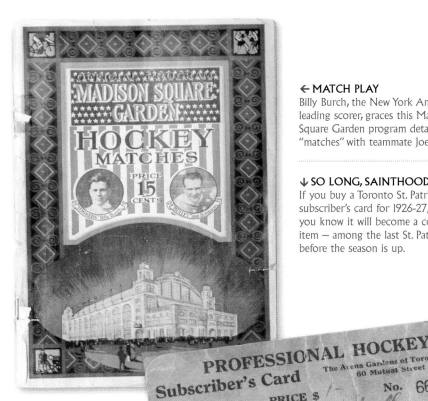

← MATCH PLAY
Billy Burch, the New York Americans' leading scorer, graces this Madison Square Garden program detailing hockey "matches" with teammate Joe Simpson.

↓ SO LONG, SAINTHOOD
If you buy a Toronto St. Patricks season subscriber's card for 1926-27, little do you know it will become a collector's item – among the last St. Pats artifacts – before the season is up.

Newsmakers & Top Headlines

1 Detroit, Chicago, Rangers awarded franchises
The NHL loses its competition when Frank Patrick, president of the rival Western Hockey League, sells the contracts of players May 4, 1926, to the NHL for $258,000. Three teams are added, the Detroit Cougars, Chicago Black Hawks and New York Rangers, and the 10-team league is divided into Canadian and American divisions. The new players have an impact – Rangers winger Bill Cook is the scoring leader, while Montreal goalie George Hainsworth (Vezina Trophy) and rearguard Herb Gardiner (Hart Trophy), win major awards.

2 St. Patricks turn over new Leaf in Toronto
As Philadelphia entrepreneurs prepare to buy the Toronto St. Patricks and move the club, Toronto hockey man Conn Smythe assembles a 16-member ownership group which purchases the club Feb. 14 for $160,000. The team is renamed the Maple Leafs and they switch their green and white colors for blue and white, launching what would become Canada's team.

3 Green's career ends after near-fatal hit
The NHL comes close to its first on-ice fatality, when New York Americans' forward Shorty Green sustains a kidney injury Feb. 27 after absorbing a clean open-ice hit from 225-pound New York Ranger defenseman Clarence 'Taffy' Abel. Green undergoes surgery March 3 to remove the damaged kidney and at one point is administered last rites. Green recovers, but never plays again.

Cup Winner
New York Rangers

Leading Scorers
1. Howie Morenz, Mtl, 51 points
2. Aurel Joliat, Mtl, 39 points
3. Frank Boucher, NYR, 35 pts
4. George Hay, Det, 35 points
5. Nels Stewart, Mar, 34 points
6. Art Gagne, Mtl, 30 points
7. Bun Cook, NYR, 28 points
8. Bill Carson, Tor, 26 points
9. Frank Finnigan, Ott, 25 pts
10. Bill Cook, NYR, 24 points

Rule Changes
Forward passes are allowed in the defending and neutral zones. Goaltenders' protective pads are reduced in width from 12 inches to 10 inches.

Significant Records
Longest shutout sequence by a goaltender: Alec Connell, Ottawa (461:29)

Nickname of the Year
Roy 'Shrimp' Worters

Worth Noting
Boston coach Art Ross, showing he's also one of the game's great innovators, creates a new model for the net, which the NHL adopts in 1927-28. Pucks, which used to bounce out of the tight twine, now stay in the loose webbing. He also redesigns the puck by getting rid of its sharp edges. He leads the Bruins to the Stanley Cup the following season...Detroit Cougars center Duke Keats receives an indefinite suspension Nov. 26, 1927, when he swings his stick at a heckling fan in Chicago. Keats is reinstated Dec. 15 and traded one day later to Chicago...Wrote New York *Times* journalist John Kieran about the last-place New York Americans: "(Coach Shorty Green) might get better results if he coached them from the mezzanine with a shotgun."

→ CATCH OF THE DAY
This puck essentially belongs to Montreal goaltender George Hainsworth, who doesn't let it get past him once during a March 24 shutout, one of his 13 on the season.

PUCK USED
CANADIEN (4) OTTAWA (0)
GAME AT FORUM
SAT. MARCH ·24ᵀᴴ 1928

Newsmakers & Top Headlines

1 Manager Patrick rescues Rangers during final
When Nels Stewart's shot strikes Rangers goalie Lorne Chabot in the eye during the second period of Game 2 of the final, it looks as if the Cup belongs to the Montreal Maroons. Montreal leads the best-of-five 1-0 and the Rangers have no backup. New York asks to use Ottawa's Alec Connell and minor-leaguer Hugh McCormick, but is turned down, so GM Lester Patrick, 44, dons the pads. He stops 17 of 18 shots and the Rangers win 2-1 in OT. Farmhand Joe Miller takes over next game as the Rangers win the Cup in five games.

2 Referee, former coach advocate use of helmets
After Chicago Black Hawks forward Dick Irvin sustains a fractured skull, two people promote the wearing of helmets. Referee Lou Marsh suggests fiber helmets similar to those worn by horse jockeys. Former Chicago coach Barney Stanley designs a pith and fiber helmet and presents it at an NHL governors' meeting, but to no avail.

3 Calder will allow no color barrier in NHL
The Boston Black Panthers are hockey's first all-African-American team. While these players are well below the caliber of teams competing for the Stanley Cup, NHL president Frank Calder insists that unlike baseball, which has a distinct color barrier, all players are welcome to play in his league. "Pro hockey has no ruling against the colored man, nor is it likely to ever draw the line," Calder says.

>1928-29

GROUND ZERO

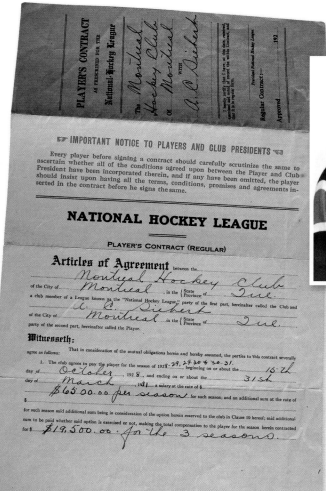

↑ MONEY PLAYER
There's a hint of a smirk in Babe Siebert's face. Does he know he's about to strike it rich with a new contract?

← LET'S MAKE A DEAL
It's no Rick DiPietro contract, but Siebert gets long-term job security with this three-year, $19,500 deal. He rewards Montreal by upping his goal total in each year of the pact.

Cup Winner
Boston Bruins

Leading Scorers
1. Ace Bailey, Tor, 32 points
2. Nels Stewart, Mar, 29 points
3. Carson Cooper, Det, 27 pts
4. Howie Morenz, Mtl, 27 points
5. Andy Blair, Tor, 27 points
6. Frank Boucher, NYR, 26 pts
7. Harry Oliver, Bos, 23 points
8. Bill Cook, NYR, 23 points
9. Jimmy Ward, Mar, 22 points
10. Frank Finnigan, Ott, 19 pts

Rule Changes
Forward passes are permitted into the attacking zone if pass receiver is in the neutral zone when the pass is made. Forward passes still forbidden in attacking zone. Ten-minute overtime no longer sudden death.

Significant Records
Most shutouts, one season: George Hainsworth, Montreal Canadiens (22)

Nickname of the Year
Lionel 'The Big Train' Conacher

Worth Noting
George Hainsworth, after his record-breaking season, speaks about his lack of flamboyance: "I can't jump on easy shots and make them look hard."...The futile Black Hawks win just seven of 44 games, while first-place Montreal loses only seven times... Boston goes a perfect 5-0 en route to its first Stanley Cup... Cy Denneny coaches the Bruins to the Cup while still suiting up as a player...Season PIM leader Lionel Conacher, named 'The Big Train' for his 6-foot-2, 195-pound frame, excels in multiple sports. He wins two Stanley Cups and a CFL Grey Cup. He goes on to be voted Canada's top athlete of the half-century in 1950...Every team posts a goals-against average below 2.00.

Newsmakers & Top Headlines

1 Year of the shutout
NHL goalies produce a record 120 shutouts in 220 games, holding shooters to a record-low 2.9 goals per game. Leading the way is Vezina Trophy-winner George Hainsworth of the Montreal Canadiens, whose 22 shutouts and 0.92 goals-against average still stand as league records. Seven other netminders, including Hart Trophy-winner Roy Worters of the New York Americans (with 13 shutouts), hit double digits in zeroes.

2 Black Hawks sleepwalk through scoring drought
Eight straight games, no goals. A Chicago Black Hawk finally scores a goal when Vic Ripley pots one three minutes into the third period of a 2-1 win March 2 over the Montreal Maroons, ending an NHL-record

scoreless streak at 601 minutes and 41 seconds — a drought that spans 28 days. Chicago scores 33 goals in 44 games, setting an NHL standard for futility, as does the Hawks' 0.75 goals-per-game average and the 20 times they are blanked.

3 Retired Winkler gets name engraved on Cup
After winning the Stanley Cup, the Boston Bruins have former goalie Hal Winkler's name inscribed on it, even though he retired before the season when he was replaced by rookie Tiny Thompson. Winkler and Detroit defenseman Vladimir Konstantinov, who sustains career-ending head injuries the summer before the Red Wings' 1997-98 Cup victory, are the only players to have their names on the Cup without playing that season.

FACTS & STATS
from 1929-30

Cup Winner

Montreal Canadiens

Leading Scorers
1. Cooney Weiland, Bos, 73 pts
2. Frank Boucher, NYR, 62 pts
3. Dit Clapper, Bos, 61 points
4. Bill Cook, NYR, 59 points
5. Hec Kilrea, Ott, 58 points
6. Nels Stewart, Mtm, 55 points
7. Howie Morenz, Mtl, 50 points
8. Normie Himes, NYA, 50 pts
9. Joe Lamb, Ott, 49 points
10. Dutch Gainor, Bos, 49 points

Rule Changes
Forward passes are permitted in all three zones but not across either blueline. The change more than doubles the number of goals scored, from an average 2.9 per game the previous year to 5.9. The rule is amended later that season to include, "No attacking player allowed to precede the play when entering the opposing defensive zone." This is similar to the modern-day offside rule.

Significant Records
Most overtime goals, one season: Howie Morenz, Montreal and Frank Finnigan, Ottawa (4).

Nickname of the Year
Carson 'Shovel Shot' Cooper

Worth Noting
The New York Rangers become the first NHL team to travel by air when they hire the Curtis-Wright Corporation on Dec. 13 to fly to Toronto for a game the following day. The Rangers lose to the Maple Leafs 7-6...Clint Benedict on the mask he wore for one game after being struck in the face: "It was leather with a big nosepiece. The nosepiece proved the problem, because it obscured my vision."...Pittsburgh goalie Joe Miller has a year to forget, suffering 35 losses in 43 starts, allowing 179 goals and posting a 4.08 goals-against average.

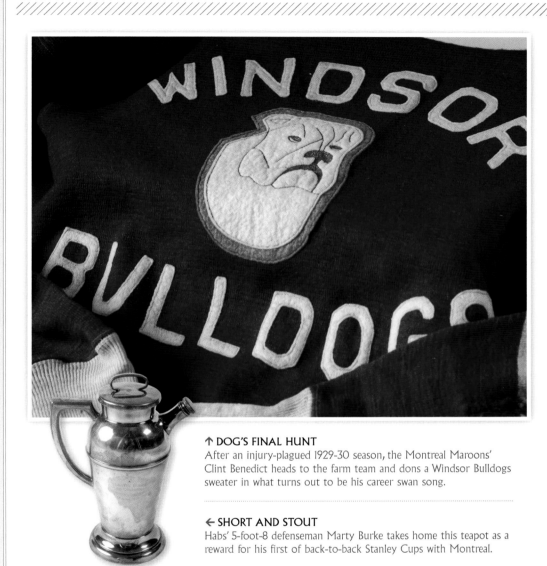

↑ DOG'S FINAL HUNT
After an injury-plagued 1929-30 season, the Montreal Maroons' Clint Benedict heads to the farm team and dons a Windsor Bulldogs sweater in what turns out to be his career swan song.

← SHORT AND STOUT
Habs' 5-foot-8 defenseman Marty Burke takes home this teapot as a reward for his first of back-to-back Stanley Cups with Montreal.

Newsmakers & Top Headlines

1 New rules produce goal rush
Alarmed by a steady decrease in scoring, which led to a record-low average of 2.9 goals per game in 1928-29, the NHL introduces rule changes that allow forward passing in all three zones, but not over either blueline. The impact is enormous. The goals-per-game average jumps to 5.9, while shutouts drop from 120 to just 26. A month into the season, NHL governors add an offside rule to prohibit attacking players from crossing the opponent's blueline before the puck.

2 Weiland smashes Morenz's scoring record
Cooney Weiland of Boston doesn't just break the points record, he shatters it. The slick center's 73 points are 22 more than Howie Morenz's old mark (51) and won't be topped for 11 seasons. Weiland (43) and linemate Dit Clapper (41) lead the NHL goal parade and the Bruins to an incredible 38-5-1 mark. Boston sets several NHL records, including most points (77), wins (38), goals (179), longest winning streak (14 games) and highest winning percentage (.875), yet fails to win the Cup.

3 Benedict NHL's first masked man
Montreal Maroons' goalie Clint Benedict sustains a broken nose in a Jan. 8 game after being struck by a shot from Montreal Canadiens' Howie Morenz. When he returns to the lineup against the New York Americans Feb. 20, Benedict becomes the first NHL netminder to don facial protection. He wears a leather mask with a big nosepiece for one game and then discards it.

STARS ARE BORN

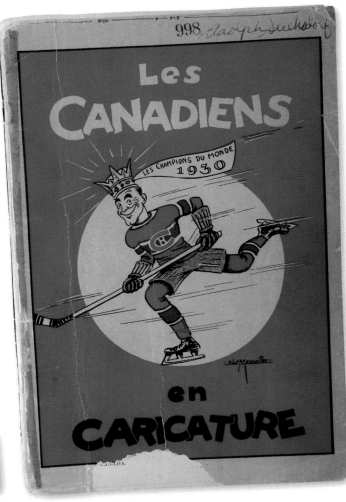

→ LIFE AT THE TOP
In the 1930s, the Montreal Canadiens are already being celebrated — even in cartoon form — as the sport's most dominant franchise.

↓ THE PUCK OF DREAMS
This is the last biscuit used in Game 5 of the Stanley Cup final, a 2-0 Habs victory in which Johnny Gagnon pots the winner.

FACTS & STATS
from 1930-31

Cup Winner
Montreal Canadiens

Leading Scorers
1. Howie Morenz, Mtl, 51 points
2. Ebbie Goodfellow, Det, 48 pts
3. Charlie Conacher, Tor, 43 pts
4. Bill Cook, NYR, 42 points
5. Ace Bailey, Tor, 42 points
6. Joe Primeau, Tor, 41 points
7. Nels Stewart, Mar, 39 points
8. Frank Boucher, NYR, 39 pts
9. Cooney Weiland, Bos, 38 pts
10. Bun Cook, NYR, 35 points

Franchise News
Pittsburgh franchise transfers to Philadelphia and becomes the Quakers. Detroit changes name from Cougars to Falcons.

Nickname of the Year
William 'Baldy' Cotton

Worth Noting
Toronto's King Clancy, Joe Primeau and **Busher Jackson** are awarded assists on Charlie Conacher's goal Feb. 14, marking the first time in NHL history three players assist on one goal…Philadelphia GM Cooper Smeaton sarcastically quips about his brutal club, "I know there are better teams than the Quakers."…Charlie Conacher hits 30-goal mark for the first time and leads the NHL in goals, which he does four more times…Conn Smythe secures funds to land King Clancy when his horse, Rare Jewel, wins a race as a 100-to-1 long shot. Legend has it Rare Jewel was fed brandy before the race.

Newsmakers & Top Headlines

1 Smythe gambles on the King
Toronto Maple Leafs' manager Conn Smythe wins nearly $15,000 betting on Rare Jewel, a thoroughbred racehorse he owns, then borrows about $20,000 and sends D-man Art Smith, forward Eric Pettinger and $35,000 to the Ottawa Senators Oct. 11 for King Clancy. The charismatic blueliner becomes the leader of a Leafs team which is the best in the 1930s.

2 Quakers win only four of 44 games
Coming off a dismal 5-36-3 season, the Pittsburgh Pirates franchise is transferred to Philadelphia and renamed the Quakers. Owned by boxer Benny Leonard, the Quakers endure a pathetic 4-36-4 campaign and .136 winning percentage, the worst in NHL history.

3 Inaugural all-star teams legendary
Every player named to the first-ever first and second all-star teams is eventually elected to the Hockey Hall of Fame, an auspicious beginning for the all-star team concept. On the first team: goalie Charlie Gardiner (Chicago Black Hawks), defensemen Eddie Shore (Boston Bruins) and King Clancy (Toronto), left winger Aurel Joliat (Montreal Canadiens), center Howie Morenz (Montreal), right winger Bill Cook (New York Rangers) and coach Lester Patrick (Rangers). On the second team: goalie Tiny Thompson (Boston), defensemen Sylvio Mantha (Montreal) and Ching Johnson (Rangers), left winger Bun Cook (Rangers), Frank Boucher (Rangers), right winger Dit Clapper (Boston) and coach Dick Irvin (Chicago).

1931-32 ‹

FACTS & STATS
from 1931-32

Cup Winner
Toronto Maple Leafs

Leading Scorers
1. Busher Jackson, Tor, 53 pts
2. Joe Primeau, Tor, 50 points
3. Howie Morenz, Mtl, 49 points
4. Charlie Conacher, Tor, 48 pts
5. Bill Cook, NYR, 48 points
6. Dave Trottier, Mar, 44 points
7. Hooley Smith, Mar, 44 points
8. Babe Siebert, Mar, 39 points
9. Dit Clapper, Bos, 39 points
10. Aurel Joliat, Mtl, 39 points

Franchise News
Philadelphia folds. Ottawa withdraws for one season. NHL shrinks from 10 teams to eight.

Nickname of the Year
Ivan 'Ching' Johnson

Worth Noting
The Leafs defeat the New York Rangers in the Cup final despite not securing Conn Smythe's top target: Howie Morenz. The Canadiens spurn a $75,000 offer for him…The Leafs' victory in the final was nicknamed 'The Tennis Series' because of its scores: 6-4, 6-2, 6-4…**Charlie Conacher** and Bill Cook become the first NHLers to tie for the league's goal-scoring lead…Joe Primeau's 37 assists set a single-season record that stands for a decade…Ivan 'Ching' Johnson finishes second in PIM with 106. His nickname wouldn't fly today: it was a derogatory reference to his supposedly "Asian-looking" facial features.

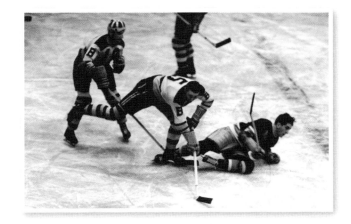

↑ HEAD OF HIS CLASS
Fittingly, Boston's Eddie Shore is among the first players to sport a primitive helmet like this one. The trailblazing blueliner is also the first NHLer to win four Hart Trophies.

← DIT HAS IT
Boston's Dit Clapper battles for a loose puck against the Rangers. He goes on to win a Cup in three different decades with the Bruins.

Newsmakers & Top Headlines

1 Toronto throws Gardens party
Toronto GM Conn Smythe is laughed at when he reveals plans to build Maple Leaf Gardens during the Great Depression, but Smythe has the last laugh. The doors open Nov. 12 and 13,233 fans watch the Chicago Black Hawks beat the Leafs 2-1. The arena is built in fewer than six months for $1.5 million. Smythe finds creative ways finish the job, using Leaf players as security guards at the job site and convincing union workers to take 20 percent of their pay in Gardens stock.

2 Senators and Quakers bow out
For the first time since 1918-19, the NHL has fewer teams than the previous season. The Philadelphia Quakers and Ottawa Senators announce Sept. 26 they will discontinue operations. Philadelphia lost more than $100,000 in 1930-31, while the Senators, who will return in 1932-33, dropped more than $50,000.

3 NHL cool to icing rule proposal
After the New York Americans ice the puck 61 times during a 3-2 win Dec. 8 at Boston, Bruins owner Charles Adams demands the NHL introduce a rule calling for a faceoff in the defending team's zone when it elects to shoot the puck the length of the ice to relieve pressure. When his pleas fall on deaf ears, Boston makes a mockery of its next game against the Americans, icing the puck 87 times in a 0-0 tie Jan. 3 at New York. Despite these tactics, the icing rule will not be adopted until 1937-38.

WING AND A PRAYER

Cup Winner
New York Rangers

Leading Scorers
1. Bill Cook, NYR, 50 points
2. Busher Jackson, Tor, 44 pts
3. Baldy Northcott, Mar, 43 pts
4. Hooley Smith, Mar, 41 points
5. Paul Haynes, Mar, 41 points
6. Aurel Joliat, Mtl, 39 points
7. Marty Barry, Bos, 37 points
8. Bun Cook, NYR, 37 points
9. Nels Stewart, Bos, 36 points
10. Howie Morenz, Mtl, 35 points

Franchise News
Ottawa rejoins league, making it nine teams. Detroit Falcons change name to Red Wings.

Nickname of the Year
Harvey 'Busher' Jackson

Worth Noting
Reg Noble, the last of the original NHLers, plays his final season, splitting the campaign between Detroit and the Montreal Maroons. Noble broke in with Toronto in 1917-18…Eddie Shore scores a career-high 35 points to become the second defenseman to win MVP. It's the first of four Hart Trophies he will earn. Only five other blueliners have ever won the award…Billy Coutu, who was expelled from the NHL in 1927 for attacking a referee, is reinstated, but never makes a return…The NHL begins to allow substitutes to serve penalties for goalies…The NHL requires a captain or alternate captain be on the ice at all times.

→ POSTER BOY
Many hockey historians call Howie Morenz the sport's first superstar. Supporting the theory: his face adorns the NHL Guide and Record Book for 1932-33.

Newsmakers & Top Headlines

1 Detroit drops Falcons for Red Wings
Things were bad in Detroit. The club had gone into receivership and was so hard up it once carved a spare goalie out of plywood because there were no funds to sign a human. They even changed names from Cougars to Falcons in 1930. But in September the team is sold to Chicago grain millionaire James Norris. Norris renames Detroit the Red Wings, feeling a winged wheel is a natural logo for a team representing the Motor City.

2 Doraty's goal ends playoff marathon
With Toronto and Boston scoreless after 100 minutes of overtime in the final game of their best-of-five semifinal April 3-4, drastic measures are considered. Maple Leafs GM Conn Smythe and Bruins GM Art

Ross suggest resuming the game the next day, but are rejected by NHL president Frank Calder. So are suggestions to remove both goalies or flip a coin. Early in the sixth overtime period, Toronto's Ken Doraty beats Boston goalie Tiny Thompson, ending what was then the NHL's longest game at 1:50 a.m., after 104:46 of overtime. Three years later, the record will be broken in a game between Detroit and the Montreal Maroons.

3 Future referee-in-chief wins first rookie award
Detroit forward Carl Voss wins the first rookie award, which is renamed the Calder Trophy in 1936-37. It's a rare achievement for Voss, who plays for eight teams in eight seasons (but gains Hall of Fame status as an official after serving as NHL referee-in-chief).

EARLY CONCUSSION VICTIM SENT TO ASYLUM

BY BOB DUFF

I t seemed such an innocuous play at first, it wasn't even treated.

When the Detroit Red Wings eliminated the Montreal Maroons from the playoffs with a 3-2 victory March 28, 1933 at Olympia Stadium, it was reported defenseman Johnny Gallagher netted the game-winning goal.

What wasn't noted in any of the game reports was Gallagher had struck his head when he tumbled into the boards, nor was he ever checked out by team medical personal for any sort of head injury.

In fact, he continued to play into the next round against the Rangers. A couple of weeks after the Wings were eliminated from the playoffs, Gallagher drove from Windsor to Toronto to watch the opening game of the Cup final between the Rangers and Maple Leafs. While in his room at Toronto's Royal York Hotel, Gallagher appeared to have suffered from post-concussion syndrome, leading to his incarceration in a psychiatric hospital.

"Johnny Gallagher critically ill," screamed the headline in the April 10, 1933 edition of the Montreal *Gazette*.

"Suffering from loss of memory, the result of injuries received several weeks ago in an NHL game, Gallagher was taken to Whitby (Ontario) Hospital Sunday afternoon for observation," reported the Border Cities *Star*.

The description of Gallagher's condition and the behavior he displayed mirrored the symptoms of post-concussion syndrome, which include headache, dizziness, fatigue, irritability, anxiety, insomnia and loss of concentration and memory. Extreme cases can include irrational acts, changes in mood and a suspicious, argumentative and stubborn nature.

"Gallagher seemed to be suffering from mental disorders Saturday night and Sunday," The *Star* reported. "He recognized friends readily and conversed with members of the Leafs and Rangers team at the hotel, but frequently lapsed into incoherent conversation.

"Twice he wandered from his room. Unobserved by friends, he left the hotel and returned minus his top coat and wrist watch. Apparently, he had given them away to persons he had encountered on the street."

Things grew even more bizarre once the decision was made to transport Gallagher to the psychiatric ward for further tests.

"He was placed in charge of a nurse and started out by automobile (for Whitby), but while on the way he jumped from the speeding car and then caught (onto) another travelling in the opposite direction while it was going 40 miles an hour," reported the *Gazette*.

Police were called in to locate Gallagher and found him a short while later. Gallagher was eventually transferred to the psychiatric ward in Penetanguishene, Ont., where more difficult cases of mental illness were treated. His absence was described in newspaper reports as a nervous breakdown caused by the strain and stress of the season and head injuries.

Gallagher arrived at training camp with the Wings in the fall of 1933, but after a few sessions, it became clear that all

↑ JACK DOESN'T KNOW
Wings coach-GM Jack Adams believes Johnny Gallagher will return to his lineup in a month and a half or less after brain surgery. He is very wrong.

was not well. Complaining of severe head pain, Gallagher discontinued workouts and X-rays revealed pressure on the brain. He underwent what was described as "a major brain operation" Oct. 30, 1933 at Detroit's Harper Hospital, performed by noted neurosurgeon Dr. Frederic Schreiber, who cut an opening through Gallagher's skull to relieve the pressure on his brain.

Border Cities *Star* sports columnist Vern DeGeer visited Gallagher in hospital a few days after his surgery and noticed a complete turnaround in Gallagher's personality. "Johnny was more like his genial self than he had been at any time since last spring," DeGeer wrote.

"Johnny should be back with us within five or six weeks at the latest," Detroit coach-GM Jack Adams boasted, but Gallagher's troubles were far from over. He sat out the 1933-34 season recuperating from surgery. When he sought to return to Detroit for the following campaign, even though a board of 12 medical examiners gave him a clean bill of health, Gallagher was informed by U.S. Immigration authorities that due to his stay in a psychiatric hospital, he would not be permitted to enter the country for a year.

In fall 1935, Gallagher appeared before a board of U.S. Immigration medical examiners and officials and was cleared to enter the country. He spent the 1935-36 campaign with Detroit's farm club, the Detroit Olympics, then was traded to the New York Americans prior to 1936-37. But the Wings reacquired him when they sustained a rash of injuries along the blueline and he helped them win the Stanley Cup that spring.

His playing days ended in 1939 and he returned to live in his birthplace of Kenora, Ont., where he died Sept. 16, 1981 at 72.

(Editor's Note: Author Susan Swan wrote a fiction novel (*The Western Light*) based on two Penetanguishene facility patients, including Gallagher. Swan had first-hand knowledge of both cases, as her father was a physician at the psychiatric ward. "It bothers me that there was such little understanding of what hockey players suffered in those days," Swan said. "I found numerous stories of men being treated badly, being forced to play with broken ankles, that sort of thing. It was like reading stories about gladiators and their mistreatment in Roman times.") THN

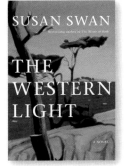

>1933-34

TRAGEDY HITS NHL

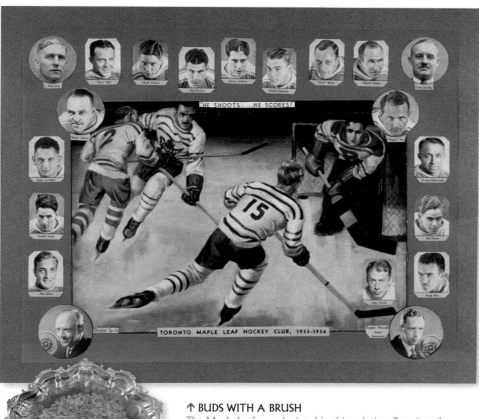

HE SHOOTS.... HE SCORES!

TORONTO MAPLE LEAF HOCKEY CLUB, 1933-1934

↑ BUDS WITH A BRUSH
The Maple Leafs are depicted in this painting. Prominently featured: Ken Doraty, No. 15, a strong playoff performer.

← GREATNESS ON A PLATE
Aurel Joliat, the Montreal Canadiens' top scorer in 1933-34, is honored with the British Consols Cigarette Trophy, a plate commemorating his efforts.

Newsmakers & Top Headlines

1 Gardiner tragedy follows triumph
Two-time Vezina Trophy winner Chuck Gardiner guides the Black Hawks to the Stanley Cup, but makes the ultimate sacrifice in the process. The four-time all-star ignores a painful tonsil infection in the spring of 1934 and it spreads through his body while he was leading Chicago to triumph. A few days after the Stanley Cup victory, Gardiner collapses and falls into coma. He dies at 29 from a brain hemorrhage, originating from the infection.

2 Bailey nearly killed in Shore attack
Boston and Toronto always have heated battles, but none can match the frightening Dec. 12 contest at Boston Garden. In the first period, Leaf King Clancy dumps Bruin Eddie Shore and heads up ice with the puck. Ace Bailey drops back to cover Clancy's defense spot while Shore, regaining his feet, mistakes Bailey for Clancy and rams him from behind. Bailey's head hits the ice. Rushed to a hospital, Bailey is listed in critical condition. His death notice is mistakenly printed in the next morning's Boston papers. Bailey recovers, but never plays again. Shore is suspended 16 games.

3 Benefit game staves off Bailey lawsuit
While Bailey considers suing Shore over his career-ending injury, the NHL offers a solution — a benefit game between the Leafs and a group of NHL all-stars Feb. 14, with proceeds going to Bailey, who shakes hands with Shore. Played in Toronto, the game raises $20,900.

FACTS & STATS
from 1933-34

Cup Winner
Chicago Black Hawks

Leading Scorers
1. Charlie Conacher, Tor 52 pts
2. Joe Primeau, Tor, 46 points
3. Frank Boucher, NYR, 44 pts
4. Marty Barry, Bos, 39 points
5. Cecil Dillon, NYR, 39 points
6. Nels Stewart, Bos, 38 points
7. Busher Jackson, Tor, 38 pts
8. Aurel Joliat, Mtl, 37 points
9. Hooley Smith, Mar, 37 points
10. Paul Thompson, Chi, 36 pts

Nickname of the Year
Frank 'The Shawville Express' Finnigan

Worth Noting
Chuck Gardiner isn't the only member of the Black Hawks to die following the season. Rookie forward Jack Leswick drowns Aug. 7...Toronto GM Conn Smythe trades 32-year-old goalie Lorne Chabot to Montreal for 38-year-old stopper George Hainsworth because Chabot threatened to quit unless he got a raise the previous season. Smythe gave him the raise, but vowed to trade him...Maple Leaf Gardens is decorated in green and orange and filled with Irish music as the Leafs salute King Clancy on St. Patrick's Day. The Irishman reveals a green jersey with a shamrock instead of a maple leaf and wears it during the first period...The New York Americans introduce new sweaters. The home uniforms use the word 'Americans' across the front with white stars over a blue area.

FACTS & STATS
from 1934-35

Cup Winner
Montreal Maroons

Leading Scorers
1. Charlie Conacher, Tor, 57 pts
2. Syd Howe, StL/Det, 47 pts
3. Larry Aurie, Det, 46 points
4. Frank Boucher, NYR, 45 pts
5. Busher Jackson, Tor, 44 pts
6. Herbie Lewis, Det, 43 points
7. Art Chapman, NYA, 43 points
8. Marty Barry, Bos, 40 points
9. S. Schriner, NYA, 40 points
10. Nels Stewart, Bos, 39 points

Rule Changes
A penalty shot is awarded when a player is tripped and thus prevented from having a clear shot on goal, having no player to pass to other than the offending player. The shot is taken from inside a 10-foot circle located 38 feet from the goal. The goalie must not advance more than one foot from his goal line when the shot is taken.

Significant Records
Most goals, one period: Busher Jackson, Toronto (4).

Nickname of the Year
Nels 'Old Poison' Stewart

Worth Noting
Long before Wayne Gretzky immortalizes No. 99, Joe Lamb, Deese Roche and Leo Bourgault all wear it at different times for Montreal during the season…Maple Leaf winger Charlie Conacher defends his NHL scoring title with 57 points and a career-high 36 goals. He also plays three minutes of shutout goaltending March 16 when George Hainsworth leaves to get a cut over his eye stitched. Boston's Eddie Shore becomes the first defenseman to win more than one Hart Trophy…Lorne Chabot wins his lone Vezina Trophy before an injury prevents him from playing another full season.

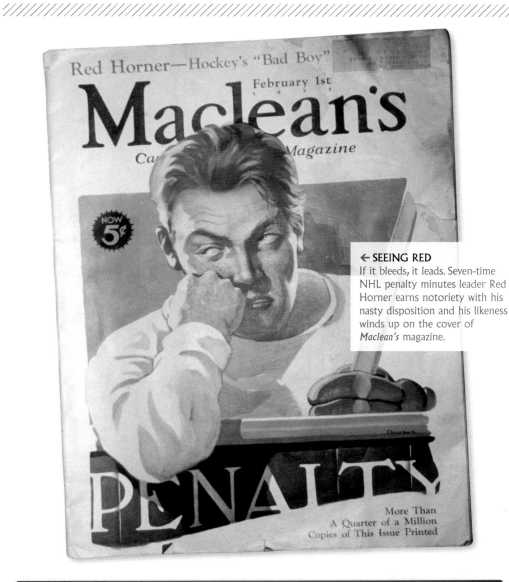

← SEEING RED
If it bleeds, it leads. Seven-time NHL penalty minutes leader Red Horner earns notoriety with his nasty disposition and his likeness winds up on the cover of *Maclean's* magazine.

Newsmakers & Top Headlines

1 Morenz among big names dealt
A hard salary cap of $62,500 per team and $7,000 per player forces NHL clubs to make difficult decisions about veterans. Goalie Lorne Chabot goes from the Canadiens to the Black Hawks, while defenseman Lionel Conacher and goalie Alex Connell wind up with the Maroons. But the most shocking move comes when the Habs ship legendary Howie Morenz to Chicago. The NHL's career scoring leader with 392 points, 'The Stratford Streak' had won two scoring titles, three Hart Trophies and three Stanley Cups with the Habs, but had finished out of the top 10 scorers since 1932-33.

2 Sens leave Ottawa and land in St. Louis as Eagles
Following three last-place finishes and a one-year hiatus, the struggling Ottawa Senators – winners of four Stanley Cups – move to St. Louis, where the team is renamed the Eagles. Two years earlier, the NHL turned down a request for an expansion franchise from the Missouri city because of the extensive travel. The team's fortunes don't improve as the Eagles finish last at 11-31-6 and fold following the season.

3 Goalies prevail in first year of penalty shot
The keepers are the victors under the new rule, stopping 25 of 29 shots. The first penalty shot takes place Nov. 10, 1934, by the Canadiens' Armand Mondou. He's stoned by the Maple Leafs' George Hainsworth. The first successful attempt comes three days later, off the stick of St. Louis Eagles D-man Ralph Bowman.

FACTS & STATS
from 1935-36

Cup Winner
Detroit Red Wings

Leading Scorers
1. S. Schriner, NYA, 45 points
2. Marty Barry, Det, 40 points
3. Paul Thompson, Chi, 40 pts
4. Bill Thoms, Tor, 38 points
5. Charlie Conacher, Tor, 38 points
6. Hooley Smith, Mar, 38 points
7. Doc Romnes, Chi, 38 points
8. Art Chapman, NYA, 38 points
9. Herbie Lewis, Det, 37 points
10. Baldy Northcott, Mar, 36 pts

Franchise News
St. Louis Eagles terminated, leaving eight teams in NHL.

Nickname of the Year
Cecil 'Tiny' Thompson

Worth Noting
Four players are part of hockey's two longest games – Lorne Chabot ('33 Leafs, '36 Maroons), Bob Gracie ('33 Leafs, '36 Maroons), Marty Barry ('33 Bruins, '36 Wings) and Joe Lamb ('33 Bruins, '36 Maroons)…A chance meeting between Wings coach-GM Jack Adams and Bruins coach Frank Patrick at the 1935 final leads to a deal sending Cooney Weiland to Boston for center Marty Barry. Adams puts Barry between **Larry Aurie** and Herbie Lewis on hockey's best line for two years. The trio leads Detroit to its first Cup…Boston's Eddie Shore is assessed a misconduct after banking a shot off the back of referee Odie Cleghorn in a playoff game.

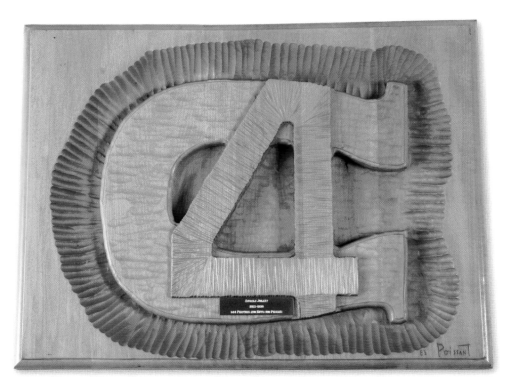

↑ CARVING OUT A ROLE
Aurel Joliat, a.k.a. 'The Mighty Atom,' is one of Montreal's first true stars and his four Stanley Cup victories are represented in this wood carving.

← TIP OF THE CAP
Just because helmets don't exist yet doesn't mean players wear nothing on their heads. Joliat regularly dons this trademark black cap during games.

Newsmakers & Top Headlines

1 Bruneteau ends longest playoff game
His name is Mud; his legend eternal. In his first Stanley Cup game, Red Wings rookie Modere 'Mud' Bruneteau beats Maroons goalie Lorne Chabot with the only goal after 176:30 of playing time, ending the longest game in Cup history March 24-25. It breaks the mark set by the Bruins and Maple Leafs in the 1932-33 playoffs by 11 minutes and 14 seconds. Detroit goalie Normie Smith, also in his first Cup game, blocks 89 shots and doesn't let in a goal for an NHL-record 248:32 until Game 3 as Detroit wins its first title.

2 Canadiens owners tempted by Cleveland
The Cleveland Canadiens? It nearly happens. With the Depression hampering attendance at NHL games in Montreal, Canadiens owners Leo Dandurand and Joe Cattarinich, who lost $40,000 the previous season, consider selling the team to parties that would relocate it to Cleveland. Montreal entrepreneurs Ernie Savard, Maurice Forget and Louis Gelinas save the day, purchasing the team Sept. 17 for $165,000.

3 NHL takes over Americans and doomed Eagles
Faced with a financial crisis, the NHL purchases the Eagles and Americans Sept. 28. President Frank Calder announces the league will operate the Amerks and names Red Dutton GM. The Eagles request a leave of absence, but the NHL folds the franchise, selling the players to the other clubs. The biggest catch is future scoring champ Bill Cowley, who goes to Boston.

1936-37 ‹

FACTS & STATS
from 1936-37

Cup Winner
Detroit Red Wings

Leading Scorers
1. S. Schriner, NYA, 46 points
2. Syl Apps, Tor, 45 points
3. Marty Barry, Det, 44 points
4. Larry Aurie, Det, 43 points
5. Busher Jackson, Tor, 40 pts
6. Johnny Gagnon, Mtl, 36 pts
7. Bob Gracie, Mar, 36 points
8. N. Stewart, Bos/NYA, 35 pts
9. Paul Thompson, Chi, 35 pts
10. Bill Cowley, Bos, 35 points

Nickname of the Year
Herbie 'The Duke of Duluth' Lewis

Worth Noting
Montreal Maroons forward Russ Blinco becomes the first NHL player to appear in a game wearing glasses...Ebbie Goodfellow, who finished second in NHL scoring in 1930-31, switches to defense after Detroit acquires Marty Barry. The move pays off as the transition helps the Red Wings to back-to-back Stanley Cups. Goodfellow earns second team all-star status on defense in 1935-36 and first-team status in 1936-37...Frank Calder purchases a trophy for the top rookie in the NHL; **Syl Apps** wins the award...Carl Voss joins the Maroons, but he comes down with influenza and cannot replace former captain Hooley Smith, who is sent to Boston. Bob Gracie steps up to fill the void... Hal Winkler of the Rangers is the first goaltender to have a shutout in his NHL debut.

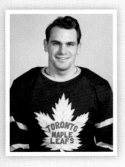

← HOWIE'S LAST STAND
Howie Morenz's final steps around a Montreal hospital are taken with the support of these crutches when he was bodychecked and broke his leg during a game.

Newsmakers & Top Headlines

1 Morenz's death stuns hockey world
Picked up by the Canadiens and reunited with old linemates Aurel Joliat and Johnny Gagnon, Howie Morenz finds new life in his 34-year-old legs. But his return is halted Jan. 28 at the Montreal Forum after he suffers four broken bones in his left leg and ankle when slammed into the boards by Chicago's Earl Seibert. Morenz suffers a nervous breakdown while in hospital, then dies of a pulmonary embolism March 8. Thousands file past Morenz's body, which lays in state at center ice of the Forum, and up to 200,000 line the streets of Montreal to watch the funeral procession.

2 'Kraut Line' leads new wave of future stars
Veteran stars King Clancy, Joe Primeau, Roy Worters, Alex Connell, George Hainsworth and Lorne Chabot all hang up their blades before, during or after the campaign. Offsetting the losses is an outstanding crop of rookies that includes Toronto's Turk Broda, Syl Apps and Gordie Drillon and Boston's 'Kraut Line' of Milt Schmidt, Woody Dumart and Bobby Bauer.

3 Chicago's all-American experiment fizzles
Bent on icing an all-American team, Chicago owner Major Frederic McLaughlin instructs coach Clem Loughlin to experiment with a lineup including nine U.S.-born players for the Black Hawks' final five league games. "I intend to throw off the traditional Canadian influence over this game," McLaughlin says. Chicago wins only one of its last five games.

FACTS & STATS
from 1937-38

Cup Winner
Chicago Black Hawks

Leading Scorers
1. Gordie Drillon, Tor, 52 points
2. Syl Apps, Tor, 50 points
3. Paul Thompson, Chi, 44 pts
4. Georges Mantha, Mtl, 42 pts
5. Cecil Dillon, NYR, 39 points
6. Bill Cowley, Bos, 39 points
7. S. Schriner, NYA, 38 points
8. Bill Thoms, Tor, 38 points
9. Clint Smith, NYR, 37 points
10. Nels Stewart, NYA, 36 points

Rule Changes
Icing rule passed, whereby teams can no longer shoot the puck the length of the ice to delay game, except during penalties.

Nickname of the Year
Larry 'Little Dempsey' Aurie

Worth Noting
A total of $20,000 is raised for the family of deceased Canadiens center Howie Morenz Nov. 2, as the NHL all-stars edge a combined Habs-Maroons squad 6-5 at the Montreal Forum…Bill Stewart, a Major League Baseball umpire, impresses Black Hawks owner Major Frederic McLaughlin with his authority and is hired to coach Chicago. He stands up for his club by getting into a punch-up with Toronto player 'Baldy' Cotton and GM Conn Smythe before Game 1 of the final. His squad wins the Cup, but he's fired 21 games into the next season…NHL takes control of the New York Americans after Bill Dwyer is unable to come up with the required capital.… Gordie Drillon's 52 points make him the last Toronto Maple Leaf to win an NHL scoring title. The drought now spans 75 years… Drillon's teammate, Syl Apps, leads the league in assists a second straight season…Four-time Cup-winner and career Montreal Canadien Aurel Joliat plays his final NHL campaign at 36.

→ **WHAT'S OLD IS NEW**
Montreal Canadiens coach Cecil Hart sports this snazzy cardigan during his nine seasons with the team. Little does he know his duds will be back in style by 2012.

Newsmakers & Top Headlines

1 Hawks scramble for goalie in final
Minor-league netminder Alfie Moore suits up and backstops Chicago to a 3-1 win over Toronto after Black Hawks goalie Mike Karakas is unable to play with a broken toe. Moore is paid $300 for the only playoff victory of his NHL career. It's a brief grasp of glory, as NHL president Frank Calder rules Moore ineligible for the remainder of the series since he's not under contract to Chicago. Karakas returns later in the series to lead the Hawks to the Cup.

2 'Old Poison' first to score 300 goals
At 36, Nels Stewart shows no signs of slowing down. The man who shared the NHL lead with 23 goals in 1936-37 follows up with 19 for the New York Americans. 'Old Poison,' so-called because of the way he stings the opposition, beats Rangers goaltender Dave Kerr March 17 to become the first NHL player to reach the 300-goal plateau. Stewart retires in 1940 with 324 career goals, a mark not surpassed until 1952 by Maurice Richard.

3 Red Wings go from best to worst
The two-time defending-champion Red Wings drop to the basement of the American Division and miss the playoffs, winning just 12 games. The Wings had finished last in 1934-35, then first overall in both of their Stanley Cup seasons. No other team in history has missed the playoffs, won consecutive Stanley Cups, then missed the playoffs again.

FACTS & STATS
from 1938-39

Cup Winner
Boston Bruins

Leading Scorers
1. Toe Blake, Mtl, 47 points
2. S. Schriner, NYA, 44 points
3. Bill Cowley, Bos, 42 points
4. Clint Smith, NYR, 41 points
5. Marty Barry, Det, 41 points
6. Syl Apps, Tor, 40 points
7. Tom Anderson, NYA, 40 pts
8. Johnny Gottselig, Chi, 39 pts
9. Paul Haynes, Mtl, 38 points
10. Roy Conacher, Bos, 37 pts

Rule Changes
One referee and one linesman replace the two-referee system.

Franchise News
Montreal Maroons withdraw from league, leaving seven teams.

Nickname of the Year
Eddie 'The Edmonton Express' Shore

Worth Noting
Rangers Muzz Patrick and Art Coulter become the first known bearded players, cashing in on a $500 bet with coach Lester Patrick. Beards later become an NHL tradition during the playoffs…Bruins rookie Frank Brimsek posts six shutouts in his first eight starts after replacing Tiny Thompson, who is dealt to Detroit. He wins the Calder and Vezina Trophies, is a first-team all-star and helps the Bruins to the Stanley Cup, four simultaneous single-season feats never matched. The nickname 'Mr. Zero' soon follows. Says Rangers coach Lester Patrick of Brimsek: "Trying to get him to make the first move is like pushing over the Washington Monument…Montreal's Toe Blake goes on to a Hall of Fame career, but wins his only scoring crown and Hart Trophy in '38-39…Eventual Hall member Sid Abel debuts with one goal in 15 games for the Red Wings.

↑ LEATHER AND LACE
Boston's Woody Dumart prefers skates that have pronounced heel and ankle guards built in to the boot. What Woody wants, Woody gets.

Newsmakers & Top Headlines

1 'Sudden Death' Hill strikes three times
A 10-goal scorer during the regular season, Boston's Mel Hill explodes for six in 12 playoff games. He scores a record three overtime goals in a seven-game semifinal win over the Rangers. Two of them come in triple OT, including the Game 7-winner on a pass from teammate Bill Cowley. Hill never scores another overtime goal, but will forever be remembered as 'Sudden Death' Hill.

2 League bids farewell to Montreal Maroons
Stanley Cup champions just three seasons earlier, the Maroons posted an NHL-worst 12-30-6 mark in 1937-38. In the summer of 1938, citing financial hardships, the Maroons take a leave of absence from the league, but they will never return. Maroons' players are divvied up among the seven remaining teams and the two-division format is dropped. Six of the seven clubs qualify for the post-season.

3 Blake scoring champ, Hart winner for dismal Habs
The Canadiens barely get their foot in the door of the Stanley Cup playoffs, thanks mainly to their big Toe. Despite the Habs finishing sixth with a record of 15-24-9, left winger Toe Blake leads the NHL in scoring with 47 points and is presented with the Hart Trophy as league MVP in his third season. It's the fourth Hart/scoring title double in NHL history. All have been turned by Montreal players — the Canadiens' Howie Morenz (1927-28, 1930-31), the Maroons' Nels Stewart (1925-26) and Blake.

FACTS & STATS
from 1939-40

Cup Winner
New York Rangers

Leading Scorers
1. Milt Schmidt, Bos, 52 points
2. Woody Dumart, Bos, 43 pts
3. Bobby Bauer, Bos, 43 points
4. Gordie Drillon, Tor, 40 points
5. Bill Cowley, Bos, 40 points
6. Bryan Hextall, NYR, 39 points
7. Neil Colville, NYR, 38 points
8. Syd Howe, Det, 37 points
9. Toe Blake, Mtl, 36 points
10. M. Armstrong, NYA, 36 pts

Nickname of the Year
Johnny 'Black Cat' Gagnon

Worth Noting
A 6-2 win by the Rangers over the Canadiens Feb. 25 at Madison Square Garden is also seen by viewers of New York television station WZXBS, making it the first NHL game to be televised...**Milt Schmidt**, center of Boston's famed 'Kraut Line' tops the NHL in assists (30) and points (52), with linemates Woody Dumart and Bobby Bauer (43 points apiece) right behind him. It's the first time linemates rank 1-2-3 in NHL scoring and one of only four times in history... The Rangers play 19 consecutive games without a loss and win their third Stanley Cup in the existence of the franchise. It would be another 54 years before their fourth...The Americans trade star winger Sweeney Schriner to Toronto for Busher Jackson, Buzz Boll, Murray Armstrong, Doc Romnes and minor-leaguer Jimmy Fowler.

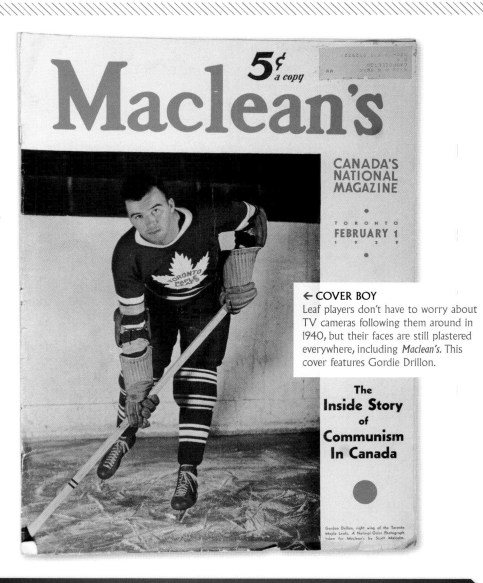

← COVER BOY
Leaf players don't have to worry about TV cameras following them around in 1940, but their faces are still plastered everywhere, including *Maclean's*. This cover features Gordie Drillon.

Newsmakers & Top Headlines

1 Bruins trade Shore to New York Americans
Four-time Hart Trophy-winner Eddie Shore and Bruins GM Art Ross are at odds at the start of the season when Shore, 37, purchases the Springfield Indians of the International-American League and asks to play for that club. Shore and Ross agree that he will play all of Boston's home and playoff games, but Ross decides, instead, to trade Shore to the Americans Jan. 25 for forward Eddie Wiseman and $5,000. The Americans agree to allow Shore to play for both teams, but he retires from the NHL at the end of the season.

2 Habs suffer through humiliating season
The season starts tragically when Babe Siebert, the Montreal Canadiens' new coach, drowns Aug. 25 before coaching a game. Under replacement Pit Lepine, the Habs finish last and equal club futility marks for fewest wins (10) and home wins (five), endure club-record seven-game losing and 15-game winless skids at the Forum and record their lowest-ever winning percentage (.260).

3 American clubs dominate individual awards
Players from American-based clubs clean up the league's individual awards. Boston's Milt Schmidt wins the scoring title, while teammate Bobby Bauer earns the Lady Byng. Ebbie Goodfellow of the Detroit Red Wings wins the Hart, Dave Kerr of the New York Rangers the Vezina and teammate Kilby MacDonald the Calder. The Maple Leafs' Red Horner leads the NHL in penalty minutes for the seventh time in eight years.

1940-41 ‹

FACTS & STATS
from 1940-41

Cup Winner
Boston Bruins

Leading Scorers
1. Bill Cowley, Bos, 62 points
2. Bryan Hextall, NYR, 44 points
3. Gordie Drillon, Tor, 44 points
4. Syl Apps, Tor, 44 points
5. Lynn Patrick, NYR, 44 points
6. Syd Howe, Det, 44 points
7. Neil Colville, NYR, 42 points
8. Eddie Wiseman, Bos, 40 pts
9. Bobby Bauer, Bos, 39 points
10. S. Schriner, Tor, 38 points

Rule Changes
Flooding the ice surface between periods is made mandatory.

Nickname of the Year
Mel 'Sudden Death' Hill

Worth Noting
Bill Cowley, a center for Boston, earns a record 45 assists – shattering Joe Primeau's mark by eight – to become the first player with more assists in a season than any other player has points. Cowley wins the scoring title by 18 with 62 points and takes the Hart Trophy…The Montreal Canadiens are in financial trouble until Frank Patrick steps in as an investor and governor. Tommy Gorman is hired as GM…Johnny Quilty wins the Calder Trophy, a prediction coach Dick Irvin made before the season via delivery of a sealed envelope to a reporter… Boston's **Bobby Bauer** repeats as Lady Byng Trophy winner. He again plays all 48 games, taking just one minor penalty.

↑ **BENTLEY WEARS THE PANTS**
Max Bentley's pants have seen better days, but he takes charge with seven goals as a rookie in 1940-41.

← **APPLAUDING 200**
This stick helps Dit Clapper pot goal No. 200. He chips in another 28 before his long career with Boston ends.

Newsmakers & Top Headlines

1 Streaking Bruins win Stanley Cup
Boston is almost unstoppable en route to its fourth straight first-place finish and third Stanley Cup. The team has an NHL-record 23-game unbeaten streak (15-0-8) which lasts two months. The Bruins also go 15 games at home without losing and have their astonishing 49-game unbeaten streak (13-0-36) in regular season overtime halted by a 3-2 loss at Chicago Dec. 8 – a streak that dates back six years to Dec. 13, 1934. The Bruins don't win the Cup again for another 29 seasons until 1970.

2 Habs grab Irvin from Leafs to take over at helm
The Canadiens scoop up veteran coach Dick Irvin, who re-signs in Toronto. Irvin has guided eight teams to the Stanley Cup final in the past decade. Although Montreal's 16-26-6 record in Irvin's first season gives no indication of things to come, he will turn a dormant Canadiens' franchise into a league powerhouse. Montreal reaches the final eight times with Irvin as coach, winning three Cups.

3 LoPresti pelted with 83 shots
Chicago Black Hawks' goalie Sam LoPresti is the target in a Boston Garden shooting gallery, facing 83 shots in a 3-2 loss March 4. LoPresti blocks 42 over the first 25 minutes before Roy Conacher scores. Milt Schmidt connects on the 59th shot and Eddie Wiseman beats LoPresti for the winner with 2:31 left. LoPresti's 80 saves are a record.

>1941-42

WAR IS UPON US

→ **AMERICAN BEAUTY**
Wearing this New York Americans cardigan, loaded with stars, stripes, red, white and blue, leaves no question of which team you support.

Cup Winner
Toronto Maple Leafs

Leading Scorers
1. Bryan Hextall, NYR, 56 points
2. Lynn Patrick, NYR, 54 points
3. Don Grosso, Det, 53 points
4. Phil Watson, NYR, 52 points
5. Sid Abel, Det, 49 points
6. Toe Blake, Mtl, 45 points
7. Bill Thoms, Chi, 45 points
8. Gordie Drillon, Tor, 41 points
9. Syl Apps, Tor, 41 points
10. Tom Anderson, Brk, 41 pts

Franchise News
New York Americans change name to Brooklyn Americans.

Nickname of the Year
Aubrey 'Dit' Clapper

Worth Noting
It's speculated (incorrectly) American teams will play in Canada in 1942-43 due to passport issues. Among the supposed changes in venue: Chicago to Montreal, the Rangers to Toronto, the Americans to Ottawa, and Boston to Hamilton, Ont...Many players answer a higher calling during the Second World War. Some are among the millions who lose their lives, including Joe Turner, Red Tilson and Red Garrett. The International League names its championship trophy in memory of Turner, an amateur goalie who plays one NHL game with Detroit. The Ontario League names its MVP award after Tilson, a junior star and Toronto prospect. The American League names its rookie award after Garrett, who plays 23 games with the New York Rangers in 1942-43...Errant pucks shot into the crowd at games have to be returned because of a WWII rubber shortage...Toronto center Billy Taylor, after the Leafs trail 3-0 in the final against the Detroit Red Wings, predicts: "Don't worry about us. We'll take them four straight."

Newsmakers & Top Headlines

1 Hockey stars join war effort
The Dec. 9, 1941 game at Boston Garden between the Bruins and Black Hawks is delayed as 10,000 fans listen to U.S. President Franklin Delano Roosevelt's declaration of war following the Dec. 7 attack on Pearl Harbor. Toronto GM Conn Smythe enlists and urges all of his players to do likewise. Boston's entire 'Kraut Line' of Milt Schmidt, Woody Dumart and Bobby Bauer joins the Royal Canadian Air Force.

2 Leafs stage amazing comeback
It's a comeback for the ages. Toronto is down 3-0 to Detroit in the Stanley Cup final. Maple Leafs' coach Hap Day benches veterans Gordie Drillon and Bucko McDonald in favor of youngsters Don Metz and Ernie Dickens.

Before Game 4, Day reads a letter from a 14-year-old girl who believes they will come back. At this time, no team has ever rallied from such a deficit. Day's new line of Syl Apps between the Metz brothers, Nick and Don, nets the game-winner in three straight Toronto victories to tie the series. A Canadian-record crowd of 16,128 packs Maple Leaf Gardens for Game 7 as Toronto wins 3-1 to capture the Cup.

3 Rangers finish first for last time in 50 years
The 29-17-2 Rangers finish atop the standings for the first time in franchise history, heights they won't reach again for 50 years. The Rangers are led by scoring champion Bryan Hextall (56 points.) No Ranger since has won the Art Ross Trophy.

↑ KID STUFF
'The Kid Line' (Charlie Conacher, Joe Primeau, and Busher Jackson) in their prime and again as oldtimers in 1953.

— 1942-1967 —

THE ORIGINAL SIX

THE START OF THE MODERN ERA LACKED GLAMOUR, BUT SPAWNED ENDURING RIVALRIES, PASSIONATE FANS AND SOME OF THE GAME'S GREAT LEGENDS

Imagine being able to see three absolutely thrilling hockey games — one being an NHL tilt — starting at 1:30 p.m. in the afternoon and finishing at 10:00 p.m. at night. And all this for a buck-and-a-quarter at the world's most famous arena, Madison Square Garden in New York.

Our hockey day was launched at noon when we got in line to see an afternoon double-header: first a Met League game, followed by an Eastern Amateur League match that featured the Rangers farm team, the New York Rovers. It cost nothing to watch because we got Police Athletic League freebies every week. For another half-dollar, Buitoni's, five blocks south of the Garden — at that time situated on Eighth Avenue between 49th and 50th Streets — served spaghetti and meatballs.

By then we were ready for the big one, which meant the Rangers against Chicago, Boston, Detroit, Toronto or Montreal in a hockey world that would seem weird to our contemporary puck-followers. At MSG, the ice was brown — no white-tinting then — because the arena floor underneath the surface happened to be brown. Protective glass was unheard of, which meant the only sanctuary from flying pucks was chicken wire that hung over both end boards.

There was absolutely no protection on either side along the end boards and that meant two things: (a) fans had to focus and be prepared to duck when pucks or players — or both — came hurtling over the wooden dashers; and (b) home loyalists such as interior designer Sally Lark, who sat next to the penalty box at all games, could stick a long hat pin into the derriere of enemy skaters. One victim was 'Wild Bill' Ezinicki of the Toronto Maple Leafs who, remarkably, didn't take the bayonetting personally.

This was the 1942-43 season — the first with the 'Original Six' — with 'Johnny Canuck' and 'Uncle Sam' well immersed in a Second

World War that looked like the Allies might even lose. Then again, that's what was said about the NHL. There was talk that league president Frank Calder might have to shut down his six-team league for the duration of the war for two reasons: it would seem patriotic to do so and because so many stickhandlers had joined the Canadian and American armed forces that rosters were decimated beyond all reason. Even Maple Leafs boss Conn 'The Little Major' Smythe went off to war — as he did in the First World War — organizing a "Sportsman's Battalion" that included athletes and media types from Toronto.

Having lost such stars as the Patrick Brothers, Muzz and Lynn, not to mention the Colvilles, Mac and Neil, to war efforts, the first-place Rangers' roster was so ravaged that when training camp opened in Winnipeg in the fall of 1942, GM Lester Patrick had a grand total of no goalies. So desperate was Patrick that he signed Steve Buzinski of the Swift Current Intermediate team whose day job was at the Saskatchewan town's agricultural station. That was bad enough, but Buzinski was, according to coach Frank Boucher, the most bowlegged fellow he had ever seen. "When his pads were on they looked like cowboy chaps," Boucher — once my boss in 1954-55 — told me. Thus, Buzinski not only had a five-hole, he added a sixth hole.

Steve was so bad — he lasted nine games — he earned one of the best nicknames ever accorded an NHLer — 'Steve Buzinski The Puck Goes Inski.' In a sense, one of his successors was worse. On Jan. 23, 1944, Ken 'Tubby' McAuley stood, or fell, between the pipes for New York at Olympia Stadium in Detroit as the Red Wings blitzed the beleaguered Edmontonian 15-0. But that didn't stop Rangers radio play-by-play man Bert Lee late in the third period from uttering his deathless line whenever the Blueshirts were losing: "Time enough for one goal; time enough for 20!"

Historians insist with good reason that the quality of play during the war years hit an all-time low and the proof is in the retreads and peach-faced rookies who emerged. The Bruins, who had lost all three members of the Kraut Line — Milt Schmidt, Bobby Bauer and Woody Dumart — to the Royal Canadian Air Force, signed 16-year-old Armand 'Bep' Guidolin to a contact. Similarly, the Maple Leafs' 1941-42 Cup-winning goalie Walter 'Turk' Broda wound up in khaki and his replacement in 1944-45 unfortunately suffered from a severe case of ulcers. Hence the obvious nickname Frank 'Ulcers' McCool. (Despite his stomach problems, he did better than Buzinski or McAuley.) McCool delivered shutouts against Detroit in the first three games of the final and helped win the Cup in Game 7. Wisely, McCool soon retired to become sports editor of the Calgary *Albertan*.

The irony of ironies is that despite the subterranean level of play, fans loved every minute of it and capacity crowds were not unusual. Another beauty part was that service teams sprinkled with NHL stars frequently played. Best of them all was the one I saw at The Garden in 1942-43. Stationed at Curtis Bay Yard in Baltimore, the Coast Guard Cutters featured Hall of Famers Frankie 'Mr. Zero' Brimsek in goal and Art Coulter, captain of the 1940 Rangers Cup-winner, on defense, along with big-leaguers Johnny Mariucci and Alex Motter among others. Over their two seasons, the Cutters won the EAHL championship each time. Their affection for brawling earned them the nickname 'Hooligan's Navy,' but fans adored them partly because they brought a 30-piece band to every game. When the Cutters scored, the band swung into a chorus of 'Semper Peratus,' the Coast Guard marching song. To me, it was one of the most fun parts of the game.

At war's end, many previous stars found their skating legs were gone. Of the 1941-42 league-leading Rangers, Muzz Patrick and Mac Colville, who played 39 games in 1945-46 and 14 games in 1946-47, called it a career and Lynn Patrick should have done so as well. His father, Lester, still Rangers major domo, told Lynn he wasn't good enough to make the big club and wouldn't give him a contact. Amazingly, Lynn outfoxed 'The Silver Fox' by

↑ RULE OF THE TURK

Goaltender Turk Broda and the Toronto Maple Leafs became the first team to three-peat and the first modern-era dynasty in the late 1940s.

invoking the U.S. G.I. Bill of Rights. It stipulated every returning soldier had to be given the job he had before enlisting and the young Patrick deked his dad. Lynn played in 1945-46 and then packed in his skates.

Peacetime hockey was punctuated by something the league had not known before: a dynasty. Among the returning veterans that Conn Smythe welcomed to Maple Leaf Gardens were 1941-42 champs such as captain Syl Apps, goalie Broda, as well as useful aces Nick Metz up front and Wally Stanowski at the blueline. "With pappy guys and some good kids," promised Smythe, "we may surprise some people." But even 'The Little Major' was stunned. The Apps-Ezinicki-Harry Watson first line was matched by his 'Kid Line' of Vic Lynn, Howie Meeker and Ted 'Teeder' Kennedy.

In a major upset, coach Hap Day's Leafs topped Montreal in the 1946-47 final and went on to win again in 1947-48 and 1948-49. No other team ever had won three straight titles, but it was the middle club that Smythe dubbed, "The best team I ever had." No Toronto fan can challenge that remark because Smythe had produced hockey's biggest trade in November, 1947, by dealing one complete forward unit and two defenseman to Chicago for center Max Bentley and minor leaguer Cy Thomas. The Blackhawks got 'The Flying Forts' — Gus Bodnar, Gaye Stewart and Bud Poile on attack with Ernie Dickens and Bob Goldham on defense. Bentley spearheaded the Leafs to the 1948, 1949 and 1951 Cups while the Hawks remained on a treadmill to oblivion with their quintet.

By today's standards, players in The Original Six were relative paupers. Managers ruled the roost at a time when rookies were tickled to be paid an annual salary of $5,000 — around $60,000 today — and if they didn't like it they could go to Springfield in the AHL and skate for martinet Eddie

Shore for less. Virtually every one of them required off-season jobs to survive. Bill Juzda, who played defense for the Rangers and then the Leafs, was a steam locomotive engineer out of Winnipeg when the hockey season ended, and Max and older brother Doug Bentley worked an eight-hour shift on the family farm in Delisle, Sask. The year I worked for the Rangers, defenseman Lou Fontinato hauled cement for contractors in his native Guelph, Ont.

If any aspect of postwar Original Six hockey was standard, it was hatred for the opposition. It was difficult to discern whether the Canadiens loathed the Leafs more than they hated the Bruins. (The notorious 1955 Rocket Richard Riot erupted from a simmering Boston-Montreal war.) When Gordie Howe was hospitalized after a controversial collision with Leafs captain Ted Kennedy in the 1950 playoffs, the mayors of Detroit and Toronto got into a furious exchange of accusations over the incident. Likewise a Jack Stewart (Detroit)-Mariucci (Chicago) fight still is regarded as the longest 1-on-1 punch-out in league annals. It helped that in the Original Six era, a penalty box consisted of one bench and when simultaneous penalties were dished out the battlers sat backside to backside. Thus, half of the Stewart-Mariucci Pier Sixer took place on the ice and the other half in the sin bin.

This was a simpler epoch where arena management did nothing to hype the crowd. All rinks had an organist who pulled the stops between periods and that was that. Smoking was permitted all over, virtually no players wore helmets and until 1959 no goalie would dare put on a mask. Names on the backs of jerseys were unnecessary because you actually could tell the players without a program, especially if they happened to be Montreal's Maurice Richard and Detroit's Howe, the marquee men who were roughly equivalent — as rivals — to Sidney Crosby and Alex Ovechkin today. At his peak, Richard earned a maximum of $25,000, but the salary tide soon would turn when Jean Beliveau showed up for a contract discussion with the Canadiens supported by a financial advisor.

The Original Six remained an all-white league through the 1940s and most of the 1950s, although good African-Canadian players starred in the minors. I saw one of them, Herbie Carnegie, play for the Quebec Senior League Sherbrooke Saints in an inter-league game at Madison Square Garden. A Toronto product, Carnegie was good enough to skate in the NHL, but the racial barrier was high (Conn Smythe once reportedly watched Carnegie in a junior game and supposedly said he'd give 25 grand if someone could change Carnegie's color.) Eventually, another black player, Willie O'Ree, crossed the color line when Boston signed him in 1957, a full decade after Jackie Robinson became a Brooklyn Dodgers regular.

Televised hockey was in its infancy and if you mentioned a Zamboni someone would think you were talking about an exotic plant. There were no overtimes and in at least one arena a limitation on playoff games. That would be MSG, which annually gave way to the circus with no interruptions in April. As a result, all Rangers playoff games in the 1950 final had to be held on the road. In this case five games in Detroit and two "home" games at Maple Leaf Gardens in Toronto.

↑ THE NHL'S GOLDEN BOY
Hockey had star players before Bobby Hull, but 'The Golden Jet' brought unprecedented charisma and excitement to the sport.

Likewise, there was no standard rink size. Montreal and Toronto featured 200- by 85-foot ice surfaces, but Boston, Chicago and New York were significantly smaller. Olympia in Detroit was distinguished by its egg-shaped design that permitted the home club to make use of billiard-style bounces off the unique boards.

If the early-to-mid-Original Six Era lacked anything, it was a truly glamorous star. The Rocket was sullen, Howe was witty but low-key and Beliveau more majestic than mesmerizing. That all changed when Bobby 'The Golden Jet' Hull took over scoring leadership of the Blackhawks at the start of the 1960s. Although Bernie 'Boom Boom' Geoffrion introduced the modern slapshot, it was Hull who turned it into the ultimate offensive weapon and himself into an idol who would help pave the way for expansion along with the arrival of Bobby Orr in Boston during the Original Six's final season (1966-67).

"The Orr Effect" could simply be explained by the fact that the defenseman who played like a forward filled every rink in which he played. One season after Orr won the Calder Trophy as rookie of the year, the NHL ballooned from six to a dozen teams and hockey as I knew it — for better and worse — never was the same THN

↑ 'The Punch Line' with (L-R) Maurice Richard, Elmer Lach and Toe Blake leading the charge and with Leo Lamoreux, Bill Durnan and Glen Harmon anchoring the defense.

→ Maurice lived up to his reputation as "The Rocket" for scoring goals and for losing his temper.

FACTS & STATS
from 1942-43

Cup Winner
Detroit Red Wings

Leading Scorers
1. Doug Bentley, Chi, 73 points
2. Bill Cowley, Bos, 72 points
3. Max Bentley, Chi, 70 points
4. Lynn Patrick, NYR, 61 points
5. Lorne Carr, Tor, 60 points
6. Billy Taylor, Tor, 60 points
7. Bryan Hextall, NYR, 59 points
8. Toe Blake, Mtl, 59 points
9. Elmer Lach, Mtl, 58 points
10. Buddy O'Connor, Mtl, 58 pts

Franchise News
Brooklyn withdraws, leaving six teams (the Original Six).

Nickname of the Year
David 'Sweeney' Schriner

Worth Noting
Max, Reggie and **Doug Bentley** form the first all-brothers line in NHL history on New Year's Day and produce two goals, including the winner, as the Chicago Black Hawks edge the New York Rangers 6-5. Reggie plays just 11 career games…NHL president Frank Calder passes away. Born in Scotland, Calder flipped a coin to pick whether he would emigrate to Canada or the U.S. It came up Canada. During his quarter-century in charge, he transformed the NHL from a tiny league based in Ontario and Quebec into one spanning much of North America. Calder is replaced by Red Dutton… Maurice 'Rocket' Richard badly breaks his leg.

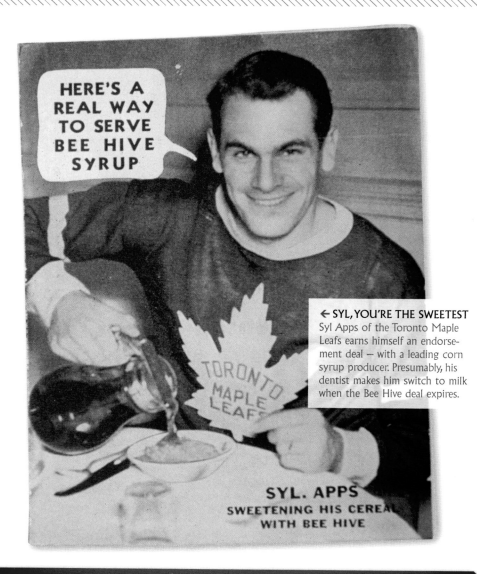

HERE'S A REAL WAY TO SERVE BEE HIVE SYRUP

TORONTO MAPLE LEAFS

SYL. APPS
SWEETENING HIS CEREAL WITH BEE HIVE

← SYL, YOU'RE THE SWEETEST
Syl Apps of the Toronto Maple Leafs earns himself an endorsement deal — with a leading corn syrup producer. Presumably, his dentist makes him switch to milk when the Bee Hive deal expires.

Newsmakers & Top Headlines

1 NHL continues despite severity of WWII
As the Second World War continues, 80 NHLers are serving in the armed services and rosters are reduced by up to 14 players per team. There are concerns the season may be cancelled, but NHL president Frank Calder announces the U.S. and Canadian governments feel hockey should continue "in the interest of public morale." His final major act as president comes Nov. 21 when he announces the 10-minute overtime period has been scrapped because of wartime travel restrictions.

2 Loss of Brooklyn leaves NHL with Original Six
Brooklyn manager Red Dutton and NHL president Frank Calder are at odds in September as the NHL drops Dutton's Americans, which the league has operated since 1936. "The Brooklyn Americans haven't quit the NHL — we've been scuttled," Dutton says in protest. "We're out of the league because Madison Square Garden forced us out." The former New York Americans shared MSG with the Rangers, but are not offered dates for the season. The loss of the Amerks leaves the NHL with six teams, later dubbed the 'Original Six,' until expansion in 1967-68.

3 Dutton succeeds Calder as head of NHL
Frank Calder, 65, who has served as NHL president since its inception in 1917, suffers a heart attack Jan. 25 while holding a meeting in Toronto and dies 10 days later on Feb. 4. Former Americans' manager Red Dutton is named interim president.

FACTS & STATS
from 1943-44

Cup Winner
Montreal Canadiens

Leading Scorers
1. Herb Cain, Bos, 82 points
2. Doug Bentley, Chi, 77 points
3. Lorne Carr, Tor, 74 points
4. Carl Liscombe, Det, 73 pts
5. Elmer Lach, Mtl, 72 points
6. Clint Smith, Chi, 72 points
7. Bill Cowley, Bos, 71 points
8. Bill Mosienko, Chi, 70 points
9. Art Jackson, Bos, 69 points
10. Gus Bodnar, Tor, 62 points

Rule Changes
Red line at center ice introduced to speed up the game and reduce offside calls. This rule is considered to mark the beginning of the modern era in the NHL.

Significant Records
Most assists by a defenseman, one game: Babe Pratt, Toronto (6).
Fastest goal by a player in his first NHL game: Gus Bodnar, Toronto (0:15).

Nickname of the Year
Frank 'Mr. Zero' Brimsek

Worth Noting
Chicago's Mike Karakas and Toronto's Paul Bibeault post shutouts and Bill Chadwick referees as the Black Hawks and Maple Leafs skate through the only scoreless, penalty-free game in NHL history Feb. 20, 1944...Reluctant to turn pro due to contract disputes, Bill Durnan finally makes his NHL debut at 27 and is an immediate success, backstopping Montreal to an excellent 38-5-7 record and victory over Chicago in the Stanley Cup final. He wins the Vezina Trophy and earns first all-star team status, honors he receives six times over the next seven seasons, an unprecedented run. Durnan's 38 wins are more than double the league's No. 2 goalie.

→ CANADIAN WAR HERO
The Toronto Maple Leafs pay tribute to farmhand Jack Fox, who is killed while serving in the Second World War. The AHL has an award in his name given to the player who combines sportsmanship and playing ability.

Newsmakers & Top Headlines

1 Center ice red line opens up game
In what is considered the beginning of hockey's modern era, the NHL changes the rules to open up the game. Previously, teams couldn't pass the puck across the blueline, which allowed forecheckers to pin opponents in their own zone by ganging up on the puck-carrier. End-to-end hockey returns, though, when the league allows defending teams to pass across their bluelines and adds a red line at center ice to which they can pass the puck from within their end. Goals per game jump from 7.2 in 1942-43 to 8.2, the league's highest total since 1920-21. "I'd say it was the biggest change hockey ever made and perhaps the best," says NHL referee and former all-star defenseman King Clancy.

2 Pratt sets defenseman scoring record
Toronto defenseman Babe Pratt is known as a high roller, but coach Hap Day senses Pratt is en route to something special and insists the playboy room with him the rest of the season. Pratt responds with 57 points, a record for a blueliner, and is awarded the Hart Trophy. Two seasons later, Pratt is suspended for life for betting on hockey, then reinstated after nine games.

3 Depleted Rangers defeated and defeated and...
The Rangers have lost 28 men to the armed forces. With only six players back from 1942-43, coach Frank Boucher, 43, activates himself, but they get off to an NHL-worst 0-14-1 start and finish 6-39-5. The misery includes an NHL-record 15-0 loss to Detroit Jan. 23.

DEFINING CHARACTERISTICS

ARTIST LARRY PURDY DRAWS HOCKEY HALL OF FAMERS LIKE THEY'RE SATURDAY MORNING CARTOON HEROES

BY TAYLOR ROCCA

It's often said the truest form of art comes from the heart. That certainly rings through for caricature artist Larry Purdy, whose early beginnings came through simple observation and the grade school tradition of exchanging valentines.

A 50-year-old native of Cornerbrook, Nfld., Purdy found it second nature to notice the defining features of the people he encountered as a young boy.

"I can remember back as early as elementary school when kids would hand out valentines," Purdy said. "There would be all these funny animal valentines. I would look at one and say, 'OK, there is an owl on this valentine and he has a round head, and (so-and-so) in my class, he has a round head and big round eyes, he looks just like that owl.' It's terrible to say that, but I would tend to notice these things."

What started as a simple game of picking out the unique physical traits of his classmates and matching them with cartoon animals eventually turned into a career. In 1994, Purdy's comic strip *The Mice Squad,* a story about a team of hockey-playing rodents, was printed in Newfoundland and eventually made its way into newspapers in Manitoba, Nova Scotia and Ontario.

As any good Canadian boy does, Purdy loves the game of hockey and took to drawing caricatures of his favorite players.

Purdy has a certain process when it comes to inking his caricatures. After settling upon his subject, he will scour and look through as many images of the player as he can get his eyes on. From there, Purdy sets forth doing simple sketches, sometimes ending up with a dozen different pieces to work with. Once he has sorted his options and determined which sketch he likes best, he moves to inking the caricature with a brush, bringing the character to life on the page.

"I try not to flatter," Purdy said. "Everybody wants to look wonderful and if I draw like that, everybody tends to look the same. I try not to draw lifelike. I ask myself, 'what would this hockey player look like if he were a cartoon character?' I try to draw them as simply as possible. I'm trying to draw as if the person was in a Saturday morning cartoon on television."

Each caricature typically takes three to four hours of total work before it is complete. For Purdy, sometimes this means putting down the pencil or brush and leaving a piece for a week before coming back to it. Other times when it jumps off the page, he starts and finalizes a piece in one afternoon.

Purdy's favorite caricature out of the set that he sketched for The Hockey News is his depiction of Foster Hewitt.

"I tried to do that one in the style of Alfred Hitchcock's self caricature," said Purdy. "Foster was just a 'voice' to most people. To be able to caricature him without drawing his full face, I believe was kind of fitting."

For this assignment, The Hockey News asked Purdy to provide one caricature from every Hockey Hall of Fame induction class — from Howie Morenz in the inaugural group of 1945 to Adam Oates in 2012. In the pages to follow, you'll see his 59 caricatures of Hall of Famers.

If the truest form of art comes from the heart, then Larry Purdy's hockey caricatures are a labor of love for the game that many, Purdy included, hold dear. Fans of the sport will certainly see that when taking in the simple detail that the artist has so excellently used to emphasize many of hockey's greatest legends. THN

FACTS & STATS
from 1944-45

Cup Winner
Toronto Maple Leafs

Leading Scorers
1. Elmer Lach, Mtl, 80 points
2. Maurice Richard, Mtl, 73 pts
3. Toe Blake, Mtl, 67 points
4. Bill Cowley, Bos, 65 points
5. Ted Kennedy, Tor, 54 points
6. Bill Mosienko, Chi, 54 points
7. Joe Carveth, Det, 54 points
8. Ab DeMarco, NYR, 54 points
9. Clint Smith, Chi, 54 points
10. Syd Howe, Det, 53 points

HHOF Inductees
Dan Bain
Hobey Baker
Chuck Gardiner
Eddie Gerard
Frank McGee
Tommy Phillips
Harvey Pulford
Art Ross
Hod Stuart
Georges Vezina
↓ Howie Morenz

Nickname of the Year
Maurice 'The Rocket' Richard

Worth Noting
While flying a transport mission to Burma (Asia), Flight Sergeant J.L. Arnett of the Royal Canadian Air Force reports he is able to pick up Foster Hewitt's broadcast of a Toronto-Chicago game on his airplane radio...NHL president Red Dutton offers to resign because of business concerns, but the league's board of governors dissuades him. Conn Smythe turns down the position. Dutton stays until 1946.

↑ CONN'S CANVAS
Leafs GM Conn Smythe adds many championship patches to this jacket, including five in the 1940s. Any Leaf who tries to mimic the trend from 1967 on has a patchless coat today.

Newsmakers & Top Headlines

1 Rocket fires 50 goals in 50 games
The Montreal Canadiens are paced by right winger Maurice 'Rocket' Richard, whose 50 goals in 50 games are an NHL single-season record. It breaks the mark of 44 set in 1917-18 by Joe Malone, who is on hand to congratulate Richard. The Canadien also sets an NHL single-season mark with eight points in one game Dec. 28 against the Detroit Red Wings, but the NHL scoring title and Hart Trophy goes to teammate Elmer Lach, who collects 80 points, including a record 54 assists. The 'Punch Line' (Lach, Richard and Toe Blake), which finishes 1-2-3 in scoring, Vezina Trophy-winning goalie Bill Durnan, defenseman Butch Bouchard and coach Dick Irvin occupy six of the seven first all-star team spots, also a new NHL standard for one team.

2 McCool overcomes ulcers to beat Red Wings
Winner of the Calder Trophy as top rookie, Toronto goalie Frank McCool is known as 'Ulcers' because of an unsteady stomach. During Game 7 of the Cup final against Detroit, he leaves the ice in pursuit of his medicine and returns to beat the Wings 2-1. His three shutouts to start the series remain a Stanley Cup record.

3 Hollett Flashes his way to goal mark
Detroit's Flash Hollett makes history when he beats Toronto goalie Frank McCool March 17 to become the first NHL defenseman to post a 20-goal campaign, earning a spot on the first all-star team. Hollett's record stands for 24 seasons until Boston's Bobby Orr scores 21 goals in 1968-69.

↑ REAL WARRIORS
Boston's 'Kraut Line' – Bobby Bauer, Woody Dumart and Milt Schmidt.

↓ THE OTHER TOE
Toe Blake is known more for his coaching prowess, but he wins three Cups and a Hart Trophy as a player with help from this stick.

Newsmakers & Top Headlines

1 League gets talent boost as WWII ends
The end of the Second World War brings many of the NHL's best players back into action. Among the returnees are Boston's 'Kraut Line' of Milt Schmidt, Woody Dumart and Bobby Bauer and goalie Frank Brimsek, Chicago's Bentley brothers (Doug and Max), New York's Patrick brothers (Lynn and Muzz), Detroit's Sid Abel, along with Syl Apps and Turk Broda of Toronto. "The caliber of play is going to make the fans forget the war years," predicts NHL president Red Dutton.

2 Hockey Hall of Fame welcomes first members
The Hockey Hall of Fame is born when the NHL approves a plan at its June, 1945 governors' meeting to honor the greats of the game. Boston GM Art Ross and former NHL stars Georges Vezina, Howie Morenz, Charlie Gardiner and Eddie Gerard are inaugural inductees, as are pre-NHLers Hod Stuart, Dan Bain, Hobey Baker, Russell Bowie, 'One-Eyed' Frank McGee, Tommy Phillips, Harvey Pulford and builder Lord Stanley of Preston, who donated the Stanley Cup.

3 Rangers experiment with two-goalie system
Rangers coach Frank Boucher tries a two-goalie system of Charlie Rayner and 'Sugar' Jim Henry. He alternates his goalies game by game, then tries shuttling them back and forth during the game every four to six minutes. "The system impressed me," says Montreal coach Dick Irvin. "We're coming into a time when goalies will be subbed as frequently as (skaters)."

FACTS & STATS
from 1945-46

Cup Winner
Montreal Canadiens

Leading Scorers
1. Max Bentley, Chi, 61 points
2. Gaye Stewart, Tor, 52 points
3. Toe Blake, Mtl, 50 points
4. Clint Smith, Chi, 50 points
5. Maurice Richard, Mtl, 48 pts
6. Bill Mosienko, Chi, 48 points
7. Ab DeMarco, NYR, 47 points
8. Elmer Lach, Mtl, 47 points
9. Alex Kaleta, Chi, 46 points
10. Billy Taylor, Tor, 41 points

Nickname of the Year
Alf 'The Embalmer' Pike

Worth Noting
Max Bentley's individual scoring title win follows his brother Doug's scoring title in 1942-43, making them the only brothers to lead the NHL in scoring, a record matched by Henrik and Daniel Sedin in 2009-10 and 2010-11. The brothers team up with Bill Mosienko to form Chicago's 'Pony Line.'...The Toronto Maple Leafs miss the playoffs after winning the Cup the previous season. It is the first time they miss the playoffs since playing at Maple Leaf Gardens... Synchronized red lights to signal goals are made obligatory for all NHL rinks...New York Rangers GM Lester Patrick retires from his position, but stays on as vice-president of MSG...Frank Patrick, former Pacific Coast Hockey Association president and former managing director for the NHL, suffers a heart attack, laying him up in hospital for several weeks.

Cup Winner

Toronto Maple Leafs

Leading Scorers
1. Max Bentley, Chi, 72 points
2. Maurice Richard, Mtl, 71 pts
3. Billy Taylor, Det, 63 points
4. Milt Schmidt, Bos, 62 points
5. Ted Kennedy, Tor, 60 points
6. Doug Bentley, Chi, 55 points
7. Bobby Bauer, Bos, 54 points
8. Roy Conacher, Det, 54 points
9. Bill Mosienko, Chi, 52 points
10. Woody Dumart, Bos, 52 pts

Significant Records
Most assists, one game:
Billy Taylor, Detroit (7)

HHOF Inductees
Dubbie Bowie
Dit Clapper
Aurel Joliat
Frank Nighbor
Eddie Shore
Cyclone Taylor
↓ Lester Patrick

Nickname of the Year
Sid 'Old Bootnose' Abel

Worth Noting
Frank Selke, who bolts Toronto to become GM of Montreal, says the Maple Leafs use wrestling tactics and suggests he'll suit up wrestler Yvon Robert against the Maple Leafs. Toronto GM Conn Smythe says he'll then dress world heavyweight wrestling champion 'Whipper' Billy Watson…Goalies Frank Brimsek, Turk Broda and Bill Durnan play every minute of all 60 games.

↑ PADDING HIS STATS
These pads help Canadiens goalie Bill Durnan play every minute of every game and capture a fourth consecutive Vezina Trophy in 1946-47.

Newsmakers & Top Headlines

1 Campbell named NHL president
Hoping to revive his inactive Brooklyn Americans' franchise, Red Dutton resigns as NHL president and touts Clarence Campbell as his successor. Campbell, named assistant to the president in June, is endorsed by NHL governors. A former NHL referee, a lawyer and Rhodes Scholar who was a lieutenant-colonel in the Canadian army during the war, Campbell was appointed Queen's Counsel and participated in the prosecution of Nazis before returning to Canada.

2 Detroit rookie Howe impresses all
At six-foot and 201 pounds, Gordie Howe physically stands out, but it is the 18-year-old Red Wing rookie's play that really sets him apart and eventually earns him the nickname, 'Mr. Hockey.' Ambidextrous and naturally strong, Howe scores on Toronto goalie Turk Broda in his NHL debut, then runs Chicago goalie Paul Bibeault in his third game, touching off a brawl. "He has a blow that can kill a man," Ab Howe says of his son's power.

3 Meeker, Taylor establish NHL records
Two single-game records are set by Toronto right winger Howie Meeker and center Billy Taylor of Detroit. On March 16, Taylor sets up seven goals in a 10-6 victory over Chicago. Meeker, who wins the Calder Trophy over Gordie Howe, sets a rookie record Jan. 8 when he scores five goals on Paul Bibeault in a 10-4 win over Chicago. Both records have since been equalled.

FACTS & STATS from 1947-48

Cup Winner

Toronto Maple Leafs

Leading Scorers
1. Elmer Lach, Mtl, 61 points
2. Buddy O'Connor, NYR, 60 pts
3. Doug Bentley, Chi, 57 points
4. Gaye Stewart, Tor/Chi, 56 pts
5. Max Bentley, Chi/Tor, 54 pts
6. Bud Poile, Tor/Chi, 54 points
7. Maurice Richard, Mtl, 53 pts
8. Syl Apps, Tor, 53 points
9. Ted Lindsay, Det, 52 points
10. Roy Conacher, Chi, 49 points

Nickname of the Year
Max 'Dipsy-Doodle-Dandy' Bentley

Worth Noting
The first hockey-only publication goes on newsstands when **The Hockey News** publishes its first issue Oct. 1...Overshadowed at center by Toronto captain Syl Apps and two-time scoring champ Max Bentley, Teeder Kennedy steps up in the playoffs, leading scorers in goals (eight) and points (14). Kennedy has a four-goal game against Boston and scores twice in the Cup-clinching win over Detroit... The Art Ross Trophy is introduced, handed out to the player with the most points...A policy whereby players raise their sticks to signify a goal is introduced, a suggestion of Frank Patrick. Canadiens forward Billy Reay is the first to do it Nov.13, 1947... Toronto goaltender Turk Broda wins a career-high 32 games and captures his second and final Vezina Trophy.

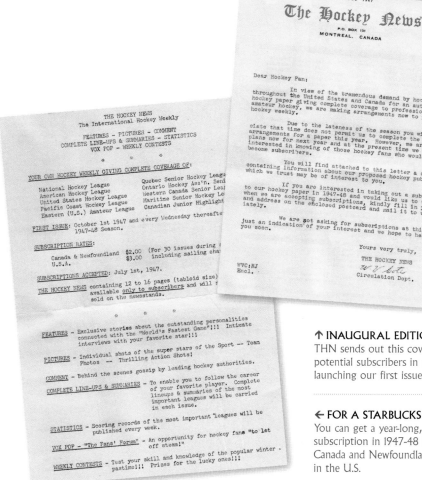

↑ INAUGURAL EDITION
THN sends out this cover letter to potential subscribers in preparation for launching our first issue Oct. 1, 1947.

← FOR A STARBUCKS COFFEE...
You can get a year-long, 30-issue THN subscription in 1947-48 for $2.00 in Canada and Newfoundland and $3.00 in the U.S.

Newsmakers & Top Headlines

1 Bentley trade keeps Stanley Cup in Toronto
In what is called the biggest trade in NHL history, the Maple Leafs deal five players — Bob Goldham, Gaye Stewart, Bud Poile, Gus Bodnar and Ernie Dickens to the Black Hawks Nov. 4 for Cy Thomas and two-time NHL scoring champ Max Bentley. Maple Leafs' GM Conn Smythe insists Bentley is worth it because Toronto is getting the league's top scorer for center-ice duties. Together with Syl Apps and Teeder Kennedy, Bentley gives the Leafs unprecedented depth down the middle and helps them retain the Stanley Cup.

2 Gambling scandal rocks NHL
After a lengthy investigation, NHL president Clarence Campbell announces March 9 that Don Gallinger of Boston and Billy Taylor of the Rangers are suspended indefinitely for "knowingly associating and communicating with James Tamer, a known criminal and gambler of Detroit." Campbell emphasizes no other players were involved and no attempt was made to fix a game. Gallinger acknowledges he spoke to Tamer, but insists he did not know of the man's background.

3 Mosienko injured in first All-Star Game
A crowd of 14,138 fills Maple Leaf Gardens to watch the Stanley Cup-champion Maple Leafs drop a 4-3 decision to the NHL All-Stars Oct. 13 in the first official NHL All-Star Game. The game isn't a complete success — Chicago's Bill Mosienko sustains a broken right ankle when checked by Toronto's Jim Thomson.

ENGLISH YOUTH AT 14 DEEMED PUCK NATURAL

DEC. 10, 1947 BY THN STAFF

LONDON, ENGLAND —

Youngster with a hockey future — that's what they call young Gordon 'Gabby' Pankhurst around Wembley these days.

The 14-year-old English boy who learned to play hockey in Canada while living there as an evacuee during the war years became the youngest player ever to represent England in an international contest as the British squad tied Sweden 3-3.

Pankhurst, born in Maidstone, England, came to Canada when he was seven years old and lived in West Kildonan, Man., and after coming into prominence as a puckchaser, the kid was called the 'Boy Wonder.' Sandy Archer, coach of the Wembley Monarchs, called him a hockey natural.

He had been playing with schoolboy teams in England, but got his big chance at fame when Doug Wilson of the Wembley team strained a thigh muscle and had to drop out of action before the international fixture against Sweden.

'Gabby' was hanging around the Wembley dressing room, his usual procedure on the night of a game, and was pressed into service as a substitute. He played only seven minutes in the second period, but showed plenty of dash and sparkle on the left wing and was right up in front on several English attacks.

He stood 5-foot-10 with his socks, and tilts the Toledo scale at around 170 pounds — a broth of a boy for a youngster not quite 15 years old. Despite his husky appearance, he has the round, chubby face of a schoolboy — a deceiving appearance when he swings into action on the ice.

Besides Archer, who is highly enthusiastic about the kid's chances, he has another strong supporter in Wembley hockey official Lou Bates. A shrewd judge of hockey talent through his many years watching Canadian imports in action, Bates says Pankhurst is the finest natural hockey player he has ever seen.

Pankhurst, even at such an early age in his hockey career, is one of the most outstanding English puck products to come along in many years. If he maintains his present pace he will undoubtedly be one of the greatest players who ever called England his home.

(Editor's Note: Gabby Pankhurst died Jan. 6, 2011 at age 78 after a long battle with dementia and is survived by his wife, Gerri, and his two sons and their families. Pankhurst returned to Canada and signed with the Montreal Canadiens, playing for the Abbott Cup-winning St. Boniface Canadiens in the Manitoba Junior League from 1952-53. The team was inducted into the Manitoba Hockey Hall of Fame in 2009. After hanging up his skates, Pankhurst moved into the hotel business and fell in love with golf. He made a hole-in-one at the Kildonan Golf Course, Winnipeg's oldest municipal golf course, in 2001 at the age of 68.)

↑ CRUISIN' FOR A BRUISIN'
Next to motorcycle racing, these reckless demons on skates are the least favorable sport to cover for insurance companies.

NOV. 26, 1947 BY THN STAFF

INSURANCE FIRMS RATE GAME'S DANGER SECOND

London, England — The game of hockey is the fastest in the world and to many it looks like the most dangerous, but insurance officials in Britain don't agree. In fact, they rate hockey second to motorcycle racing. The helmeted speed demons who plant themselves in motorcycle saddles and whirl through the dust are given top billing by the English insurance magnates.

One of the insurance brokers who handles the business in the two sports said, "Payments to speedway riders are much greater than to hockey players." He did remark, however, that the companies did have a bad time with hockey payments in the days before the war when the English teams were manned with Canadian players.

Insurance rates took a decided drop and the injury lists were also cut when the Canadian players who arrived in Britain in 1946 were warned by league officials to cut out all the rough stuff. The rink owners pay the premium on all players and the approximate cost is fifty cents a game and the insurance covers injuries received by players on both teams.

The payoffs are as follows: The dependents of a player killed in a game or practice receive $2,000. The same dividend is paid to a player if he loses both eyes or two limbs. If a player loses one eye or a limb he pockets £250.

The insurance companies balk at one common accident in hockey and that is the players' teeth and dentures. The players are on their own as far as teeth are concerned because the companies figure it happens far too often for them to cover.

The referees also come under the insurance act, but an insurance official couldn't say what would happen if a referee was skulled with a bottle or other missile thrown by some excited fan. **THN**

>1948-49

LEAF THREE-PEAT

↑ BLACK HAWK GOWN
Bill Gadsby's Black Hawks jacket borrows its color scheme from a couple other Original Six clubs. Gadsby spent the first eight-and-a-half of his 20 NHL seasons with Chicago.

← RARE SIGHT
The Rangers' Don Raleigh beats Montreal goalie Bill Durnan here, but that doesn't happen often. Durnan posts a league-best 10 shutouts in '48-49.

Cup Winner
Toronto Maple Leafs

Leading Scorers
1. Roy Conacher, Chi, 68 points
2. Doug Bentley, Chi, 66 points
3. Sid Abel, Det, 54 points
4. Ted Lindsay, Det, 54 points
5. Jim Conacher, Det/Chi, 49 pts
6. Paul Ronty, Bos, 49 points
7. Harry Watson, Tor, 45 points
8. Billy Reay, Mtl, 45 points
9. Gus Bodnar, Chi, 45 points
10. Johnny Peirson, Bos, 43 pts

Nickname of the Year
Eddie 'The Great Gabbo' Dorohoy

Worth Noting
Detroit's Bill Quackenbush is the first defenseman to win the Lady Byng Trophy, playing all 60 games without a penalty minute...The season marks the fourth time Leafs goalie Turk Broda backstops Toronto to the Cup. He loses just once in the playoffs, posts a 1.57 goals-against average and allows more than two goals only once in nine games...Don Gallinger of Boston is expelled from the NHL for life after finally admitting to gambling...A league record of 10 major penalties is set Nov. 25, 1948 in front of 11,000 fans at the Montreal Forum...Gordie Howe undergoes knee surgery, while Montreal loses **Elmer Lach** when he fractures his jaw in a collision with Toronto's Bob Goldham...The 'Durnan Rule' states goalies cannot be the captain or wear the 'C' or 'A.'

Newsmakers & Top Headlines

1 **Maple Leafs turn first Stanley Cup natural hat trick**
It doesn't look like the Maple Leafs will triumph as Stanley Cup champs a third straight time. Captain Syl Apps and Nick Metz retire before the campaign and Toronto stumbles through the regular season, finishing fourth with a mediocre 22-25-13 record. "If the Leafs get in there sound, they'll take it all," says Toronto GM Conn Smythe just before the playoffs. Toronto ousts the Bruins in five games and sweeps the Red Wings to become the first NHL team to three-peat.

2 **Durnan lays goose eggs on opposition**
Bill Durnan becomes a brick wall in the Canadiens net, stopping everything he faces for 309 minutes and 21 seconds — a modern era record at the time. After the Hawks' Roy Conacher beats him at 16:15 of the first period in a 3-1 Habs win Feb. 24, Durnan whitewashes Detroit 2-0, blanks Toronto 1-0 and posts back-to-back shutouts against Boston before Black Hawk Gaye Stewart scores at 5:36 of the second period March 9.

3 **Rangers injured in auto accident**
Six days prior to the start of the season, four Rangers are injured when their car crashes near Rouses Point, N.Y., en route to training camp at Saranac Lake. Buddy O'Connor breaks several ribs, Frank Eddolls has a knee tendon severed, Edgar Laprade is left with a broken nose and Bill Moe sustains head lacerations requiring stitches. A fifth player, Tony Leswick, escapes the mishap uninjured.

GAME'S ONLY ALL-BLACK LINE THRILLS FANS

JAN. 26, 1949 BY FRED ROBERTS

MONTREAL, QUE. –

Sunday, April 13th, 1947, was an unforgettable day in the minds of 12,000 leather-lunged hockey fans, whose privilege it was to attend one of the most thrilling encounters ever staged in the spacious Montreal Forum, home of the Canadiens.

Yet, oddly enough, those spine-tingling episodes were not supplied by the parent club, but by their No. 1 farm team, the Montreal Royals, and more particularly, by an unheralded triumvirate of black players.

The setting was perfect on that sunny afternoon. The Royals and Sherbrooke Red Raiders were teeing off in the Eastern Canada Allan Cup playoffs, a tournament that moves the amateur fans to mass hysteria.

The Royals had won the first game by a score of 8-3 and were favorites to win the series, a 3-of-5 affair, and nobody was ready to bet a dime that they wouldn't sink the lowly Red Raiders once the series returned to Montreal. The pattern seemed to follow form as the Royals, a powerful outfit driven by a dynamic set of forwards, quickly built a first-period lead of 4-1.

When Montreal proceeded to extend the count to 6-1 in the first few minutes of the second frame, the Sherbrooke diehards shook their heads collectively and mumbled, "poor Sherbrooke, they tried so hard."

A pair of Sherbrooke goals in the same period only seemed to prolong their downfall. A valiant effort seemed destined to end in defeat. Yet sometimes destiny walks hand in hand with Lady Luck, and on this memorable afternoon, the fair lady was to smile benevolently on the Red Raiders.

The final period opened with the Red Raiders trailing 6-3. Sherbrooke's followers seemed discontented and resolved to their fate until it happened – and when it did, the Forum roof vibrated to their whoops and cheers.

A trio of windmills, fighting with all the fire and fury of prehistoric dragons, broke through with a barrage of scoring, the likes of which kept the Royals and spectators spellbound. The line, led by smooth-skating Herbie Carnegie, banged in five goals in the wild-scoring period to shoot the Red Raiders ahead 8-6. Two other Montreal goals were neutralized by 'Torpedo' Tony Demers and Bernie Lauzon and the Red Raiders skated off the ice with an unbelievable 10-8 victory.

The 'Dark Destroyers,' as they became known after that epic display of courageous hockey, were the toast of the town. When the final tally had been made, Herbie Carnegie finished with two goals and three assists, brother Ossie Carnegie had four goals and one assist and Mannie McIntyre pitched in with a goal and an assist.

Together they had amassed 12 scoring points in a 10-goal game, and seven of those points were goals. As it later turned out, the Royals, with a wider range of reserves and power, won the series anyway, three games to one. They went on to win the Allan Cup from the Calgary Stampeders.

↑ ATTEMPTING TO BREAK THE COLOR BARRIER
Herb Carnegie goes on to star with the Quebec Aces in the early 1950s after wowing the crowd in Montreal while playing for Sherbrooke.

Yet, fans will spend many a night around a barroom table reminiscing about the feat of the Dark Destroyers. Everybody who saw that dream game will unanimously agree that the victory was most deserving.

The Carnegies and McIntyre are unique in that they represent the only colored line in the boundaries of organized hockey today. They first played as a unit around Ontario and came to Quebec during the 1944-45 season where they lined up with the Shawinigan Cataractes, then members of the Senior B Provincial League. The next season Shawinigan joined the Quebec Senior League and the Destroyers switched their allegiance to Sherbrooke where they played bang-up hockey under the shrewd guidance of coach Yvon Dugre. They finished high up in the scoring bracket that season and hit even greater heights the following year.

An itch to see the world broke up the trio in 1947 when McIntyre and Ossie Carnegie, both bachelors, sped off to Paris where their ability was only surpassed by their popularity. They played for the Paris Racing Club in the French League. During their absence, Herbie, father of two children and described as the "brain" of the trio, picked up two new linemates and had an equally good year.

The year Sherbrooke joined the Quebec Senior League, they were badly in need of the best material available. In rebuilding, Dugre laid the foundation when he persuaded the "Parisian" members of his famous line to return to the fold.

Herbie and McIntyre were both 27 while Ossie was the senior member of the trio at 31. The Carnegie brothers hail from South Porcupine, Ont., whereas McIntyre was raised in Devon, N.B.

In their spare time the boys play a little baseball, a game which McIntyre excels. Playing in Ontario, he was voted the most valuable player in the league the year Phil Marchildon was signed by the Philadelphia A's. No mean feat at that. **THN**

GORDIE GROUNDED

FACTS & STATS
from 1949-50

Cup Winner
Detroit Red Wings

Leading Scorers
1. Ted Lindsay, Det, 78 points
2. Sid Abel, Det, 69 points
3. Gordie Howe, Det, 68 points
4. Maurice Richard, Mtl, 65 pts
5. Paul Ronty, Bos, 59 points
6. Roy Conacher, Chi, 56 points
7. Doug Bentley, Chi, 53 points
8. Johnny Peirson, Bos, 52 pts
9. Metro Prystai, Chi, 51 points
10. Bep Guidolin, Chi, 51 points

60 Moments
that changed the game
No. 53: League officials paint the ice surface white to create more contrast and make the game easier to follow.

HHOF Inductees
Scotty Davidson
Charles Drinkwater
Mike Grant
Si Griffis
Newsy Lalonde
George Richardson
Harry Trihey
↓Joe Malone

↑ FIRE AND ICE
Toronto's Max Bentley takes home this lighter after his third of four career All-Star Game appearances.

Nickname of the Year
Bill 'The Honest Brakeman' Juzda

Worth Noting
"The Lord and 12 apostles couldn't have kept the Red Wings under control tonight," says Toronto Maple Leafs GM Conn Smythe after Detroit seeks retribution in the first game following Gordie Howe's devastating head injury.

Newsmakers & Top Headlines

1 Howe almost dies after on-ice mishap
Detroit not only loses Gordie Howe for the playoffs, it almost loses him for good. During a playoff game loss, Howe has Teeder Kennedy of Toronto lined up. "I saw Howe coming," Kennedy says. "I stepped aside and he crashed into the boards." Wings coach Tommy Ivan claims Kennedy butt-ended or elbowed Howe. Howe sustains a concussion, nose and cheekbone fractures and a lacerated eyeball. Doctors drill through his skull to relieve pressure on the brain. Howe's family is rushed to his bedside, and to everyone's relief he recovers.

2 Smythe tells Broda to cut the fat
With his team mired in a six-game winless skid Nov. 29, Toronto GM Conn Smythe decides his Leafs are fat cats and goalie Turk Broda is the poster boy for their complacency. "We are not running a fat man's team," Smythe says. "He is off the team until he shows some common sense." Smythe demands Broda get down to 190. Broda loses 10 pounds to meet Smythe's deadline.

3 Reardon bites tongue and lays off Gardner
Injured by Toronto's Cal Gardner in a game Jan. 1, 1949, Ken Reardon of the Canadiens has a long memory. "Even if I have to wait until the last game I ever play, Gardner is going to get it good and plenty," Reardon says. President Clarence Campbell forces Reardon to put up a $1,000 good-conduct bond. When he retires at the end of 1949-50 without harming Gardner, Reardon petitions for a refund and gets his money back.

DEBATE FLARES OVER CONACHER, WALTER AFFAIR

FEB. 18, 1950 BY THN STAFF

DETROIT, MICH. —

Rumored threats of a "boycott" of Detroit games by the Motor City's hockey writers followed in the wake of the "Battle of the Century" between coach Charlie Conacher and writer Lew Walter of Detroit. According to the grapevine, the Detroit scribes were planning a meeting for this week, threatening to give NHL games the brush-off unless heavy justice was meted out to the Hawks coach.

The whole affair started in Detroit Feb. 8 after the Wings had laced Chicago 9-2, in a game which saw Conacher involved in a dispute with referee Bill Chadwick. Conacher had claimed that Detroit's George Gee should have been given a penalty for knocking down Doug Bentley and leaving him with a badly damaged optic.

In the dressing room afterwards, Walter, a Detroit *Times* newsman, tangled with the Chicago coach and former star with Toronto's famed Kid Line. In the fracas, Walter was punched on the face by Conacher, raising a black and blue bump on his cheek in testimony. Accounts of the battle varied widely, but Walter had a warrant sworn out charging Conacher with assault. The warrant will be served when Chicago next visits the Michigan auto center March 11, and the pros and cons will be threshed out then.

Conacher claimed Walter called him a vile name — Walter denied it. Walter said Conacher threw a "sneak punch" at him, then grabbed him by the throat while he was on the floor — Conacher said he threw one punch and walked out.

Text of Conacher's statement, witnessed by eight players in the dressing room, and the rebuttal made by the Detroit writer, are as follows: "When Walter came into the dressing room, I asked if he came to gloat over the victory and that I never saw him come in when we beat Detroit. He got sarcastic and said: 'I'll come in here any ------ time I please.' I said 'Oh no you won't! Get out of here." With that he turned to speak to a player. "Walter then came back at me and said, 'what the ------ is wrong with you?' I told him to go ahead and print some more lies like last year when he said Roy (Conacher) and Bentley had all their points given to them in Chicago. He said 'You are the worst ----- of a coach to speak to,' and with that I struck him and that's the end of it."

From Walter: "It isn't in my character to use profanity in talking to any hockey coach and I called him no names. Neither was I angry when I talked to him. He accused me of lying in a couple of stories I had written about Chicago. When I went to leave, he said 'So you boys come and see me when we've taken a licking. You sneak away when we win one.' I told him he was one of the toughest coaches in the whole league to find after a game. Then he nailed me. It was a sneak punch. We intend to bring suit. I never saw the punch coming. The next thing I knew I was lying on the floor, with Conacher on top of me clutching my throat."

↑ TALK ABOUT AN EXCLUSIVE
Chicago coach Charlie Conacher engages Detroit journalist in "conversation," then delivers a stiff haymaker to the cheek.

JAN. 21, 1950 BY THN STAFF

DAN AND FRANK ARE UNUSUAL HOCKEY DUO

HERSHEY, PA. —

The most unusual brother combination in hockey now decorates the Hershey Bears' lineup. The unusual combo is that of Dan and Frank Porteus, the only twins playing professional hockey.

However, more unusual than the fact they are twins, is their contracts. One clause in their contracts says that where one brother goes the other will follow. In other words, they can't be split up. It is said that their money arrangement with their clubs is exactly the same. Some fun, eh kid?

The Porteus brothers, Daniel Frederick and Thomas Francis, were born in Kirkland Lake, Ont., on Sept. 10, 1923, where their father was, and still is, in the gold mining business. Business interests moved the Porteus family to Montreal when the twins were young and that's where they started to play hockey.

Before the pair joined forces in the pro loops, they wore the colors of Valleyfield Braves of the Quebec Senior League. In 1946, Frank turned pro for Omaha in the United States League, his service being acquired by Detroit. That left Dan at home alone. He decided he'd like to enter college and enlisted at McGill University.

While there, Dan played for the college team that included John Peirson and Jack Gelineau of the current Boston Bruins.

During the 1947-48 season, the brothers hooked up again. Dan left McGill and signed with the now defunct Washington Lions, as did Frank. In 1948-49, the pair were sent to the Cleveland Barons and at the beginning of this season, they were bought by the Hershey Bears. **THN**

LEGEND OF BARILKO

FACTS & STATS
from 1950-51

Cup Winner
Toronto Maple Leafs

Leading Scorers
1. Gordie Howe, Det, 86 points
2. Maurice Richard, Mtl, 66 pts
3. Max Bentley, Tor, 62 points
4. Sid Abel, Det, 61 points
5. Milt Schmidt, Bos, 61 points
6. Ted Kennedy, Tor, 61 points
7. Ted Lindsay, Det, 59 points
8. Tod Sloan, Tor, 56 points
9. Red Kelly, Det, 54 points
10. Sid Smith, Tor, 51 points

Nickname of the Year
Wally 'The Whirling Dervish' Stanowski

Worth Noting
The league implements a rule requiring teams to provide an extra goalie for every game for use by either team in case of emergency or illness...Before perishing on an ill-fated fishing trip, defenseman Bill Barilko's final game-winning goal gets his name engraved on Lord Stanley's Cup for the fourth time in his five-year career...Goaltender **Terry Sawchuk** captures the Calder Trophy, winning an NHL-best 44 games for Detroit in his rookie campaign...On the other hand, the Black Hawks' Harry Lumley suffers a forgettable season, allowing 246 goals and posting a miserable 3.90 goals against average...Future NHL superstars and Hall of Famers Jean Beliveau and Bernie 'Boom Boom' Geoffrion make their NHL debuts with the Montreal Canadiens.

↑ LEATHER LARCENY
Gerry McNeil plays 70 games for the Canadiens in his first full season as their starter, robbing shooters with this trapper.

← GRAND FINALE
The last puck to ever touch Bill Barilko's stick finds twine in overtime to win the Leafs the Cup in 1951.

Newsmakers & Top Headlines

1 Barilko's farewell goal wins Cup for Leafs
Toronto returns to the top in unique fashion after a one-year absence, alternating Turk Broda and Al Rollins in goal. Rollins, who plays in 40 of 70 games, earns the Vezina. The Leafs top the Canadiens in an exciting five-game final, with every game decided in overtime. Defenseman Bill Barilko nets the Cup winner at 2:53 of extra play. On Aug. 26, a plane carrying Barilko, 24, and pilot Dr. Henry Hudson disappears on a Northern Ontario fishing trip. Their remains aren't found until 1962.

2 Howe stages amazing comeback
Rebounding from a near-fatal head injury in the 1950 playoffs, Detroit's Gordie Howe is a headache for NHL goalies. Wearing a helmet as a precautionary mea-sure, Howe sets an NHL scoring record with 86 points while topping the league in goals (43) and assists (43). He's the first player to lead in all three categories since the Montreal Canadiens' Howie Morenz in 1927-28.

3 Adams pulls trigger on record deal
Detroit GM Jack Adams makes a nine-player trade with Chicago, the largest in NHL history. Goalie Harry Lumley, defensemen Jack Stewart and Al Dewsbury, and forwards Pete Babando and Don Morrison go to Chicago. In return, the Wings get goalie Jim Henry, defenseman Bob Goldham and forwards Metro Prystai and Gaye Stewart. Lumley has taken Detroit to the final four times since 1945, but Adams feels he has a ready replacement in Terry Sawchuk.

BLONDES, BRUNETTES, YANKS, CANUCKS – WHO CARES – WE WANT GOOD LOOKERS WHO KNOW HOW TO COOK

FEB. 10, 1951 BY PAUL CHANDLER

DETROIT, MICH. –

It has been published that there are 10 Red Wing bachelors but not why. All 10 were in the Olympia dressing room. "Fellows," said the one who wanted to write the story, "I've got to find out if you are women-haters or whether the 'right one' just hasn't come along."

Laughter, somewhat embarrassed…wisecracks…blushes…

"Only been in love once in my life – that was with my first car, a '34 Chevy," said Gordon Howe. Someone whistled: "I want a girl just like that girl that married dear old dad." Another chanted: "Some Sunday morning when the weather is…"

Altogether, the early moments were not comfortable, though it was curious that half the club so far had escaped the vows and odd that the Detroit club had 35 percent more unmarried players than any other team in the NHL. As a group, it was plain the 10 "had everything" – rugged, good looks, substantial income. Modesty, manners, character and good habits.

They had to be interviewed individually. This is no boast – they were.

In summation, only two admitted having "a best girl." They were Gerry Couture, who said he was engaged, and Marty Pavelich, who was flushed to confessing "there is a girl in Windsor." There was grave suspicion that the interviews did not provide the whole truth, for when Ted Lindsay, who drives a Cadillac, denied he had a girl, his buddy, Howe, interrupted: "Come on, Ted, you don't think you can get away with that?" All were chary about declaring for or against Canadian or American girls as preferred types.

There could be only one conclusion: They're all lonely hearts.

Each bachelor was asked the same questions – why are you waiting? Do you prefer Canadian girls or American? Brunettes or blondes or red-heads? Is a good cook more important than good looks?

Here are the answers:

Leonard Patrick Kelly (red-head, 23, 5-foot-11, 180, plus a bewitching smile): "I'll marry anytime now. I'm just waiting for the right girl. On the average, there's no difference between Canadian and American girls. Brunettes or blondes are fine, but I can't get along with another red-head. We always clash. I want a wife who's a good cook, but I hope she's good-looking, too."

Terry Sawchuk (charming grin, 21, 5-foot-11, 195): "I'm too young to get married. I'm going to wait until I'm 30, no matter who comes along. No comment on Canadian girls compared to Americans. I'll want a good-looking wife. You can always hire a cook. Brunettes for me."

Ted Lindsay (perfect manners, 25, 5-foot-8, 165): "It's not fair to marry a girl when you're playing hockey. We're on the road

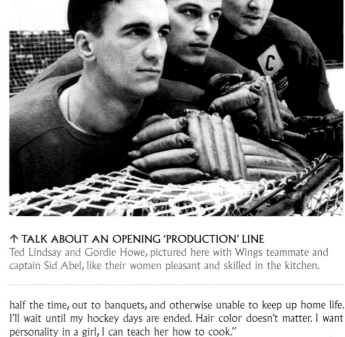

↑ TALK ABOUT AN OPENING 'PRODUCTION' LINE
Ted Lindsay and Gordie Howe, pictured here with Wings teammate and captain Sid Abel, like their women pleasant and skilled in the kitchen.

half the time, out to banquets, and otherwise unable to keep up home life. I'll wait until my hockey days are ended. Hair color doesn't matter. I want personality in a girl, I can teach her how to cook."

Marty Pavelich (great sense of humor, 23, 5-foot-11, 170): "I'm too young to be married. I thought the right girl came along a couple of times, but I caught myself. Don't care about those chemistry blondes. I'll find a girl who can cook and look good – both."

Gordon Howe (quiet and modest, 22, 6-foot-1, 185): "I'll be married five years from the time I first think about the big step. I like Canadian girls. My mother is Canadian. When the right girl comes along I guess she'll make the decision. I want a pleasant girl who can cook a steak. Otherwise all she needs is a good can opener."

Gerry Couture (college student, 25, 6-foot-2, 185): "A girl in Toronto has the ring. Met her at the University of Saskatchewan when she was studying to be a nurse and I was in pre-med. Don't know when we'll be married. I think she can cook."

Jim McFadden (Irish-born, 29, 5-foot-7, 180): "I'll wait till I'm through with hockey. Give me the Canuck girls, good-looking brunettes. I want a cook with looks, if I can get one."

Metro Prystai (strong and silent type, 23, 5-foot-9, 170): "Give me a chance, I'll marry the right girl. I've wanted to get a little money in the bank. American girls seem a little more forward than Canadians. How about a pretty brunette who can cook spaghetti?"

Clare Ragian (big and blond, 23, 6-foot-1, 190): "Haven't found her yet. Detroit girls seem a little nicer than the ones in Chicago. Brunettes for me."

That's the story, anyway, and any maiden fair who doubts it will have to do further research on her own. ⊤ℍℕ

1951-52

BANG, BANG, BANG

↑ LOST ART
This painting depicts the dominant, Ted Kennedy-captained Leaf teams of the late 1940s and early '50s. Toronto wins five Stanley Cups during a seven-year stretch in that era.

→ SWEET STABILITY
'Sugar' Jim Henry, the subject of this illustrated card, begins a four-year run as Boston's goalie in 1951-52. The season ends with a memorable, seven-game playoff setback to Montreal.

Newsmakers & Top Headlines

1 Mosienko bags NHL's quickest hat trick
Browsing through a record book late in the season, Chicago Black Hawks star Bill Mosienko says, "It would be nice to have my name in there." On the last day of the campaign, he arranges for it. With both teams out of playoff contention, he puts three goals past New York Rangers' goalie Lorne Anderson March 23 in the third period in a record 21 seconds. He scores at 6:09, 6:20 and 6:30. Mosienko almost adds a fourth off the next faceoff when he rings a shot off the post.

2 'Kraut Line' reunited in fairy-tale ending
The Bruins honor the 'Kraut Line' before a game with Chicago March 18 and the line returns the favor. Bobby Bauer ends a four-season retirement to rejoin linemates Milt Schmidt and Woody Dumart and gets a goal and an assist in a 4-0 win. A magical moment comes when they set up Schmidt's 200th goal. Schmidt finishes with a goal and three assists, while Dumart has an assist as Boston clinches the final playoff spot.

3 Hawks forced to put 46-year-old in net
After 18 years, trainer Moe Roberts finds himself between the pipes again. When Chicago goalie Harry Lumley is injured during a game with the Red Wings Nov. 25, former NHL goalie Roberts takes over and plays a shutout period. At 46, he's the oldest player in NHL history. Roberts debuted in the NHL Dec. 8, 1925, for the Boston Bruins, posting 35 shutout minutes, and last played in 1933-34 for the New York Americans.

Cup Winner
Detroit Red Wings

Leading Scorers
1. Gordie Howe, Det, 86 points
2. Ted Lindsay, Det, 69 points
3. Elmer Lach, Mtl, 65 points
4. Don Raleigh, NYR, 61 points
5. Sid Smith, Tor, 57 points
6. Bernie Geoffrion, Mtl, 54 pts
7. Bill Mosienko, Chi, 53 points
8. Sid Abel, Det, 53 points
9. Ted Kennedy, Tor, 52 points
10. Milt Schmidt, Bos, 50 points

60 Moments
that changed the game
No.16: Bernie 'Boom Boom' Geoffrion is the first player to regularly use a slapshot in games and scores two goals in the season opener.

Significant Records
Fastest three goals: Bill Mosienko, Chicago (0:21).

HHOF Inductees
Dickie Boon
Moose Goheen
Moose Johnson
Mickey MacKay
↓ Bill Cook

Nickname of the Year
Bill 'Bashing Bill' Barilko

Worth Noting
The NHL changes its All-Star Game format, pitting the 1950-51 first-team selections against the second-teamers. Players from all six NHL teams are selected.

MEET MY PRICE AND I'LL PLAY, 'GEL' TELLS ROSS, WHO SAID NO

OCT. 20, 1951 BY LEN BRAMSON

MONTREAL, QUE. –

Jack Gelineau, home from the Boston Bruins training camp at Hershey, Pa., has settled down to making a career in the insurance business. The Bruins third-year goaler failed to come to a mutual contract agreement and Gelineau decided rather than play in the NHL for less than what he thinks he's worth, he'll go into retirement.

However, Gelineau, 26, has not quit the game. If the Bruins should see fit to change their mind and meet Jack's terms then he would return to Boston where he won the rookie-of-the-year honors in the 1949-50 season.

Gelineau reported that he and the Bruins parted company under friendly conditions.

"Mr. (Art) Ross and I had a long talk in Boston before I came home. He told me that I was possibly making the right decision. We failed to see eye-to-eye and I would not sign for anything less than what I asked for and what was promised me when I turned pro two years ago.

"That season the Bruins made certain promises to me regarding my contract and I asked that they be kept this season. However, they failed to live up to those promises and I decided not to play. I thought about this move all summer, so you see it wasn't made on the spur of the moment. I have given it plenty of thought.

"It is my own decision. I would love to play hockey this season, but not for anything less than what I think I'm worth. I have spent quite a long time in hockey and what I've got out of it has not compensated for those years. I never earned any money in junior and certainly never got a nickel at McGill. I told Mr. Ross that I had to save more money to compensate for those years I spent in amateur and college hockey."

Although rumors were current that Gelineau left the Bruins because he refused to go to the minors, he denies them.

"The Bruins never offered nor even mentioned sending me to the minors. The only time it was ever mentioned was when I first turned pro and it was thought that I might have to spend a year in the lower league to gain experience. They never threatened or even mentioned it at camp or when I talked contract with Mr. Ross."

As for Gelineau's career, which rose and fell like a meteor in two seasons, well, it's up to the game itself. If they want him, he'll play, but for his price.

"It is my life and I must decide for myself," says Gelineau. "Only time will tell whether I made the right decision. I have a good job with better earning potential than hockey. I have weighed both sides of the situation and decided than I cannot take a chance each year waiting until August rolls around to

↑ TRADING IN PADS FOR A DESK
A little more than a year after winning the Calder Trophy, Jack Gelineau leaves the Bruins to take a position as an insurance salesman.

find out if I'm going to be offered a 30-week guarantee to play the game of hockey.

"Many people have often mentioned I never wanted to play hockey in the first place. They were wrong. I love the game and have always wanted to play professional. I had never thought about retiring until last summer and then I wrote Mr. Ross and told him. Two weeks before camp, I received a letter and was asked to report to see if contract details could be worked out."

It was at camp where Gelineau first heard that the Bruins had brought in their present goaler, Sugar Jim Henry.

"I was eating dinner one day when somebody approached me and asked if Henry had arrived yet. I didn't know what he was talking about so I said 'report,' where is he supposed to be reporting to?" Then I found out that the Bruins had bought him.

"Mr. Ross had phoned from Boston and told (coach Lynn Patrick) that they could not meet my terms. Patrick told me. Then I went to Boston and talked over the situation with Ross himself. He told me that I may be making the right decision and that he was sorry it was to be this way. We parted the best of friends."

As for his future, Gelineau is uncertain as far as hockey goes. His job with the Sun Life Insurance Company is his future, he says, and unless he can mix hockey with his job and the money is right, he'll stick by it. He will not leave the job for hockey again unless it's at his price.

(Editor's Note: Gelineau spent a few seasons playing in the Quebec Senior League, while holding down the insurance job, and returned to the NHL for just two games at age 29 in 1953-54. He resumed his desk job thereafter. Gelineau died in 1998, one day after his 74th birthday.) THN

BLAST OFF

FACTS & STATS
from 1952-53

Cup Winner
Montreal Canadiens

Leading Scorers
1. Gordie Howe, Det, 95 points
2. Ted Lindsay, Det, 71 points
3. Maurice Richard, Mtl, 61 pts
4. W. Hergesheimer, NYR, 59 pts
5. Alex Delvecchio, Det, 59 pts
6. Paul Ronty, NYR, 54 points
7. Metro Prystai, Det, 50 points
8. Red Kelly, Det, 46 points
9. Bert Olmstead, Mtl, 45 points
10. Fleming Mackell, Bos, 44 pts

60 Moments
that changed the game
No. 9: The first televised game in Canada brings hockey and the NHL to the masses.

Nickname of the Year
Ted 'Teeder' Kennedy

Worth Noting
Gordie Howe makes a run at Rocket Richard's 50-goal season record. Howe enters the final game of the season with 49 goals, but is held off the scoresheet by the Canadiens, who check vigorously to protect their teammate's mark. Nonetheless, Howe shatters his own NHL points record by nine with 95, winning the Art Ross and Hart Trophies…The American League champion Cleveland Barons issue a Stanley Cup challenge to the NHL. They're turned down, as is the city's bid for an NHL expansion franchise when it cannot come up with the necessary working capital.

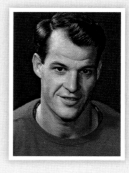

↑ TERRIBLE TWO
Detroit's Gordie Howe (right, white jersey) and Ted Lindsay bully the Bruins. They finish 1-2 in league scoring three times in the 1950s.

← SPANDEX TILT
These body-hugging uniforms on women players look like they were designed by Lululemon, but wouldn't pass the safety standards of today. Back in 1953, however, the Williams Silver Skates pinball machine is a big hit with men.

Newsmakers & Top Headlines

1 Rocket dethrones Stewart as scoring king
Ten years to the day that he scored his first NHL goal, Montreal's Rocket Richard beats Black Hawks goalie Al Rollins to become the league's all-time goal-scoring king. Richard's record 325th goal moves him past Nels Stewart. Richard finishes with 28 goals, 21 behind Detroit's Gordie Howe, who just misses joining Richard in the exclusive 50-goal club by one.

2 Saturday night hockey debuts on TV
Following weeks of experimentation, NHL hockey hits the small screen in Canada for the first time. Montreal beats Detroit 2-1 Oct. 1 in the first televised game, a French-language broadcast with Rene Lecavalier calling the play-by-play. On Nov. 1, the first English-language broadcast airs, with Foster Hewitt at the mic from midway through the second period as the Maple Leafs beat the Bruins 3-2. Leafs owner Conn Smythe fears that showing the entire game will cut into crowds at Maple Leaf Gardens.

3 Shakeup in Chicago makes Black Hawks Abel
Chicago acquires Sid Abel from Detroit July 22 and names him player-coach. Then, on Sept. 11, the franchise is purchased by Arthur Wirtz and Bruce and James D. Norris. The club ships all-star goalie Harry Lumley to Toronto for goalie Al Rollins, defenseman Gus Mortson and forwards Cal Gardner and Ray Hannigan. The Hawks hold first place early in season and make the playoffs for the first time since 1946.

← **MR. HOCKEY'S MITTS**
These gloves help Gordie Howe dazzle his way to a scoring title in 1952-53. Still, he finds time to drop them and remind his opponents who's boss now and then.

1953-54
PHENOM SIGNS

Cup Winner
Detroit Red Wings

Leading Scorers
1. Gordie Howe, Det, 81 points
2. Maurice Richard, Mtl, 67 pts
3. Ted Lindsay, Det, 62 points
4. Bernie Geoffrion, Mtl, 54 pts
5. Bert Olmstead, Mtl, 52 points
6. Red Kelly, Det, 49 points
7. Dutch Reibel, Det, 48 points
8. Ed Sandford, Bos, 47 points
9. Fleming Mackell, Bos, 47 pts
10. Ken Mosdell, Mtl, 46 points

Significant Records
Most power play goals,
one game: Camille Henry,
NY Rangers (4).
Most assists by a player,
first NHL game:
Dutch Reibel, Detroit (4).

Nickname of the Year
Gaye 'Box Car' Stewart

Worth Noting
Red Kelly, 26, is the first winner of the James Norris Trophy as the NHL's top defenseman, named in honor of the former Red Wings owner. The Detroit blueliner finishes sixth in league scoring with 49 points (16 goals and 33 assists) and also wins the Lady Byng Trophy for the second consecutive season. No defenseman wins the Lady Byng again until Brian Campbell of the Florida Panthers in 2011-12... Chicago Black Hawks goalie Al Rollins loses 47 games, setting a league record that lasts nearly two decades.

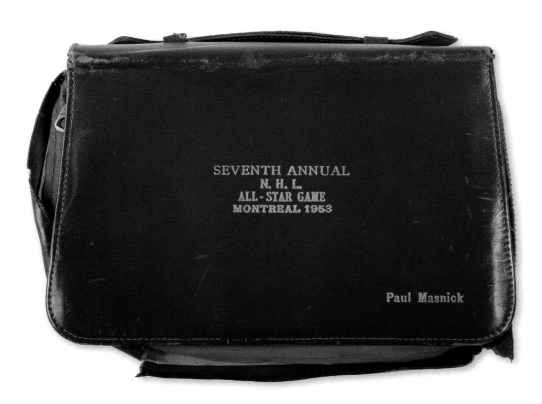

SEVENTH ANNUAL
N. H. L.
ALL-STAR GAME
MONTREAL 1953

Paul Masnick

↑ SWAG TO SPARE
All-Star Game participants in 1953 receive this nifty pouch as a perk. Journeyman center Paul Masnick doesn't suit up, but gets the gift anyway as a member of the '53 Habs.

Newsmakers & Top Headlines

1 Canadiens sign phenom Beliveau
With TV cameras on hand to record the moment and a financial advisor and tax specialist at his side to make sure he gets the best deal possible, Quebec Aces superstar Jean Beliveau signs a five-year, $100,000 contract with the Canadiens. "It's the highest contract ever given any player — by a city block," proclaims Habs managing director Frank Selke. A broken ankle limits Beliveau to 44 games and 34 points as a rookie. In short order, he will prove to be worth the investment.

2 Canadians absorb first setback to Soviets
It's raining and the outdoor ice at the World Championship in Stockholm turns to slush. But Soviet players use their soccer skills to kick the puck to teammates. They trounce the Toronto East York Lyndhursts 7-2 to win the gold medal in the first match of a long-running cold war between the two countries. "The worst thing that ever happened to me was standing on the blueline in pouring rain and watching that Russian flag go up," said coach Greg Currie. "A lot of guys were crying. They felt they'd let Canada down."

3 Rocket told to put away poison pen
Writing a column Jan. 9 in the Montreal weekly Samedi-Dimanche, Rocket Richard blasts NHL president Clarence Campbell, labeling him a dictator. Richard is ordered to write an apology and deposit a $1,000 cheque as a good-conduct bond with the NHL and is instructed to refrain from sportswriting.

FULL-BLOODED NATIVE COULD BE CHIEF IN CHICAGO

OCT. 31 1953 BY BUD BOOTH

CHICAGO, ILL. –

When the late Maj. Frederic McLaughlin guided the destiny of the Chicago Black Hawks, he often expressed a fervent desire to ice a capable team made up entirely of Americans. He did eventually see the idea put to the test, but it failed miserably. While he so much wanted a winning squad of United States skaters, it is doubtful McLaughlin ever went so far as to consider someday having a real American native — an Indian — in Hawk regalia. Although the club was named after a famed warrior, this seemed just a little bit too much to ask.

Last month, at the Chicago training camp, however, the "impossible" popped up in the person of a young center, Fred Sasakamoose (pronounced Saska-Moose). He, it was revealed, is a full-blooded member of the Cree tribe of Saskatchewan and bears the honorary title of Chief 'Running Deer.'

He emerged as a standout from the very first day of drills. Coach Sid Abel, GM Bill Tobin and other Hawk officials unanimously tabbed Fred as the possessor of a definite future in the big time.

"He's been sensational from the time he's been in organized hockey and should be the first Indian to ever play in the National League," exclaimed Tobin. "While he won't make the complete jump this season, we do plan to bring him up for at least a three-game tryout."

George Vogan, Chicago's scout at Moose Jaw, Sask., first spotted Fred one day juggling a puck about with fellow skaters on the Cree reservation at nearby Duck Lake. The discoverer of Metro Prystai, he brought him to Moose Jaw, where he has starred with the junior squad for two years.

As a chief of the Cree tribe, Sasakamoose annually receives $5 in treaty money from the Canadian government. His outstanding work among the non-professionals at training camp earned him the distinction of being picked as the top youngster over highly rated goaler Hank Bassen.

(Editor's Note: Sasakamoose was indeed the first Canadian aboriginal player in the NHL, but played just 11 games for Chicago in 1953-54 and another 45 games in various leagues the following two seasons. He later became a band councillor and chief on his reserve.)

OCT. 31, 1953 BY MARSHALL DANN

HECTIC HUNT FOUND GATHERUM DEEP IN SLUMBER

There may have been players more excited for their first NHL game than Davey Gatherum was, but there never was one sleepier than Davey when he hit the big-time.

Gatherum had to make a hectic cross-country dash to get into the Red Wing nets after Terry Sawchuk was injured and it meant a sleepless night of travel. The story had a happy ending since the baby-faced 21-year-old native of Fort William, Ont., shut out Toronto in his debut. And he stayed on for two more games in his emergency stint, allowing three goals.

↑ 'RUNNING DEER' RUNS AWAY WITH JOB
Fred Saskamoose, a.k.a. Chief 'Running Deer' of the Cree Tribe, becomes the first Canadian aboriginal NHLer after impressing the Hawks in camp.

But a part of the Detroit farm system was kept hopping the night of Oct. 10 and the morning of Oct. 11 to plant Davey in the Detroit goal. It all happened in this sequence: Sawchuk was hurt in the Montreal Forum about 9:55 p.m. (It was a three-stitch wound on his knee cap).

Jake Forbes, coach of Detroit's farm club at Sherbrooke in the Quebec League, was on hand as a spectator. Detroit coach Tommy Ivan asked Forbes if he could reach Gatherum and get him on a Detroit-bound plane. Gatherum was at Sherbrooke, more than 100 miles away. He and his wife had retired without knowledge of Sawchuk's injury and they have no telephone.

So Forbes phoned Tod Campeau, another Sherbrooke player, and Campeau enlisted teammate Moe Irving to assist in the search. Shortly after midnight, Campeau and Irving roused Gatherum out of bed and after taking 15 minutes to convince him it wasn't a joke, they got Davey started.

The Sherbrooke trainer rushed to the rink to open the dressing room so Gatherum could get his equipment. Then he waited until 2:15 a.m. until Forbes and Kenny Brown, a Wings' scout, arrived from Montreal by auto.

Brown and Gatherum took off in Gatherum's car for Dorval Airport at Montreal, arriving at 5:15 a.m. Davey caught a 6 a.m. flight and arrived at a Detroit hotel shortly after noon. So far he'd had fewer than 30 minutes sleep and the jitters had hit him so hard that there was no sleep that afternoon.

"I was so nervous that there was no use thinking about sleep," Davey recalls. "Lucky for me the jitters always go away after I handle my first shot. But they came back this time in the last period. I never had had a shutout in pro hockey and I started thinking about what a thrill it would be to get one in my first NHL game — and against Toronto."

The Wings gave a terrific defensive showing in front of Gatherum and he made 22 saves — the toughest of all by Ted Kennedy late in the final period. Detroit won 4-0. **THN**

>1954-55

RICHARD RIOT

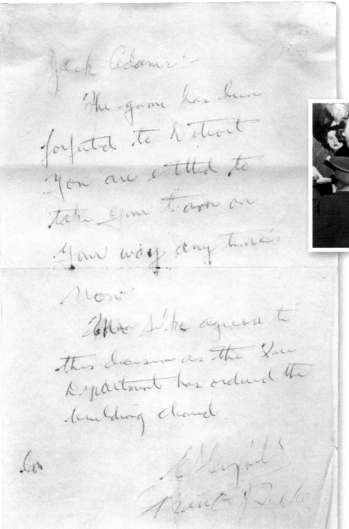

↑ MOB MENTALITY
Enraged Montreal fans swarm NHL president Clarence Campbell at the Forum after he suspends Maurice Richard for the season.

← GET IT IN WRITING
Its legibility rivals a doctor's prescription, but this note, addressed to Detroit GM Jack Adams, details the Canadiens' forfeiture of a game to the Red Wings following the Richard Riot.

Cup Winner
Detroit Red Wings

Leading Scorers
1. Bernie Geoffrion, Mtl, 75 pts
2. Maurice Richard, Mtl, 74 pts
3. Jean Beliveau, Mtl, 73 points
4. Dutch Reibel, Det, 66 points
5. Gordie Howe, Det, 62 points

60 Moments
that changed the game
No. 14: Smooth-skating Doug Harvey wins his first Norris Trophy and ushers in an era of the offense-minded defenseman.
No.19: Zamboni resurfacing machine introduced during intermission of a game in Toronto, replacing old practice of men pushing snow shovels.
No. 51: Fans make a stand against NHL president Clarence Campbell suspending Maurice Richard with the Richard Riot.

Nickname of the Year
Joe 'The Duke of Paducah' Klukay

Worth Noting
Seven members of the Cup-champion Detroit Red Wings – John Wilson, Bill Dineen, Marcel Pronovost, Ted Lindsay, Alex Delvecchio, Vic Stasiuk and Red Kelly – become NHL head coaches in the future, but none will coach a Cup winner…NHL president Clarence Campbell receives many death threats following his decision to suspend Rocket Richard. The ban (15 total games) is the longest ever handed out by Campbell.

Newsmakers & Top Headlines

1 Richard Riot rocks Montreal
Reacting to a high stick from Boston's Hal Laycoe in a March 13 game, Montreal's Rocket Richard attacks Laycoe with a stick three times and linesman Cliff Thompson with his fists and is ejected. NHL president Clarence Campbell suspends Richard for the rest of the season, costing him a shot at what would have been his one and only scoring title. The next night, as Montreal plays Detroit, fans move towards Campbell's seats in the Forum, hurling insults and debris. A tear gas bomb explodes, sending people rushing for the exits. The game is forfeited to Detroit, the crowd spills onto St-Catherine Street and rioting begins. When it's all over, the damage inflicted on local businesses is estimated in the hundreds of thousands of dollars.

2 Big changes at top of NHL ladder
Despite a Stanley Cup win in 1954, Tommy Ivan resigns as coach of Detroit to take a position as GM of the Black Hawks. While Ivan is about to launch a long career as an NHL executive, two others bring theirs to a close. GM Art Ross ends his 30-year association with the Bruins and Conn Smythe retires as managing director of the Maple Leafs.

3 Zamboni makes clean sweep at Gardens
A new ice re-surfacing machine, the Zamboni, makes its NHL debut March 10 as Montreal battles Toronto at Maple Leaf Gardens. Zambonis quickly become standard equipment at NHL rinks. The fresh ice makes little difference as this game ends scoreless.

RICHARD RIOT: THE GIST AND JEST OF IT

MARCH 26, 1955 BY ELMER FERGUSON

MONTREAL, QUE. –

There never was anything like this in the long history of Montreal sport. And we hope there never will be again. For a band of young hooligans who climaxed a disgraceful display of mob-hatred directed against president Clarence Campbell by exploding a tear-gas bomb in the Forum might have caused a panic and cost scores of lives.

But amazingly, such panic as developed was limited. From where this observer was stationed, high up in the press box, there was some rushing for the south end exits, but the main body of customers were cool. Some ran but the poise, the undismayed spirit of other thousands who stood blinking as the acrid fumes brought tears from their eyes, who gagged and choked as the smoke hit their throats, was astonishing. A few minutes before, they were in the throes of excitement, as the Red Wings roared over the stricken Habs. Yet, when something real came, most of them met it with cool, almost dare-devil indifference.

You may not agree with his judgment, but you can't but admire the superb courage of Clarence Campbell, a man who faced death throughout World War II, to whom the heckling and the minor missiles and the torrents of verbal abuse ranging from stupid to obscene hurled his way bounced like thistle-down off one who had faced shells and shrapnel. Here was a man caught between two extremes. If he avoided the game, he would be listed as a coward. If he went, he was inciting a riot. So he went. On physical injury, he took his chances, came through a gentleman.

Rocket Richard sat only a few yards from the NHL president, whose harsh ruling against the greatest of all hockey players started the fearsome display that dealt Montreal sport a black, as well as a tearful eye.

The Rocket sat behind the south-end nets. It was just behind him but a few feet away that the tear-gas bomb exploded after the first period. After the excitement had died somewhat, the Rocket, almost unnoticed in the milling mob, walked half-way around the rink to where his wife was sitting, took her arm, helped her down into the aisle. They walked slowly around. "This is a terrible thing," said the Rocket, shaking his head, unsmilingly. "It was terrible, awful. People might have been killed."

Curiously, no one seemed to notice the broad-shouldered Richard in his dark street clothes, and grey hat. He and Mrs. Richard walked quietly to the side-entrance and left.

When Pres. Campbell entered, after the game had started, with his blonde secretary Phyllis King, the verbal storm broke. It halted then resumed in full fury when the period ended with the Canadiens in arrears 4-1, their championship chances fading fast as the Wings ploughed through a team that seemed bewildered and disorganized. Hundreds swarmed near the box where he sits, hurled insults. A tomato hand landed on the presidential hat early in the proceedings. After a time, he took off the hat, wiping it carefully. Rubbers flew through

↑ THE MORNING AFTER

Damage is severe outside the Montreal Forum the first game after Rocket Richard is suspended by NHL president Clarence Campbell.

the air. Twice Miss King was struck on the side of the face with these missiles, merely straightened her white hat, paid no further attention. Programs, rolled-up newspapers were flung.

A few marauders sought to get up the short stairway to his seat, were thrown back by ushers and firemen. Then a skinny little fellow came along, meekly asked the usher if he might shake the president's hand. The usher, surprised to find a sporting spirit, agreed. The shrimp walked up, stretched out his hand, then hurriedly slapped at the president's face. Jimmy Orlando, former hockey star and wrestling referee, leaped up the short stairway, caught the belligerent one, and yanked him down the steps. The attacker fought, kicked and punched, but Orlando was too much for him.

"He didn't hit me," said Campbell afterwards. "He made some flapping motions, but I pushed him back with my foot and someone caught him. "

Then came the bomb. Pres. Campbell gathered in Miss King, they hustled around the corner, out into the passage where the air was cleaner.

Inside, the acrid fumes drifted high and wider. Smaller glass-tubed tear-gas bombs exploded on the ice, with short, sharp barks. Outside, the mob was roaring, windows crashed as bottles and chunks of ice flew. Bullets too streaked through the glass into the brick walls of the empty lobby. Inside, Campbell and his friends, with Bill and Mrs. Wray, sat in Bill Head's clinic.

We asked Campbell first about the game. "It's forfeited to Detroit," he said. "Anytime conditions such as prevailed tonight make it impossible to go on with the game, it is forfeited to the visiting team, no matter which club is ahead."

Police Chief Tom Leggett stood by until midnight. Outside the crowd on St. Catherine Street was still roaring, glass was smashing. After 11 o'clock, Leggett consulted with the Forum's Jim Hunter, and said: "I think you can go home now, Mr. Campbell. There's no one around the back entrance."

Then the Selkes left quietly. And your agent and Les Daly stepped out the rear door and hailed a passing taxi.

Out in front, the crowd still roared, the missiles still flew.

So ended, we hope, a disgraceful incident in the history of Montreal sport. **THN**

DYNASTY SEED

↑ EARLY PROTECTION
Jacques Plante, one of the game's great innovators, toys with the idea of wearing a mask in a game for many years prior to the famous 1959-60 debut. This is his prototype mask from 1955.

→ I'LL HAVE A VEZINA TO GO
Players are given personal trophies when they win a major NHL award. Hall-of-Famer to be Plante finds room for seven of these "personal" Vezinas on his fireplace mantle at home.

FACTS & STATS
from 1955-56

Cup Winner
Montreal Canadiens

Leading Scorers
1. Jean Beliveau, Mtl, 88 points
2. Gordie Howe, Det, 79 points
3. Maurice Richard, Mtl, 71 pts
4. Bert Olmstead, Mtl, 70 points
5. Tod Sloan, Tor, 66 points
6. Andy Bathgate, NYR, 66 pts
7. Bernie Geoffrion, Mtl, 62 pts
8. Dutch Reibel, Det, 56 points
9. Alex Delvecchio, Det, 51 pts
10. Dave Creighton, NYR, 51 pts

60 Moments
that changed the game
No. 29: Detroit opens the door for Glenn Hall to be its No.1 goalie. He's the originator of the butterfly style of goaltending.

Nickname of the Year
Gus 'Old Hardrock' Mortson

Worth Noting
Toe Blake makes the transformation from star player to coach smoothly, guiding Montreal to an NHL-record 45 wins and a 100-point season, the club's first, in his debut behind the bench. When the Habs capture the Cup, Blake joins Eddie Gerard and Hap Day as the only NHLers to captain and coach teams that win the Cup...NHL president Clarence Campbell asks for a revision to the penalty rule that will see a penalized player return to the ice when a power play goal is scored. The Canadiens are the lone club to vote against the idea.

Newsmakers & Top Headlines

1 Wings trade Sawchuk in favor of rookie Hall
After winning the Stanley Cup, Red Wings GM Jack Adams engineers a seven-player deal with the Black Hawks May 28, then stuns the hockey world by shipping star goalie Terry Sawchuk to Boston in a nine-player trade June 3, feeling rookie Glenn Hall is ready for the big time. When he's done, just nine players are left from the 1954-55 Cup squad. Detroit's record of seven consecutive first-place finishes is halted and so is the Wings' two-year reign as champions.

2 Blake takes helm of fab Habs
Montreal coach Dick Irvin moves to Chicago and former Canadiens captain Toe Blake is named coach June 9. Jean Beliveau wins the Hart and Art Ross Trophies, Doug Harvey wins the Norris, Jacques Plante takes the Vezina and rookies Claude Provost, Jean-Guy Talbot, Don Marshall, Bob Turner and the Rocket's younger brother Henri suit up as the Habs capture the Stanley Cup, the first of a record five straight.

3 Howe and Lindsay receive death threats
Anonymous calls to Toronto papers before a March 24 semifinal game between the Red Wings and Maple Leafs state Ted Lindsay and Gordie Howe will be shot if they play. GM Jack Adams suggests rookie Cummy Burton start the warmup wearing Lindsay's No. 7, and if all goes well, then put on Howe's No. 9. Burton refuses. In the end, both men play and are not harmed. Lindsay scores the overtime winner.

FACTS & STATS
from 1956-57

Cup Winner
Montreal Canadiens

Leading Scorers
1. Gordie Howe, Det, 89 points
2. Ted Lindsay, Det, 85 points
3. Jean Beliveau, Mtl, 84 points
4. Andy Bathgate, NYR, 77 pts
5. Ed Litzenberger, Chi, 64 pts
6. Maurice Richard, Mtl, 62 pts
7. Don McKenney, Bos, 60 pts
8. Dickie Moore, Mtl, 58 points
9. Henri Richard, Mtl, 54 points
10. Norm Ullman, Det, 52 points

Rule Changes
Player serving a minor returns to the ice when opponent scores.

60 Moments
that changed the game
No. 15: Montreal's proficiency on the power play prompts the league to amend a rule to have the penalty end when a power play goal is scored.
No. 24: Detroit trades Ted Lindsay to Chicago, rebuffing Lindsay's attempt to win a Red Wings vote to proceed with creating a union.

Nickname of the Year
Lou 'Leapin' Louie' Fontinato

Worth Noting
Teeder Kennedy ends an 18-month retirement on Jan. 6, trimming down from 206 pounds to 185 to help a struggling Toronto Maple Leafs squad stay in the hunt for the playoffs. The Leafs miss the post-season by nine points…Frank Mahovlich, 19, gets his first cup of coffee in the NHL, scoring once in three games with the Leafs…Says Ted Lindsay on what sparked plans to create a players' union: "Actually, we don't have many grievances. We just felt we should have an organization of this kind."… Maurice Richard hits the 30-goal plateau for the ninth and final time in his career.

↑ ELBOWS AND LEATHER
At 6-foot-2 and 182 pounds, rugged defenseman Allan Stanley doesn't need a hard, plastic cap shell on his elbow pads to inflict damage. Stanley carves out a Hall of Fame career with five teams in the 1950s and '60s.

Newsmakers & Top Headlines

1 Lindsay attempts to organize players
A group of players led by the Detroit's Ted Lindsay, Montreal's Doug Harvey and Toronto's Jim Thomson and Tod Sloan begin the process of unionizing the players, revealing plans to form a labor association. The idea does not sit well with Toronto GM Conn Smythe, who labels his captain Thomson "a traitor and a quisling." Smythe trades Thomson and Sloan to Chicago. Detroit GM Jack Adams also dislikes the idea and ships fan favorite and team leader Lindsay and goalie Glenn Hall to Chicago.

2 Powerful Habs force power play rules
The potent power play of the Stanley Cup-champion Montreal Canadiens leads to a rule change that allows penalized players to return to the ice immediately after the opponent scores. Previously, teams spent the entire two minutes shorthanded, which was of massive benefit to the talent-laden Habs. Jean Beliveau, for example, scored three times in just 44 seconds against Boston on Nov. 5, 1955.

3 Sawchuk walks out on Bruins
Suffering from infectious mononucleosis and saying, "I'm fed up, I'm quitting," Boston goalie Terry Sawchuk walks away from the game Jan. 16. "My nerves are shot," he says. "I'm just edgy and nervous all the time." He sits out the remainder of the season, but returns next year following a trade back to Detroit. He continues his career for more than a decade.

1957-58

SCUPPERED UNION

← ROCKET'S RED GLARE
Armed with that trademark fire in his eyes, Maurice Richard racks up 34 points in just 28 games as a 36-year-old in 1957-58. However, an Achilles injury costs him much of the year.

↓ FIRST TO 500
Richard starts the season in style, blasting this puck past Chicago's Glenn Hall Oct. 19, 1957 for career goal No. 500. 'The Rocket' is the first member of the exclusive club.

FACTS & STATS
from 1957-58

Cup Winner
Montreal Canadiens

Leading Scorers
1. Dickie Moore, Mtl, 84 points
2. Henri Richard, Mtl, 80 points
3. Andy Bathgate, NYR, 78 pts
4. Gordie Howe, Det, 77 points
5. Bronco Horvath, Bos, 66 pts
6. Ed Litzenberger, Chi, 62 pts
7. Fleming Mackell, Bos, 60 pts
8. Jean Beliveau, Mtl, 59 points
9. Alex Delvecchio, Det, 59 pts
10. Don McKenney, Bos, 58 pts

60 Moments
that changed the game
No. 47: Willie O'Ree breaks the color barrier in hockey, suiting up for Boston against Montreal.

Significant Records
Fastest goal from start of period: Claude Provost, Montreal (0:04)

HHOF Inductees
Frank Boucher
King Clancy
Sprague Cleghorn
Alec Connell
Red Dutton
Frank C. Foyston
Frank Fredrickson
Herb Gardiner
George Hay
Dick Irvin
Duke Keats
Hughie Lehman
George McNamara
Paddy Moran
↓ Ching Johnson

Nickname of the Year
Harry 'Whipper' Watson

Newsmakers & Top Headlines

1 NHLPA suffers setback
Ted Lindsay's hopes for a player union take a hit when, fearing retribution from the NHL, his former Detroit teammates back out of the certification bid. Lindsay had been traded to Chicago earlier in the year after he spearheaded a $3-million anti-trust lawsuit against the league, primarily over player pensions. While the union bid fails, the lawsuit has a positive impact: it scares the NHL into increasing the minimum salary to $7,000, improving the pension plan and allowing players to decide themselves when they're ready to return to action following an injury.

2 Black Hawks surrender Rocket's 500th goal
Fittingly, the Black Hawks are the victims as Rocket Richard becomes the first player in NHL history to score 500 goals. The historic marker comes at 13:52 of the first period of Montreal's 3-1 win Oct. 19, with Richard beating Glenn Hall. The Black Hawks were also Richard's victims for Nos. 100, 200, 400 and 325, the tally which moved him past previous goal-scoring leader Nels Stewart.

3 O'Ree NHL's first black player
Boston's Willie O'Ree becomes the first black player in NHL history when he debuts Jan. 18 in the Bruins' 3-0 win at the Montreal Forum. O'Ree plays the next night in Boston against the Habs, then is returned to the minors. His NHL career concludes with 43 games in 1960-61 when he scores four goals and 14 points.

O'REE'S TWO GAME STAND: HE'LL BE BACK

FEB. 1, 1958 BY LEN BRAMSON

MONTREAL, QUE. –

Willie O'Ree became the first Negro to play in the NHL, but his presence on the scene didn't mean that a barrier had been broken, as was the case of Jackie Robinson, the first Negro to break into major league baseball. NHL owners have never discriminated against race, color or creed. All they have ever asked for was ability on skates.

There have been other Negro players in organized hockey. Most prominent were the Carnegie Brothers, Ossie and Herbie. They played most of their hockey in Quebec for the now defunct Sherbrooke Saints of the old Quebec Amateur Hockey League. When the club folded, Herbie moved over to the Quebec Aces before retiring. The Aces can boast the use of more Negroes than any other hockey club. Carnegie was the first, before O'Ree and a third, Stan Maxwell, is presently with the Aces as well. Maxwell, like Willie, is a Boston chattel and is highly regarded by the Bruins.

Willie's debut in Montreal didn't cause too much excitement. Most Montreal fans had either seen or heard of him in the Quebec League. But they did appreciate the fact he was the first Negro to break into the NHL and they applauded him accordingly.

As to his hockey ability, most of the Montreal experts like the way he handled himself at left wing and were impressed with his speed. But he seemed to freeze around the nets. He had a sure goal on his stick in the 3-0 Boston win, but he took too long to fire the puck and before he made his move defenseman Tom Johnson had draped himself all over him.

O'Ree showed great spirit and hustle and in his very first turn on the ice he carried Bert Olmstead into the boards and left him hanging on the rail.

The consensus of opinion is O'Ree will be back, but next time to stay.

Willie, a native of Fredericton, N.B., told reporter Dick Bacon he was really nervous in the first period of his first game.

"But I was much better as the game went on. I had a real good chance to score in the third period when Gerry Toppazzini gave me a pass in close. I thought I had (Jacques) Plante deked pretty good, but Johnson hooked me," said O'Ree.

Coach Milt Schmidt said he was happy with Willie's showing. "I knew he was nervous, that's one of the reasons I alternated him with Pierson. But who wouldn't be nervous in their first game. I knew I was plenty nervous in mine," said Milt.

Willie, christened William Eldon O'Ree, admitted "I hardly slept at all after my coach, Joe Crozier, called me at my boarding house and told me I was supposed to report to the Bruins at the Mount Royal Hotel in Montreal. I got a little rest on the train down from Quebec City, but that was all."

O'Ree is one of several Negroes to perform in the minors, but his debut in the NHL marks the lowering of the last color line among major sports in North America. However, some

↑ **"GREAT SPIRIT AND HUSTLE"**
After breaking the color barrier in the NHL with Boston, Willie O'Ree spends most of his career in the Western League with San Diego.

hockey observers point out that the only reason a "Color Line" existed was the fact that there hasn't been a Negro player qualified to make the NHL. Several colored hockey players have played in the minors, in fact, O'Ree has been a linemate of one – Stan Maxwell.

"I was the most surprised guy in the world when I found out I was going to play for the Bruins," O'Ree said. "In fact, I still am. After all, I thought there were several other guys Boston would have called up before me. I've been having trouble scoring (seven goals in 32 games) ... I've been having trouble around the cage... hitting the post or just missing the net."

The 5-10, 175-pound winger has been playing hockey ever since his father built him a backyard rink in his pre-teenage days.

"I've always hoped some day I might make the NHL," he continued. "I've thought about it ever since I began listening to the Saturday night broadcasts from Toronto by Foster Hewitt."

The closest he came before his debut was a three-week training stint with the Bruins last September.

O'Ree is the youngest of eight children — four boys and four girls. The only other skater in the family is one of his brothers who "fools around in a commercial hockey league back home." The quiet-spoken athlete has been pro for two years. Before that he played for the Kitchener Junior Canucks where he said coach "Black Jack Stewart helped me a lot." The year before that he was with the Quebec Frontenacs, another junior team) then coached by Phil Watson, now coach of the New York Rangers.

A summertime shortstop with hands like meat-hooks, O'Ree also played rugby, the English variety, in his school days at Fredericton High. **THN**

(Editor's Note: The views expressed and language in the story were mostly left intact to reflect the tone of the times).

>1958-59

PACKING PUNCH

↑ CASH TO CUPS
The Toronto Maple Leafs pluck Johnny Bower from the Cleveland Barons of the AHL after the New York Rangers had traded him away for scratch. Bower goes on to win four Stanley Cups and two Vezina Trophies in Toronto.

← ALL GUTS, ALL GLORY
Given the paltry padding his chest protector provides, Bower uses guts more than gear to stop pucks in his second season with the Maple Leafs. Bower plays until he's 45 years old.

Newsmakers & Top Headlines

1 Imlach rallies Leafs to playoff spot
Toronto is seven points out of a playoff spot with nine days left in the season. Coach Punch Imlach boasts he'll not only get his club into the playoffs, but also to the Stanley Cup final. The Leafs pass the faltering Rangers on the final day of the season to make the big dance. The Leafs sideline the Boston Bruins in the semifinal before bowing to Montreal in the final.

2 Storey quits as NHL referee
Longtime referee Red Storey doesn't know it, but when he takes the ice April 4 for Game 6 of the Stanley Cup semifinal between Montreal and the Chicago Black Hawks, it will be his last game. Montreal wins 5-4 to oust Chicago and Black Hawks' coach Rudy Pilous

raps the redhead, saying he "didn't have the guts" to call two late fouls by the Habs. A 25-minute protest, in which two fans attack Storey, follows Claude Provost's winning goal. The worst comes the next day, when NHL president Clarence Campbell claims Storey "froze." Storey resigns as a result of the comments.

3 Newcomers spark Chicago turnaround
With young stars Bobby Hull, Glenn Hall, Stan Mikita, Eddie Litzenberger, Eric Nesterenko and Pierre Pilote joining veterans Ted Lindsay, Tod Sloan and Dollard St-Laurent, long-dormant Chicago is suddenly a force to be reckoned with in the NHL. The Black Hawks finish third and their 69 points equal a club record as they makes the playoffs for the first time since 1952-53.

FACTS & STATS
from 1958-59

Cup Winner
Montreal Canadiens

Leading Scorers
1. Dickie Moore, Mtl, 96 points
2. Jean Beliveau, Mtl, 91 points
3. Andy Bathgate, NYR, 88 pts
4. Gordie Howe, Det, 78 points
5. Ed Litzenberger, Chi, 77 pts

60 Moments
that changed the game
No. 32: Full-time air travel replaces train transportation prior to the playoffs.

HHOF Inductees
Jack Adams
Tiny Thompson
↓ Cy Denneny

Nickname of the Year
Harry 'Apple Cheeks' Lumley

Worth Noting
Montreal's Dickie Moore wins his second straight scoring title. His 96 points eclipse Gordie Howe's single-season record by one… On "Gordie Howe Night" in Detroit March 3, Howe skates out to receive a new car and finds his parents in the backseat, in town for their first NHL game…Rangers coach Phil Watson, mocking Punch Imlach's bold predictions and bald head: "The only crystal ball he's got is on his shoulders. What a beautiful head of skin."… Tom Johnson ends Doug Harvey's Norris Trophy streak at four. He goes on to be the only D-man besides Harvey to win it in an eight-season stretch.

HOWE RETAINS 'FIST' TITLE AT LOUIE'S EXPENSE

FEB. 14, 1959 BY MARSHALL DANN

DETROIT, MICH. —

Gordie Howe has a crown he doesn't want, a title he didn't seek and an honor he doesn't like. The durable Detroiter is king of hockey's fist-fighters. "Don't say that," Howe insists in a pleading manner. "I get paid for hockey, not fighting. I don't like fighting and I hope I never have another fight."

Regardless of Howe's own opinions, the fistic ability of the rugged Red Wing captain no more can be questioned today than his all-around greatness in every department of hockey. That was settled a few nights ago when Howe stood with Lou Fontinato in a toe-to-toe slugging match at Madison Square Garden, a free-swinging young challenger to the 'Top Cop' title.

"The fiercest fist fight I've seen since that great battle between Jack Stewart and Johnny Mariucci maybe 15 years ago," is how Detroit coach Sid Abel described the brawl that overflowed into the St. Clair Hospital.

That was where Fontinato woke up the next morning. He went for repairs because his facial features were rearranged by Howe's pumping right hand. The doctors held Fontinato overnight for observation.

The fight came after 17 minutes of wild action during which New York jumped to a 4-1 lead. Several times Howe and Rangers rookie Eddie Shack came close to tangling, and Fontinato appeared on the scene as a policeman.

To make sure Howe understood how he felt for grievances against Shack, Fontinato took an open stand seconds before the fight exploded. At a faceoff, he skated over and gave Howe a warning visible to all 15,168 patrons.

"I don't know what he said," Howe commented later. "He was trying to say something, but just kept spewing all over my uniform. I finally told him to go mind his own business."

Just 13 seconds later, Shack and Red Kelly tangled behind the Detroit net. Howe got into it and all the players fell against the cage. They were getting up peacefully when Fontinato exploded. Standing some 20-25 feet away, Louie dropped his stick, shucked off his gloves and headed for the action.

"I saw him coming like a mad man and put out my left arm to stop him," Howe detailed. "He took it on the chops and then started swinging. I had trouble getting my gloves off for an instant. Then I got rid of them and was busy for a while."

Fontinato, a rangy defenseman, tried overhand bolo punches for a while and connected steadily on the side of Howe's head. Finally, Howe managed to get a grip on the front of Fontinato's jersey with his left hand and, holding Louie in front like a punching bag, started pumping in solid uppercut rights.

"I could hear those punches landing whop-whop-whop just like someone chopping wood," says Jack McIntyre, who guarded Howe's flank throughout.

The normal guardwork by teammates was not needed in this case. Everyone paired off to make sure there was no interference, and the two linesmen — Bill Morrison and Art Skov — let the fight run its course. While linesman are instructed to intervene promptly in all fights, this was one they couldn't or wouldn't. Showing instincts toward self-preservation, neither chose to step between the pair of 200-pound giants as they flailed freely with their fists.

"I never saw a fight like that since I've been in hockey," claimed goalie Terry Sawchuk, who had a ringside seat. "They just stood there slugging each other with all they had."

This slugfest went 30 seconds, maybe 40 seconds — it's hard to guess. Wise old Bill Gadsby, veteran Ranger rearguard, finally gave the signal to call it off. He leaped on Howe, and Andy Bathgate slid ahead of Fontinato.

It wasn't a hard fight to stop. Both warriors were completely spent.

Referee Frank Udvari rewarded each with a fighting major, but excused them to the powder rooms. Neither Howe nor Fontinato gave each other as much as a dirty look the rest of the game. Howe sparked Detroit's comeback try with a second goal, but the Rangers prevailed 5-4. Fontinato had enough zip left to pick up a couple more minor penalties.

There are a few footnotes to this fight. While Fontinato was defeated in injury, he was a game goer who gained considerable respect in defeat. Louie finished the game before heading to the hospital ward for treatment to massive facial bruises and a nose flattened and bent grotesquely. Howe got a mouse over his right eye and a badly sprained little finger on one hand.

In the pressbox, where Fontinato was a sentimental favorite, some called it a draw. That was before they looked at or inquired about Fontinato. There is great sentiment among Ranger followers that Fontinato was the uncrowned king of the fighters and his defeat was not taken easily by his followers.

Howe has had a strong fighting reputation ever since he broke into the league as a heavily muscled 18-year-old westerner from Saskatoon. In his first three seasons he had a half-dozen bouts, only two of which were more than one-punch affairs. He flattened Gaye Stewart in a wild fight along the boards, and he battered Rocket Richard in a lively brawl.

Fontinato has learned from himself why rival players, who always have respected Howe for his playing skill, also have deep regard for the power and speed in his ham-like hands and sledgehammer arms. **THN**

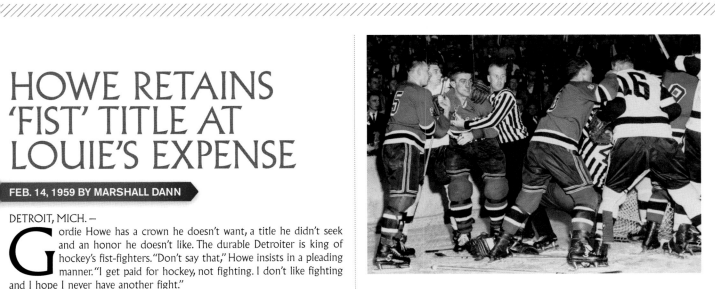

↑ LOOKING FOR MORE TROUBLE

Sporting a rearranged nose, New York's Lou Fontinato is held back trying to get at Detroit's Gordie Howe. The tilt is a hockey classic battle.

FACTS & STATS
from 1959-60

Cup Winner
Montreal Canadiens

Leading Scorers
1. Bobby Hull, Chi, 81 points
2. Bronco Horvath, Bos, 80 pts
3. Jean Beliveau, Mtl, 74 points
4. Andy Bathgate, NYR, 74 pts
5. Henri Richard, Mtl, 73 points
6. Gordie Howe, Det, 73 points
7. Bernie Geoffrion, Mtl, 71 pts
8. Don McKenney, Bos, 69 pts
9. Vic Stasiuk, Bos, 68 points
10. Dean Prentice, NYR, 66 pts

60 Moments
that changed the game
No. 4: Jacques Plante dons a mask for the first time in a game and the face of goaltending changes forever.

HHOF Inductees
Buck Boucher
Jack Walker
↓ Sylvio Mantha

Nickname of the Year
Johnny 'Iron Man' Wilson

Worth Noting
Down one point in the scoring race heading into the last game, Bobby Hull overtakes Bronco Horvath with two points in a head-to-head matchup to win his first Art Ross Trophy with 81 points…This season is the first of the Original Six era during which every active player has played for Original Six teams only – since 1942-43…Phil Watson sustains an ulcer and is replaced by Alf Pyke as Rangers coach.

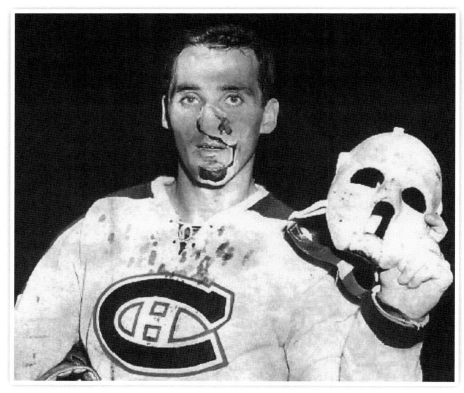

↑ STITCH WORK
Jacques Plante invents a mask to prevent further facial injuries.

Newsmakers & Top Headlines

1 Fifth straight Cup for 'best-ever' Canadiens
The Canadiens sweep to their record fifth consecutive Stanley Cup, taking care of the Black Hawks and Maple Leafs in eight straight games. In its five-season reign as champion, Montreal never trails in a playoff series and is not pushed to a single Game 7. During the regular season, the Habs average more than 40 wins per campaign and cop 15 individual awards.

2 Masked marvel gives goalies new life
A day after Halloween, Jacques Plante dons a mask and changes the game forever. After being cut for seven stitches by an Andy Bathgate shot during a Nov. 1 game against the Rangers, Plante returns wearing a custom-made fiberglass mask he has been experiment-ing with in practice. He stops 29 of 30 shots in a 3-1 win. Montreal goes unbeaten in its first 11 games with its masked netminder. "If they let me wear it all the time, I can play until I'm 45," Plante says.

3 Kelly traded twice in five days
Unhappy with an article which suggests he forced Red Kelly to play with a broken ankle, Detroit GM Jack Adams trades his all-star defenseman and forward Billy McNeill to the Rangers Feb. 5 for Bill Gadsby and Eddie Shack. Both Detroit players balk and announce their retirements, so the trade is rescinded. On Feb. 10, Adams then trades Kelly to Toronto for defenseman Marc Reaume. This time, Kelly approves the deal and reports to the Maple Leafs.

GO WEST YOUNG MAN, BUT CAHAN FINDS IT IS A LOT TOUGHER BY CAR THAN BY HORSE

OCT. 10, 1959 BY THN STAFF

Defenseman Larry Cahan, former New York Ranger, was late for the opening of Vancouver Canucks' Western League training camp. But he had some good reasons. Driving from Toronto through the United States, a tie rod in his car broke at Superior, Wisc.

In an attempt to fix the rod, he scooted past a motorcycle policeman while doing 90 miles an hour. He was brought to a halt further down the road by a roadblock consisting of five police cars and six constables armed with shotguns and drawn pistols.

He was put in jail and fined $100. That was $15 more than he had on him so he had to stay in jail until Canucks coach Art Chapman wired him some loot. On the road again, he had three flat tires. When he was changing one of them outside Spokane, Wash., his jack slipped and the car crunched down on some household goods he had removed to lighten the load.

JAN. 30, 1960 BY JOHN KUENSTER

LITZ TRAGEDY CAME JUST WEN HE WAS SHAKING SEASON SLUMP

Captain Ed Litzenberger will be lost to the Black Hawks for the remainder of the season, according to a report. Physicians who examined the veteran right winger said he "cannot play hockey again this season."

Litzenberger, 27, was injured and his wife, Doreen, 26, was killed in an auto crash northwest of Chicago early Monday morning. The crash occurred at 4:30 a.m. after the Litzenbergers had been with friends following the Hawks-New York Rangers game at Chicago Stadium Sunday night.

They were driving to their home in suburban Glenview, where their son Dean, 2, was being minded by a baby-sitter when their car apparently skidded on ice and struck the side of an overpass on Edens Expressway. The car did not overturn, but its right side was caved in.

Mrs. Litzenberger was thrown from the auto and died shortly after arrival at Covenant hospital. The investigating officer found her husband in the back seat moaning, "I was hurt on the ice." Litzenberger suffered head lacerations and internal injuries. There were no broken bones, although it was first feared he might have a broken pelvis.

Litzenberger was put under heavy sedation and not told about his wife's death until Tuesday. He was still suffering some shock effects at the time and, according to the doctor, did not seem to comprehend when told the complete story.

GM Tommy Ivan and coach Rudy Pilous both visited Litzenberger. Ivan said he and other Black Hawks officials were so shocked by the tragedy that they hadn't given any thought to bringing up a replacement for Litzenberger, who had been the Hawks leading scorer for three years prior to this season.

Pilous sent the Hawks through an hour and half scrimmage using Eric Nesterenko in Litzenberger's right wing post on a line with left winger Ted Lindsay and center Stan Mikita.

↑ **TRAGIC TIMES IN WINTRY CHICAGO**
Black Hawks captain Ed Litzenberger is never the same following a Chicago-area car crash that claims the life of his wife.

FEB. 6, 1960 BY JACK BERRY

EEL GETS HIS MAN IN CHASE TO THE STREET

Camille Henry shows promise of becoming a candidate for the Mounties. He got his man — and four stitches in his face.

Just when Red Wings fans and the management were congratulating themselves on the complete suppression of trash throwers at the Olympia, a rowdy element planted itself along the aisleway from the Rangers' bench to the dressing room. After a 2-2 tie Jan. 24, the Rangers were filing back to the dressing room when rowdies started taunting the Blues and throwing programs, cups, peanuts and other trash at them.

"Lou (Fontinato) was in front of me and stopped to argue with someone," Henry related. "Then someone threw something at me and I made a run for him. As soon as I went off the rubber walkway my skates hit the concrete, I fell on the seat of my pants and my stick fell. A man — not the one I was after — reached over, grabbed my stick and hit me with it. Then he threw down the stick and ran.

"I took off after him," said the smallest player in the NHL, nicknamed 'The Eel' because of his talents for slipping away from checks. "But I fell down a couple more times and then Red (Sullivan), Lou and Gump (Worsley) were chasing me. I grabbed him on the sidewalk outside the building and yelled to some policemen and they came and got him," Henry said.

The stick-swinger turned out to be a 37-year-old dry goods salesman, Eric H. Steiner. "I was carried away by the excitement. It was a thing of impulse," said Steiner, who later shook hands with Henry after the Red Wings doctor put four stitches under his eye. Henry and Rangers coach Alf Pike decided not to press charges and Steiner was released. **THN**

FACTS & STATS
from 1960-61

Cup Winner
Chicago Black Hawks

Leading Scorers
1. Bernie Geoffrion, Mtl, 95 pts
2. Jean Beliveau, Mtl, 90 points
3. Frank Mahovlich, Tor, 84 pts
4. Andy Bathgate, NYR, 77 pts
5. Gordie Howe, Det, 72 points
6. Norm Ullman, Det, 70 points
7. Red Kelly, Tor, 70 points
8. Dickie Moore, Mtl, 69 points
9. Henri Richard, Mtl, 68 points
10. Alex Delvecchio, Det, 62 pts

HHOF Inductees
Syl Apps
Charlie Conacher
Hap Day
George Hainsworth
Joe Hall
Percy LaSueur
Frank Rankin
Maurice Richard
Olivier Seibert
Bruce Stuart
↓Milt Schmidt

↑ EARLY BATTLE, LATE VICTORY
Black Hawks' future Hall of Famer Pierre Pilote fights for the puck with Henri Richard early in the 1960-61 season — a season in which Pilote goes on to win his only Stanley Cup while while Richard goes on to win eleven Stanley Cups.

← ONE OF WORSLEY'S WORST
Gump Worsley doesn't get much help out of these pads in 1960-61. He posts the second-highest goals-against average of his career (3.28).

Nickname of the Year
Johnny 'The China Wall' Bower

Worth Noting
Montreal coach Toe Blake receives a $2,000 fine, the largest in NHL history, for slugging referee Dalton MacArthur after losing Game 3 of the Habs' Stanley Cup semifinal against Chicago on Murray Balfour's power play goal…Bernie Geoffrion joins Maurice Richard as the NHL's second-ever 50-goal man, but can't eclipse the single-season record, failing to find the net his final two games of 1960-61.

Newsmakers & Top Headlines

1 Hawks end Canadiens dynasty
It seems like a mismatch — the five-time Stanley Cup-champion Canadiens against a Black Hawks team that hasn't won the Cup since 1937-38. But the Black Hawks pound the smaller, more skillful Canadiens into submission, then beat the Red Wings in the final.

2 Rocket calls it quits after 18 years
Montreal superstar Rocket Richard ends months of speculation when he announces his retirement Sept. 15 before the start of the 1960-61 season. "I guess I finally realized the game is getting too fast for me," says the 39-year-old Richard, whose 18-season career leaves him with 17 NHL records. He's the all-time leader in goals with 544, including a record 82 game-winners.

Richard's additional 82 goals and six overtime winners in the playoffs are also league marks. The Hockey Hall of Fame waives its three-year waiting period to admit Richard immediately.

3 'Boom Boom,' 'Big M' shoot for 50 goals
It looks certain the NHL will have its second 50-goal-scorer and it does — but not the guy everyone is watching. Toronto Maple Leafs' sniper Frank 'The Big M' Mahovlich has 26 goals after 29 games and 41 by his 59th game. However, Mahovlich scores just seven times the rest of the season to finish with 48. Meanwhile, Montreal's Bernie 'Boom Boom' Geoffrion blasts past him with 22 goals in his last 21 games and reaches the magical 50-goal plateau in his 62nd game.

BRUINS GOALER SIMMONS TOSSED FOR FLIPPING DISC

OCT. 22, 1960 BY RED FISHER

Hockey players, somebody once mentioned, are just like human beings. In other words, they're learning something new from time to time, just like the man paying his way into the rink.

There was the episode on the weekend at Boston, when referee Frank Udvari administered a two-minute penalty to Boston goalie Don Simmons. It happened this way:

The Canadiens had put together a rush into the Boston zone. Goalie Simmons grabbed the puck and instead of throwing it to the side of the net, he hurled it several feet in front of him onto the stick of one of his teammates. That's when Udvari whistled down the play and stuck Simmons with a two-minute penalty.

Simmons raced all the way to the blueline to protest the call, as if he didn't know the ruling was in the book. Simmons, as a goalie, knew all about it, but most of the men on the Canadiens didn't realize that a penalty covered the manoeuvre. Neither did most of the people in the rink.

The reason for this, of course, is that the infraction has been rarely called. Udvari, for example, told me after the game that the occasion was the first time he called it in pro hockey. Doug Harvey, who's been around for a few years, doesn't remember a similar call in his entire career. And referee Eddie Powers, who handled last night's game here, called the penalty once last season — the only time he has whistled it down since joining the NHL staff.

"We've always given the goalie a lot of room on that particular play," says Powers. "But last year, I had to call it in a game at Detroit when the goalie threw it 10 feet in front of him onto the stick of one of his men."

The culprit? Yeah, you guessed it: Don Simmons.

AUG., 1961 BY JEANE HOFFMAN

NO HANDICAP FOR EX-CANADIAN

You pause to wonder, sometimes, what Lyle LeBere could do if he had two hands…Lyle has only one you see.

A crane accident during a summer job on the St. Lawrence Seaway cut off his arm four inches below the elbow. If the crane wheel had not been turned the wrong way, Lyle could have extricated himself with only broken bones. "That's life," shrugged Lyle philosophically, "at least I wasn't a piano player…"

He was a hockey player — the best juvenile hockey player in the province of Ontario. A trophy, awarded to him as the "Most Valuable Player of Ontario" in 1957 proved that.

So what was a guy to do? Quit?

"Quit?" the 21-year-old pronounces the word as if he'd never heard it before. "Why should I quit? I knew I could keep on playing hockey. All I wanted was the chance to prove it."

He's had the chance in the California League, and if you

↑ THROWING IT ALL AWAY
Goalie Don Simmons may lose this encounter with Jean Beliveau, but his glove hand is free to toss the puck down the ice just in case.

want to know what he's proven as a goalie, take a look: LeBere backed his team, Long Beach Paramount, to the 1961 championship with a total of only 79 goals — a 3.7 per game average — well ahead of the league's other three net tenders. He won the Hamman Trophy as the league's best goalie, beating out the U.S. Olympic team goaler, Gene Catchine, for the prize.

"I like the sport too much to give it up," smiled good-humored Lyle, who recently moved here with his family. "I just bolted the goalie stick on to the end of my artificial arm and kept going. The game is more of a challenge now.

"I've had to rely on my body English more. Turk Broda, one of the game's immortals, paid me a hospital visit and told me he figured I'd have to play a 'stand up' game. He thought I wouldn't be able to get off the ice fast enough.

"First time I went down, I'll admit it took three guys to get me up. But I've learned to spring up, using my legs. I can handle angle shots fine. What bothers me is dropping to one knee to clear the puck in front of the net. I use my gloved hand to retrieve it because I don't have that much stick control.

"My main worry is that some guy, tearing down the ice, may get his stick caught and yank my arm out of my shoulder socket. I've learned to twist my body and release the stump from the artificial arm in a spit second.

"Occasionally a puck will slam into the wooden arm, and give off with a hollow sound that echoes all over the arena. You should see the spectators' amazement when that happens. I've played entire games without fans or rivals realizing I have a wooden arm — until that puck hits it."

Lyle, who's looking for a job as a bookkeeper or accountant, hasn't let the handicap bother him off-season. Guess what? He plays baseball… THN

1961-62
LEAFS BACK ON TOP

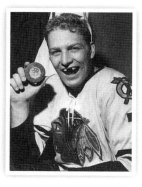

↑ TOOTHLESS WONDER
All I want for Christmas... Bobby Hull scores 50 goals.

← CHICAGO HOPE
Bobby Hull (left) and Stan Mikita have the Windy City abuzz after leading the Black Hawks to a Cup in 1960-61, but never repeat the feat despite posting dominant offensive numbers throughout the decade.

→ AHEAD OF THE CURVE
Mikita's molded blade helps him blossom into a four-time league scoring champion and stands as one of the game's greatest innovations.

Newsmakers & Top Headlines

1 Hull ties Bathgate in Art Ross race
For the first time in NHL history, there's a tie for the individual scoring title, as Chicago's Bobby Hull and New York's Andy Bathgate both finish with 84 points. Hull, the third 50-goal-scorer in NHL history, is awarded the Art Ross Trophy because he has more goals than Bathgate (50-28). Hull scores No. 50 on New York's Gump Worsley in the season finale.

2 Leafs end 11-year Stanley Cup drought
A groin injury to 1960-61 Vezina Trophy-winner Johnny Bower thrusts Don Simmons, who backstopped the Bruins to the Stanley Cup final in 1957 and 1958, into the spotlight. Simmons posts victories in Games 5 and 6 to bring the Maple Leafs the Cup in the last playoff action of his NHL career. With the series tied 2-2, the Leafs explode for an 8-4 victory over the Black Hawks at Maple Leaf Gardens, then get goals from Bob Nevin and Dick Duff in the final 10 minutes for a 2-1 win at Chicago Stadium. The Cup triumph is Toronto's first since 1951, marking the longest championship drought in franchise history.

3 Habs trade all-star Harvey to Rangers
Looking to add more toughness to the Canadiens, Frank Selke trades six-time Norris Trophy-winner Doug Harvey to the Rangers for Lou Fontinato. Harvey, named player-coach in New York, earns the Norris again and helps the Rangers make the playoffs. Fontinato leads the league with 167 penalty minutes.

FACTS & STATS
from 1961-62

Cup Winner
Toronto Maple Leafs

Leading Scorers
1. Bobby Hull, Chi, 84 points
2. Andy Bathgate, NYR, 84 pts
3. Gordie Howe, Det, 77 points

60 Moments
that changed the game
No. 46: In the early 1960s, Stan Mikita and Bobby Hull are credited with coming up with the curved hockey stick.

HHOF Inductees
Punch Broadbent	Billy McGimsie
Harry Cameron	Reg Noble
Rusty Crawford	Jack Ruttan
Jack Darragh	Sweeney Schriner
Jimmy Gardner	Joe Simpson
Billy Gilmour	Alf Smith
Shorty Green	Barney Stanley
Riley Hern	Nels Stewart
Tom Hooper	Marty Walsh
Bouse Hutton	Moose Watson
Harry Hyland	Harry Westwick
Jack Laviolette	Fred Whitcroft
Fred Maxwell	Phat Wilson
↓ Didier Pitre	

Nickname of the Year
Glenn 'Mr. Goalie' Hall

Worth Noting
Seven weeks after the Maple Leafs win their first championship since 1951, when Bill Barilko scored the Stanley Cup winner in overtime and then was lost in a plane crash, the wreckage of Barilko's plane is found in dense bush in Northern Ontario, 35 miles off course.

FACTS & STATS
from 1962-63

Cup Winner
Toronto Maple Leafs

Leading Scorers
1. Gordie Howe, Det, 86 points
2. Andy Bathgate, NYR, 81 pts
3. Stan Mikita, Chi, 76 points

60 Moments
that changed the game
No. 23: NHL puts an end to the sponsorship system to procure players by introducing the amateur draft.
No. 37: Dawn of scouting follows Boston's signing of 14-year-old Bobby Orr to a C-form contract.

Significant Records
Most consecutive complete games by a goaltender: Glenn Hall, Detroit, Chicago (502).

First Draft Pick, 1963
Garry Monahan, LW, Montreal

HHOF Inductees
Ebbie Goodfellow
Earl Seibert
↓Joe Primeau

Nickname of the Year
Ted 'Terrible Ted' Lindsay

Worth Noting
Leafs president Stafford Smythe on Chicago's $1-million offer for Frank Mahovlich: "No human being is worth $1 million — to buy or sell. I consider this to be a publicity stunt."…Gordie Howe wins his sixth and final scoring title.

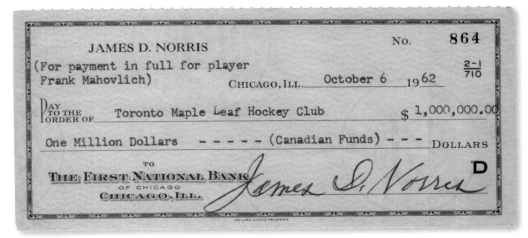

JAMES D. NORRIS No. 864

(For payment in full for player Frank Mahovlich) CHICAGO, ILL. October 6 19 62 2-1/710

PAY TO THE ORDER OF Toronto Maple Leaf Hockey Club $ 1,000,000.00

One Million Dollars ----- (Canadian Funds) --- DOLLARS

TO THE FIRST NATIONAL BANK OF CHICAGO CHICAGO, ILL. James D. Norris D

↑ THE MILLION-DOLLAR DREAM
Chicago steps up with this $1-million check for Frank Mahovlich, but the Leafs decide they're better off with 'The Big M' — and are rewarded with Lord Stanley's mug.

← MONEY ISN'T EVERYTHING
Leaf fans don't care if their team's pockets get deeper. They value Mahovlich far more and publicly voice their sentiment.

Newsmakers & Top Headlines

1 Hall halted at 502 straight games
He hasn't missed a game since the start of 1955-56, but Glenn Hall knows he's in trouble when he pinches a nerve in his back during a Nov. 6 practice. The Chicago goalie dresses for the next game against Boston, but after the first shot beats him, he gives way to Denis DeJordy. Hall can't play the next game, ending his consecutive game streak at 502 — an NHL record for goalies. "I knew almost as soon as the game started that I couldn't finish," says Hall, who plays all 502 games and 49 more in the playoffs without a mask.

2 Adams leaves Red Wings after 35 years
A fixture in Detroit since he was hired as manager in the spring of 1927, Jack Adams retires as GM of the Red Wings April 25, 1962. He leaves behind a legacy of seven Stanley Cups. 'Jolly' Jack, 66, has another job lined up. He takes over as president of the newly organized Central Professional Hockey League.

3 First amateur draft held
Although one day it will become a major event on the NHL calendar, the first amateur draft is shrouded in secrecy. It's held behind closed doors June 5 and the names of the 21 players selected are not revealed. Eligible to be drafted are 17-year-olds not currently playing with an NHL-sponsored amateur club. Eventually it's discovered the Montreal Canadiens take Garry Monahan first overall, while Detroit grabs Peter Mahovlich with the second pick.

>1963-64 THREE FOR LEAFS

↑ TOE'S LAST CRUSADE
Toe Blake wears a fedora that would make Indiana Jones proud. His Habs fall short in '63-64 despite a first-place finish, but win three titles in four years after that.

↓ SEVENTH HEAVEN
Tim Horton raises this stick in triumph after his Maple Leafs outlast the Red Wings in Game 7 of the Stanley Cup final. The victory nets him a third ring.

Newsmakers & Top Headlines

1 Howe, Sawchuk share historic day
Two magical moments occur in the same game as the Red Wings blank the Canadiens 3-0 at the Olympia Nov. 10. Gordie Howe beats Montreal goalie Charlie Hodge for his 545th career goal, moving him past Maurice Richard as the NHL's all-time leading goalscorer. No one beats Red Wing netminder Terry Sawchuk, who stops 39 shots for his 94th career shutout, tying George Hainsworth's NHL record. Sawchuk breaks it Jan. 18 with a 36-save performance in a 2-0 win over the Canadiens.

2 Habs and Rangers make blockbuster deal
Montreal and New York pull off an unexpected seven-player deal June 4 which sees the Habs part with six-time Vezina Trophy-winner Jacques Plante, Don Marshall and Phil Goyette in return for goalie Gump Worsley and youngsters Dave Balon, Leon Rochefort and Len Ronson.

3 Courageous Baun Stanley Cup hero
With his team down 3-2 in games to Detroit in the Stanley Cup final, Toronto defenseman Bob Baun is carried from the ice on a stretcher after being hit in the right ankle by a Gordie Howe shot during Game 6. But Baun returns and is a hero when his shot beats Terry Sawchuk 1:40 into overtime. Baun plays Game 7 as Toronto wraps up the title with a 4-0 win. Only after that game does he go for X-rays, which reveal he has a cracked bone.

Cup Winner
Toronto Maple Leafs

Leading Scorers
1. Stan Mikita, Chi, 89 points
2. Bobby Hull, Chi, 87 points
3. Jean Beliveau, Mtl, 78 points
4. A. Bathgate, NYR/Tor, 77 pts
5. Gordie Howe, Det, 73 points
6. Kenny Wharram, Chi, 71 pts
7. Murray Oliver, Bos, 68 points
8. Phil Goyette, NYR, 65 points
9. Rod Gilbert, NYR, 64 points
10. Dave Keon, Tor, 60 points

First Draft Pick, 1964
Claude Gauthier, RW, Detroit

HHOF Inductees
Bill Durnan
Babe Siebert
Black Jack Stewart
↓ Doug Bentley

Nickname of the Year
Andy 'Spuds' Hebenton

Worth Noting
No hockey legend is ever treated as poorly late in his career as Doug Harvey with the Rangers. New York demotes the 39-year-old Harvey – ranked the No. 2 defenseman of all-time by The Hockey News in 2010 – to Quebec of the AHL in November, 1963. Harvey plays five seasons in the AHL before returning for one with St. Louis in 1968-69 at 44…Goalie Eddie Johnston plays every minute of all 70 games for Boston, marking the final time in NHL history a goaltender plays every minute of every game.

ACE STARTLES GARDENS CROWD BY SHOWING UP FOR NHL GAME

DEC. 14, 1963 BY THN STAFF

Former NHL hockey star Ace Bailey tossed the sports world and the people around Maple Leaf Gardens for a loop the night of Dec. 4 when he walked into the big hockey rink very much "alive."

Hockey officials and fans alike couldn't believe their eyes when Ace showed up in the Gardens to take his regular position as penalty timekeeper one night after he had been reported dead.

But Ace had been mistaken for Harold Bailie, a 64-year-old city parks employee who died of a heart attack as he inspected damage to his car following a minor traffic accident.

Harold Bailie was known to his fellow workers as 'Ace' — and when some confusion as to identity arose at the hospital, it led to an erroneous report.

Thirty years ago this month, the hockey Ace hovered on the brink of death for weeks after being checked by Eddie Shore in a game at Boston, ending his brilliant career. His obituary was written then, too.

At Maple Leaf Gardens, the sole topic of conversation was his "passing." There was even talk of observing a period of silence for the 60-year-old before the game between the Leafs and Canadiens started.

"There were some surprised looking people when I walked in," Ace said. "Most people had heard it. A lot of them blinked and shook their heads."

One of the first to encounter Bailey was Conn Smythe, former president of the Maple Leafs and now a member of the board of directors, who had stayed at Ace's bedside in Boston during his valiant fight for life in 1933.

"My driver had picked me up to go to the game," said Mr. Smythe.

"He told me Bailey had died and it was a big blow. When I saw him alive as we drove into the Gardens, it was a happy moment."

NOV. 30, 1963 BY JIM PROUDFOOT

BOWER ONCE RELUCTANT ABOUT JUMPING TO NHL; NOW HE'S GLAD HE DID

Johnny Bower's day of decision arrived in 1958.

He had just returned to Cleveland, his hockey home, after a discouraging tryout with the New York Rangers, followed by sojourns in Vancouver and Providence. Now he was back in the city where he'd turned professional in 1945, where so many of his friends were located and where good friend, the late Jim Hendy, was GM. Bower was a comfortable, contented man and his outlook was reflected in his brilliant 1957-58 achievements — eight shutouts and a 2.18 GAA netminding in the American League.

Poor goalkeeping was a major problem with the Toronto Maple Leafs, who had finished last in the National League that season, and at the insistence of coach Billy Reay, they drafted Bower for $15,000. At 33, he was quite happy to make his home in Cleveland and stay there. This acquisition by the Maple Leafs didn't produce the type of reaction you'd normally expect when a minor league player is secured by a major league club.

↑ YOU'RE NOT IN CLEVELAND ANYMORE
Toronto goalie Johnny Bower forges a Hall of Fame career not long after making the tough decision to move up from the minor leagues.

"I honestly didn't want to go," Bower says now. "I was happy in Cleveland and I wanted to stay there. But the draft rule was in effect then and I actually had no choice. Besides, Mr. Hendy convinced me it was an excellent opportunity. He was right, too."

Bower estimates he's earned more than $50,000 above his anticipated AHL wages in the five seasons since he joined the Leafs. This is his sixth year with the Leafs. Moreover, he's gained glory and satisfaction beyond his wildest hopes. He's been first-string goalie for two world championship clubs as well as a first place team; he's won the Vezina Trophy as hockey's foremost goaltender and has been chosen all-star goalie as well.

Above all that, too, Bower is perhaps the most popular player who plays for NHL pay. Teammate Dick Duff once explained this: "John symbolizes the type of guy who can't quite make the grade in the NHL, then did make it after it seemed to be too late. And he's been so grateful in everything he does that everybody's got a soft spot in their heart for him."

Sentiment of this sort never is expressed in the Leafs dressing room. Bower is the focal point of team morale and good spirit and this is developed by good-natured barbs mostly centered around the subject of his age.

According to the record book, Bower celebrated his 39th birthday Nov. 8. Some people claim this is sheer fiction. Reliable authorities have placed his age at 45 and even the team physician, Dr. Jim Murray, figures he's over 40. Bower enjoys the controversy and feeds it, saying: "I've lied about my age so much I've forgotten what it actually is."

Compounding the mystery is the fact Bower served in the Canadian Army during World War II. He says he joined in 1942 and was posted in England. In 1945, coming out of junior hockey in Saskatchewan, he signed his first professional contract with Cleveland.

Punch Imlach, Leafs coach and GM, has the proper attitude. When the jibes get thickest, he tells Bower: "I don't care how old you are. As long as you can stop the puck, you've got a job." **THN**

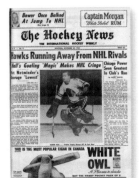

1964-65

SEEDS OF CHANGE

→ VIRTUOSO OF VOICE
This microphone belongs to legendary broadcaster Foster Hewitt, inducted into the Hall of Fame as a builder in 1965.

Newsmakers & Top Headlines

1 Lindsay stages remarkable comeback
Ending a four-season retirement, 39-year-old Ted Lindsay earns a spot with the Red Wings. 'Terrible Ted' produces 14 goals and 28 points in 69 games and shows he hasn't lost his edginess, doing battle with NHL president Clarence Campbell over $75 in fines he receives following a Jan. 2 game against Toronto. "I'm not going to sit for Campbell's kangaroo court," says Lindsay, who eventually apologizes and pays the fines.

2 Swede's debut precursor of European invasion
Swedish forward Ulf Sterner becomes the first European-trained NHLer, debuting with the Rangers Jan. 27 against Boston. Sterner, 24, discards his helmet and mouthguard to fit in with North American play-ers. "Maybe people would look at it and say: 'Swede, go home,'" Sterner says. He fails to pick up a point in four games and is farmed out to Baltimore of the American League. He returns to Sweden after the season.

3 NHL opts for two-goalie system
Tired of waiting for spare goaltenders to don pads and warm up after an injury to the No. 1 man, NHL governors adopt a rule Feb. 2 which requires two goal-ies to suit up for every game of the 1965 playoffs. It becomes a regular season practice in 1965-66. Mean-while, replacing the legendary Terry Sawchuk, Detroit goalie Roger Crozier leads the NHL with 40 wins and six shutouts, wins the Calder Trophy and is the last stopper to appear in all his team's games (70).

FACTS & STATS
from 1965-66

FACTS & STATS
from 1965-66

Cup Winner

Montreal Canadiens

Leading Scorers

1. Bobby Hull, Chi, 97 points
2. Stan Mikita, Chi, 78 points
3. Bobby Rousseau, Mtl, 78 pts
4. Jean Beliveau, Mtl, 77 points
5. Gordie Howe, Det, 75 points
6. Norm Ullman, Det, 72 points
7. Alex Delvecchio, Det, 69 pts
8. Bob Nevin, NYR, 62 points
9. Henri Richard, Mtl, 61 points
10. Murray Oliver, Bos, 60 points

First Draft Pick, 1966

Barry Gibbs, D, Boston

HHOF Inductees

Max Bentley
Toe Blake
Butch Bouchard
Frank Brimsek
Teeder Kennedy
Ted Lindsay
Babe Pratt
Kenny Reardon
↓Elmer Lach

Nickname of the Year

Bernie 'Boom Boom' Geoffrion

Worth Noting

Toronto coach Punch Imlach employs three goalies in a season-ending 3-3 tie at Detroit, marking the first time that has happened. He uses Johnny Bower, Terry Sawchuk and Bruce Gamble… Jack Kent Cooke after being awarded an NHL franchise in Los Angeles: "I feel like I'm now one echelon above the president of the United States."

↑ FOLLOW THE LEADER

Canadiens captain Jean Beliveau keeps guiding his team to Stanley Cups as he reaches his mid-30s.

↓ GORDIE'S GLORY

Continuing to rewrite the record books, Gordie Howe nets career goal No. 600 with this unassuming stick.

Newsmakers & Top Headlines

1 Golden Jet first to top 50 goals
It's just another typical Bobby Hull goal — except it gives him more than any other player has scored in one season. Trailing the New York Rangers 2-1 in the third period March 12, the Chicago star blows a slapshot by goalie Cesare Maniago on the power play for goal No. 51 — breaking the record held by Rocket Richard, 'Boom Boom' Geoffrion and himself. Hull receives an eight-minute standing ovation. He finishes the season with 54 goals.

2 NHL announces expansion plans
The NHL announces Feb. 9 it will double in size for the 1967-68 season, adding franchises in Philadelphia, Pittsburgh, Minnesota, Oakland, Los Angeles and St. Louis at a cost of $2 million each. St. Louis hasn't officially applied, but the St. Louis Arena is owned by Chicago owners Arthur Wirtz and Jim Norris, sparking cries of cronyism from Vancouver and Buffalo, two overlooked cities. Buffalo bidders Seymour and Northrup Knox say they are "bitterly disappointed."

3 Adams first Lester Patrick winner
Jack Adams is named the first winner of the Lester Patrick Trophy for outstanding hockey service in the U.S. The former Detroit coach and GM guided the Red Wings from the verge of bankruptcy to their position as an NHL powerhouse. The award is introduced by the New York Rangers, for whom Lester Patrick coached and managed.

1966-67

ORR'S ARRIVAL

← PRAISE IS IN ORDER
Maurice Richard is among the first group of people to receive the Order of Canada, represented by this medal.

↓ DOZENS OF DONUTS
The Toronto Maple Leafs honor Terry Sawchuk with this plaque after he records career shutout No. 100 in March 1967.

FACTS & STATS
from 1966-67

Cup Winner
Toronto Maple Leafs

Leading Scorers
1. Stan Mikita, Chi, 97 points
2. Bobby Hull, Chi, 80 points
3. Norm Ullman, Det, 70 points
4. Kenny Wharram, Chi, 65 pts
5. Gordie Howe, Det, 65 points
6. Bobby Rousseau, Mtl, 63 pts
7. Phil Esposito, Chi, 61 points
8. Phil Goyette, NYR, 61 points
9. Doug Mohns, Chi, 60 points
10. Henri Richard, Mtl, 55 points

60 Moments
that changed the game
No. 13: Bobby Orr makes his NHL debut and goes on to change the way defensemen play the game.

First Draft Pick, 1967
Rick Pagnutti, D, Los Angeles

HHOF Inductees
Neil Colville
Harry Oliver
↓ Turk Broda

Nickname of the Year
Bobby 'The Golden Jet' Hull

Worth Noting
Suffering from tracheitis, an inflammation of the breathing tube, Detroit's Paul Henderson wears a surgical mask while playing to keep cold air out of his lungs… Chicago center Stan Mikita becomes first NHLer to win the Lady Byng, Hart and Art Ross Trophies in one season.

Newsmakers & Top Headlines

1 Orr's arrival signals dawn of new era
Defenseman Bobby Orr, 18, makes his NHL debut with Boston after signing a two-year, $75,000 contract with the Bruins. He does not disappoint. Orr finishes with 41 points in 61 games and is named the NHL's top rookie. "Bobby Orr was a star when they played the national anthem before his first game," says Boston coach Harry Sinden. Orr's skating and offensive talents expand the role of defensemen in the game, leading to a generation of imitators.

2 Leafs oldest Stanley Cup winners in history
With Johnny Bower, Red Kelly and Allan Stanley all in their 40s and nine players in their 30s, the Maple Leafs look to be over the hill as they struggle to make the playoffs. But they stun the first-place Black Hawks in the semifinal, then down the Canadiens to take the Stanley Cup, despite an average age of 31.4 years, making the Leafs the oldest champs in NHL history. "Hockey is an old man's game in the head, where it matters," says Leaf coach Punch Imlach.

3 Black Hawks break 'Muldoon's Curse'
The mythical 'Muldoon's Curse' comes to an end March 12, as Chicago blanks Toronto 5-0 to clinch first place for the first time in franchise history. Legend has it Pete Muldoon, Chicago's first coach, cursed the team to never finish first after he was fired in 1927. The truth is the story was the product of writer Jim Coleman's fertile imagination.

CANADIENS' STARS BECOME PERMANENT HELMET USERS

DEC. 10, 1966 BY GIL SMITH

MONTREAL, QUE. –

Two leading Canadiens have decided head-pieces will form part of their equipment, from now till the end of their careers. Bobby Rousseau, the team's highest scorer, and J.C. Tremblay, the outstanding defenseman, are both sporting head-covers these days in the pursuit of their trade.

Rousseau was actually the first to put on a helmet, though his thinking was influenced to some extent by a head injury to Tremblay. The injury occurred during a game against the Rangers last month, when J.C. struck his head heavily on the ice after being bodychecked by Reg Fleming. Tremblay suffered a concussion, plus an ugly gash on the back of his head that required eight stitches. He was sidelined two weeks and missed six games.

A week after J.C.'s injury, Rousseau skated out wearing a white helmet which he says he'll wear "for the rest of my career." The starry Hab forward stated that Tremblay's injury had partly influenced his decision to don a helmet, "but that he had been thinking of wearing one for some time." He claims that the helmet in no way interferes with his ability to see the puck.

Tremblay began wearing his helmet immediately upon his return to action after the injury. "If I'd been wearing one when Fleming hit me, I wouldn't have had a concussion or a cut," he said. "Helmets are a protection against things like that and I also wish I'd had one the night Ed Van Impe, of Chicago, smashed into me and my head struck the boards."

Tremblay was referring to a Montreal-Chicago game in October, when he was knocked senseless after being charged into the board.

Like Rousseau, J.C. feels the headguard is no handicap to his play. "I can see perfectly well with it," he says, "and, I don't find it too heavy. I'll admit it's a bit hot, but it's hot playing hockey anyway, especially when you're under those lights. Perhaps the only thing that's bothersome about it is the chin-strap that sort of tugs a bit during play. But, that can be corrected."

The wearing of helmets has long been a point of contention among hockey players, many of whom feel "sissified" to wear one. Such theories go out the window when it's recalled that one of the first players to ever wear a headguard in the NHL was the tough-as-nails Eddie Shore. According to Elmer Ferguson, dean of Canadian sportswriters, Shore wore one for years playing for Boston and New York.

Ferguson says as far back as 1933, following the tragic incident between Shore and Ace Bailey, that resulted in the near-death of the latter, the NHL suggested all players wear helmets for their own protection. For awhile, some players did sport the headpieces, but they gradually abandoned them.

DEC. 31, 1966 BY WILLIAM SANTANIELLO

PLAYER REVOLT ROCKS HOCKEY

SPRINGFIELD, MASS. – The mutinous Springfield Indians went back to the business of playing hockey after staging an

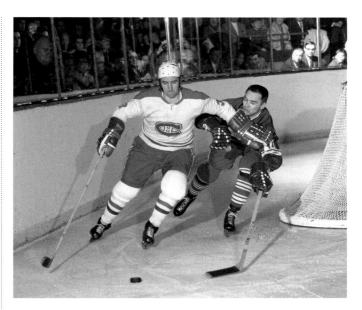

↑ STARTING THE BUCKET LIST
Montreal's J.C. Tremblay isn't the first player to put on a helmet, but his reasoning gets a bunch of other players doing the same thing.

unprecedented team walkout that involved all 23 players and ended with four of their set being placed under suspension by owner Eddie Shore.

The Springfield executive solicited the help of other professional teams and came up with five replacements as the Indians resume their American League schedule. Shore defiantly announced he would organize a completely new club after his players staged their mass strike, the first full-scale player rebellion since 1925.

The Indians' chief refused to give ground and Shore appeared to win his point when the players' legal advisor – Alan Eagleson, a Toronto lawyer hired by the players to defend them – told the team members to end their strike. The players reluctantly agreed with Eagleson and went back to practice under coach Harry Pidhirny, the first for the club in nearly five days prior to the game with Providence Dec. 23. However, Eagleson told the Indians he had no intention of dropping the matter and would fight for their rights from his Toronto home and would return to Springfield after the Christmas holidays.

A full-scale investigation by the AHL will undoubtedly be launched to get at the root of the trouble in Springfield.

The 64-year-old Shore, hardnosed owner of the AHL club and one of hockey's all-time great defensemen, rejected demands that he reinstate suspended defensemen Dale Rolfe, Bill White and Dave Amadio and veteran forward Brian Kilrea.

He also insisted that the team's 19 other players honor contracts. The 19 threatened to continue the walkout until their four teammates were reinstated.

The three defensemen were suspended by Shore after the Indians suffered their fourth straight defeat in a loss to Quebec Aces last weekend. Kilrea, who acted as team spokesman, was suspended for indifferent play when the players walked out the next day.

Shore said he suspended the players mostly because he was unhappy with their overall play. THN

BY KEN CAMPBELL

— 1967-1979 —

GRAND EXPANSION

THE NHL LOST ITS INNOCENCE BY DOUBLING IN SIZE, WATERING DOWN THE TALENT. THE GAME GREW, BUT SHOULD HAVE BECOME MUCH MORE

At a time when billionaires are at odds with millionaires on how to parse the revenues of a $3.3-billion industry, it's entirely understandable to view those who run hockey as myopic and greedy. Perhaps the only consolation can come in the knowledge that the highest powers in the game were even more so five decades ago, in the time before the league doubled in size and underwent a frenetic transformation. Nothing of its kind was seen before or since.

About the only thing that remained constant in the NHL between 1967 and 1979 was the excellence of the Montreal Canadiens, who captured eight of the 13 Stanley Cups. After the Toronto Maple Leafs upset the Canadiens in the final in 1967, The Hockey News declared: "The Toronto Maple Leafs are becoming almost as proficient at winning the Stanley Cup as the Montreal Canadiens."

Like the Maple Leafs, the NHL began another modern era with such hope and promise. Also like the Maple Leafs, the NHL under-delivered, disappointed its fans and failed to capitalize on its potential. There was a feeling in the sporting world that the NHL, which had doubled in size in 1967, was an entity on the cusp of becoming a major player on the professional landscape. Roone Arledge, who grew to become the most innovative and influential sports broadcasting pioneer in history, opined in the 1960s that the NHL had, "all the potential of pro football."

And like pro football, which had until the emergence of television been dwarfed by the college game's enormous shadow, hockey was beginning to feel its oats. Benefitting from commercial flight that turned marathon train rides into hours, sports were beginning to see the bonanza that existed to the south and west. The Brooklyn Dodgers and New York Giants were the first to realize it, moving to Los Angeles and San Francisco in 1958, while the Milwaukee Braves left for an expanding TV market in Atlanta in 1966.

That the NHL was late to come to the party should come as no surprise. Almost since its inception, the NHL has been dominated by owners whose self-interests always trumped those of the collective. That was no more evident than in the early days of the NHL, a league that was operated under the iron grip of five old-money families whose monopoly over the sport brought them enormous riches. There were the Molsons in Montreal,

the Norris family in Detroit and Chicago, the Adams family in Boston, the Kilpatricks in New York and the Smythe family in Toronto. Despite opportunities and no shortage of suitors, those who ran the league rebuffed all interlopers, largely because they didn't think it would be in their best interests to expand. NHL president Clarence Campbell often pointed out that making the league bigger would not sell a single ticket in the Original Six markets because all those tickets had been sold anyway.

But the NHL did finally decide to expand in an effort to achieve two goals — to thwart any possibility of a rival league and to pursue a national television contract. It failed miserably on both accounts. By 1972, the World Hockey Association was born and began to poach established, star players, along with opening the door to European talent. The NHL, meanwhile, has never been able to gain a legitimate foothold on network television in the United States.

But after years of stubbornly maintaining only six teams, the NHL grew at a dizzying rate. Three years after the league doubled in size, the Buffalo Sabres and Vancouver Canucks were added, followed by the New York Islanders and Atlanta Flames two years after that. In 1974, the Kansas City Scouts and Washington Capitals came aboard and within eight years the league had tripled in size. After the Cleveland and Minnesota franchises merged, the NHL absorbed the four healthy franchises from the dying WHA to bring its membership to 21.

There were both benefits and growing pains to the maturing process. For the players, it planted the seeds of autonomy and freedom and started the pendulum swinging enormously in their favor. Wildcat strikes by players on the Springfield Indians in 1966 and 1967 against tyrannical owner Eddie Shore gave rise to the NHL Players' Association. The WHA and the courts' rulings against the reserve clause, which tied players to NHL clubs, gave players the freedom to shop their services and cut their own deals and many of them hired agents to do that for them. Stan Mikita, one star player who did not jump to the WHA, said every morning he bowed in homage to Bobby Hull for securing his million-dollar contract with the Winnipeg Jets and raising the wages of every player in the game.

The NHL, meanwhile, was witness to a mind-boggling amount of change.

The Summit Series in 1972 altered the landscape forever, forcing Canadians to objectively examine their place in a game they once dominated. No longer could they lay claim as the sole producer of NHL talent. More and more was coming from Europe and much of it was prodigious.

But the Euro influx still wasn't enough to support the need for quality players in two bloating professional leagues in North America. In just eight years in North America, professional hockey had grown from six teams in one league employing 120 players to 32 teams in two leagues with 640 players. There is little doubt the product was diluted, but it also led to marginal players having a much bigger mark on the game.

And as a result, the Broad Street Bullies were born. The Philadelphia Flyers were an up-and-coming team that had some impressive top-end talent, but also a roster that was chock full of lesser talents who could intimidate. Sensing he could gain a competitive advantage, coach Fred Shero went out to indelibly change the complexion of the game with that team.

Fighting and intimidation were undoubtedly a staple in the game, but until then the vast majority of fights and acts of violence were the products of an emotional game played at a high speed by men with an abundance of competitive juices. Gordie Howe was just as likely to fight as John Ferguson. But Shero and the Flyers were the first team to use fists and fear as a tactic to win games, giving birth to the goon or enforcer, a role still prominent in today's game. It brought the Flyers instant success in the form of two consecutive Stanley Cups and created a culture of violence that is still the norm in the game almost 40 years later. In his book, *The Game*, Hall of Fame goaltender Ken Dryden gave his appraisal of what the Flyers did to the game: "They were bullies. They showed contempt for everyone and everything. They took on the league, its referees and teams; they took on fans, cops, the courts and politicians. They searched for weakness, found it, trampled it, then preened with their cock-of-the-walk swagger. For two years, they were kings of the mountain. Not many years from now, those two years will be symbols of the lost decade."

The late 1960s and 1970s will be remembered as a period of unbridled and unprecedented growth for the NHL. But they'll also be remembered as an opportunity lost, probably forever. THN

↑ **ADAPT AND THRIVE**
Expansion didn't stop Ken Dryden and the Montreal Canadiens from dominating the NHL. They won six Stanley Cups in the 1970s.

↑ **HERE COME THE '70s**
Phil Esposito became the spiritual leader of the Cup-winning Boston Bruins and Team Canada.

1967-68

AN EVEN DOZEN

↑ NEW KIDS ON THE BLOCK
These patches show off the NHL's six new teams. Bright colors are certainly the flavor of the day.

← PUT A CAP IN YOUR...
Early Pogs? Not really. These Coke bottle caps, featuring stars of the Montreal Canadiens and Toronto Maple Leafs, sure do pop, however.

Newsmakers & Top Headlines

1 Original Six welcome six more
The largest single-season growth in NHL history takes place June 6, when six expansion franchises – the Los Angeles Kings, Minnesota North Stars, California (Oakland) Seals, Philadelphia Flyers, Pittsburgh Penguins and St. Louis Blues – stock their rosters. Each of the six established teams protects one goalie and 11 skaters. Among the veteran players selected are three Vezina Trophy winners – first overall pick Terry Sawchuk, 37, (Los Angeles), Charlie Hodge, 33, (California) and Glenn Hall, 35, (St. Louis).

2 Masterton dies in on-ice collision
Hit by California defensemen Larry Cahan and Ron Harris in a Jan. 13 game, Minnesota center Bill Master-ton, 30, strikes the back of his head on the ice, suffers massive brain injuries and dies two days later. It's the NHL's only on-ice fatality and many players don helmets as a result. The Bill Masterton Memorial Trophy is introduced and awarded for the first time to Montreal's Claude Provost.

3 Blockbuster trades rock the league
The Bruins make the playoffs for the first time since 1958-59 after getting Phil Esposito, Ken Hodge and Fred Stanfield from the Black Hawks for Pit Martin, Gilles Marotte and Jack Norris. The Maple Leafs deal Frank Mahovlich to the Red Wings, with Garry Unger, Pete Stemkowski and the retired Carl Brewer for Paul Henderson, Floyd Smith and Norm Ullman.

FACTS & STATS
from 1967-68

Cup Winner
Montreal Canadiens

Leading Scorers
1. Stan Mikita, Chi, 87 points
2. Phil Esposito, Bos, 84 points
3. Gordie Howe, Det, 82 points
4. Jean Ratelle, NYR, 78 points
5. Rod Gilbert, NYR, 77 points
6. Bobby Hull, Chi, 75 points
7. Norm Ullman, Tor, 72 points
8. Alex Delvecchio, Det, 70 pts
9. John Bucyk, Bos, 69 points
10. K. Wharram, Chi, 69 points

Rule Changes
Limit of curvature of hockey stick blade is set at 1-1/2 inches.

Franchise News
Six teams added.

60 Moments
that changed the game
No. 1: The NHL expands its universe when it doubles in size.
No. 35: Minnesota center Bill Masterton dies of head injuries sustained in a fall, prompting a shift towards head protection.
No. 59: The first series of private boxes are created, at MSG, as another source of revenue.

First Draft Pick, 1968
Michel Plasse, G, Montreal

HHOF Inductees
↓ Bill Cowley

Nickname of the Year
Jean 'Le Gros Bill' Beliveau

↑ BATTLE-TESTED ARMOR
Goalie Ed Chadwick gets a taste of the NHL, playing every game of two non-playoff seasons with the Toronto Maple Leafs from 1956 to 1958. But he and this equipment spend most of his days bouncing around the AHL. Chadwick finishes with the Buffalo Bisons.

1968-69

ESPOSITO BLOSSOMS

↑ ESPO'S EXCALIBUR
This stick, custom-taped by Bruins trainer 'Frosty' Forristall, is Esposito's weapon of choice and helps him net point No. 100.

→ THE 700 CLUB
Mr. Hockey becomes the first 700-goal scorer with this disc. No one threatens the total for another two-plus decades.

↓ HEAVY METAL
As bands like Led Zeppelin top the charts with a new sound, Brad Park is one of the first to play with an aluminum stick.

GORDIE HOWE 700TH GOAL WINGS 7 — PENGUINS 2 DEC. 4, 1968

Cup Winner
Montreal Canadiens

Leading Scorers
1. Phil Esposito, Bos, 126 pts
2. Bobby Hull, Chi, 107 points
3. Gordie Howe, Det, 103 pts
4. Stan Mikita, Chi, 97 points
5. Ken Hodge, Bos, 90 points
6. Yvan Cournoyer, Mtl, 87 pts
7. Alex Delvecchio, Det, 83 pts
8. Red Berenson, StL, 82 points
9. Jean Beliveau, Mtl, 82 points
10. Frank Mahovlich, Det, 78 pts

Significant Records
Most goals, one road game:
Red Berenson, St. Louis (6)

First Draft Pick, 1969
Rejean Houle, LW, Montreal

HHOF Inductees
Sid Abel
Bryan Hextall
Roy 'Shrimp' Worters
↓ Red Kelly

Nickname of the Year
Frank 'The Big M' Mahovlich

Worth Noting
Montreal goalie Tony Esposito makes his first NHL start Dec. 5 at the Boston Garden in a 2-2 tie against the Bruins. Tony stops 33 shots and both Boston goals are scored by his older brother, Phil...Minnesota's Danny Grant and Oakland's Norm Ferguson tie Nels Stewart's 40-year-old NHL record for most goals by a rookie with 34.

Newsmakers & Top Headlines

1 Espo, Hull, Howe surpass 100 points
It takes 51 years for one NHL player to score 100 points. Within a month, three have done it. Boston center Phil Esposito leads the way with two goals March 2 against Pittsburgh to hit the 100-point plateau and finishes with a record 126 points. Chicago left winger Bobby Hull joins his former teammate 18 days later and then breaks his own goal record with 58 to go along with 107 points. Detroit right winger Gordie Howe scores his 100th point March 30, one day before his 41st birthday, and remains the oldest player to hit triple digits. Howe winds up with a career-high 103 points.

2 Howe scores goal No. 700
In a 7-2 win Dec. 4 at Pittsburgh, Detroit's Gordie Howe fires a shot from the slot through the legs of Pittsburgh goalie Les Binkley for the 700th goal of his NHL career. Howe's only disappointment is that the record tally does not come on home ice. "They had (700) balloons ready for me in the rafters," he says.

3 Plante comes back to win seventh Vezina
Lured out of retirement by St. Louis, Jacques Plante teams with fellow veteran Glenn Hall to bring the Vezina Trophy to the second-season Blues. It's the seventh time Plante's name goes on the award, more than any other goalie. Any trophy case for these two future Hall of Famers would be quite full. They've combined for 10 Vezinas, one Hart, a Calder, a Conn Smythe Trophy and 17 first- or second-team all-star selections.

REGAN FINED $1,000 FOR PUNCHING REFEREE

NOV. 9, 1968 BY BILL LIBBY

LOS ANGELES, CALIF. –

The head on the wire-service release said, "Punch a referee and see the world."

Behind the scenes, Clarence Campbell, NHL president, huddled with Jack Kent Cooke, owner of the Los Angeles Kings, to determine a proper punishment for Kings' manager Larry Regan.

Early this season, after a game in Oakland, Regan cornered referee Bruce Hood and after an exchange of words threw a punch at him. Later, the tempermental Irishman had a bruised hand and admitted he'd connected. Most expected Campbell to levy the maximum $2,000 fine. However, Campbell indicated he also wanted to suspend him, but felt it would be difficult to enforce a suspension of a manager without the help of the team's owner.

After Campbell and Cooke huddled, it was announced Regan had been fined $1,000 and been sent to Czechoslovakia for two weeks, where he can presumably polish up his punching on Russian invaders. Regan was due to spend the early part of November there on full salary, scouting prospects for the NHL. "The referees represent the authority in the NHL," Campbell declared. "They must retain the superior hand."

Coach Red Kelly has assumed additional duties as acting GM.

In 1961, Montreal coach Toe Blake chased a referee across Chicago ice. He threw a punch but missed. He was fined $2,000 and was given a holiday in Europe. Obviously, Blake was ahead of his time.

APRIL 19, 1969 BY THN STAFF

POLICE RECOVER NHL'S STOLEN HART, CALDER, SMYTHE TROPHIES

Playoff action in the NHL always brings out some unusual happenings and this year was no exception. Three of the most coveted trophies in pro hockey were stolen from the Hall of Fame in Toronto. Last week, thieves broke into the building and smashed open cases containing the Calder, Hart and Conn Smythe Trophies. Also taken were two sets of medals from the Sport Hall of Fame in the same building.

Police wasted little time in tracking down the culprits, however, and two days later the trophies were found in a green plastic bag in a shed behind a vacant house in the Toronto suburb of Etobicoke, following an intensive investigation.

Police said the three trophies, unofficially valued at $10,000 (the equivalent of roughly $63,000 today), were being well looked after and would be returned to the NHL whenever they were called for. NHL president Clarence Campbell indicated the trophies would only return to the Hall after increased security is discussed with the Canadian National Exhibition, which houses the Hall of Fame.

Also recovered by police: about 100 speedskating medals won by Fred J. Robson around the start of the 20th century.

↑ CZECHING OUT
Part of Kings GM Larry Regan's punishment is being "banished" to Czechoslovakia to scout prospects for two weeks.

OCT. 12, 1968 BY THN STAFF

LARKIN SUFFERS FATAL HEART ATTACK ON ICE

Tragedy struck the Buffalo Bisons fewer than 30 minutes after their opening skating drill in the Kitchener Memorial Arena when Wayne Larkin, a 29-year-old right winger, collapsed on the ice and died of an apparent heart attack.

Larkin, embarking on his third season with the Bisons, passed the customary training camp physical examination the previous day after driving here from his Winnipeg home with teammates Dennis Hextall and Allan Hamilton and former Bison Ray Brunel.

Coach Fred Shero directed the squad through a series of skating exercises before Larkin, circling near the goal, collapsed. He received attention immediately on the ice and later was removed to St. Mary's Hospital, where he was pronounced dead. A coroner's inquest decided a coronary thrombosis was the cause of death. It was the second death on the ice in pro hockey this year. Bill Masterton of the Minnesota North Stars died of head injuries after being hurt in an NHL game Jan. 15.

The skating session was conducted without pucks and Larkin wasn't involved in any body contact prior to his collapse.

Larkin, purchased by the Bisons two years ago from the Montreal Canadiens, played with Winnipeg and Vancouver in the Western League and with Cleveland, Springfield and Providence in the American League.

He is survived by his wife, Winona, and two daughters, Karen, 8, and Kelly, 6.

Larkin was regarded as one of the game's better fist-fighters. Two years ago he collected 18 goals in 72 games.

"I coached Wayne in St. Paul in his last season as an amateur and he was a close personal friend," Shero said. **THN**

1969-70

YEAR OF THE 'O'

↑ GONE TOO SOON
1969-70 marks Terry Sawchuk's final season, as a tragic altercation with a teammate leads to his death.

....

← IN MY DAY...
Today's goaltending equipment looks like medieval armor compared to this arm pad worn by Sawchuk.

FACTS & STATS
from 1969-70

Cup Winner
Boston Bruins

Leading Scorers
1. Bobby Orr, Bos, 120 points
2. Phil Esposito, Bos, 99 points
3. Stan Mikita, Chi, 86 points
4. Phil Goyette, StL, 78 points
5. Walt Tkaczuk, NYR, 77 points

Rule Changes
Limit of curvature of hockey stick blade is set at one inch.

60 Moments
that changed the game
No. 50: Montreal becomes the first team to pull its goalie in favor of an extra attacker to create more offense.

First Draft Pick, 1970
Gilbert Perreault, C, Buffalo

HHOF Inductees
Babe Dye
Tom Johnson
↓ Bill Gadsby

Nickname of the Year
Gordie 'Mr. Hockey' Howe

Worth Noting
With the Montreal Canadiens and Toronto Maple Leafs out, 1969-70 marks the first time all participating playoff teams are from the United States...The St. Louis Blues record the only winning record in the West division. The Blues are swept in the Cup final a third straight season.

Newsmakers & Top Headlines

1 Orr and Tony 'O' assault record book
Boston's Bobby Orr sets scoring marks for rearguards in all categories with 33-87-120 totals, becoming the first defenseman to win the Art Ross Trophy. Meanwhile, Tony Esposito, an intra-league draft pick by the Black Hawks from the Canadiens, posts 15 shutouts, an NHL record for rookies and the highest number since the NHL introduced the red line in 1943. Tony 'O' wins both the Vezina and Calder Trophies.

2 Sawchuk dies following freak injury
An altercation between New York teammates Terry Sawchuk and Ron Stewart April 29 leaves Sawchuk — at the time the NHL's all-time leader in shutouts (103) and games by a goalie (971) — with a critical injury. He undergoes surgery to remove his gall bladder and then two more operations after complications arise. Shortly after the third one, Sawchuk, 40, dies of cardiac arrest. A Nassau County, N.Y., grand jury investigation is held, but no charges are laid against Stewart.

3 Maki fractures Green's skull
Boston's Ted Green and Wayne Maki of the Blues engage in a vicious duel in a Sept. 21 exhibition game. Green hits Maki with his stick, then the Blues player retaliates by striking Green in the temple with his stick, fracturing Green's skull. Green undergoes five hours of surgery and misses the entire season. Criminal charges are laid, but both players are exonerated. The NHL suspends Maki for 30 days and Green for 13 days.

← LEAGUE LEADERS
Bobby Orr and Phil Esposito turn the Boston Bruins into world champions. Orr scored 130 points while Esposito contributed 99 points in 1969-70.

↓ GROOMING
Coach Harry Sinden works on the finer points of the game with a young Bobby Orr.

↑ A SEAL IN SKATES?

Now we've seen everything.
Morris Mott of the California
Golden Seals sports this bold
boot design from 1972 to 1974.

FLYERS' BOB CLARKE AN INSPIRATION TO DIABETICS

NOV. 28, 1969 BY JACK CHEVALIER

PHILADELPHIA, PA. —

It takes courage to wake up every morning, stick a needle in your arm and give yourself 55 units of insulin.

It takes will power to adhere to a diet that eliminates rich desserts and limits the amount you can eat at every meal.

It takes determination to practise and play big-league hockey every day when you realize that you're burning up blood-sugar like engine fuel.

And it takes guts to risk head and facial cuts when every medical dictionary says you're very vulnerable to infection.

The man with all these unusual problems and admirable qualities is Bob Clarke, the Flyers' 20-year-old rookie center and the only known diabetic in the history of the National Hockey League.

"Bob is very self-conscious about the disease and hates to be looked upon as someone special," Flyers trainer Frank Lewis said, "but his courage should be a great example to others afflicted."

"We like to think diabetics can do anything," added Dr. Stanley Spoont, the Flyers physician. "With careful thinking and certain daily precautions, Bob Clarke can enjoy a normal and useful career in the NHL. He is not in any grave danger."

The American Diabetic Association reports only two pro athletes — Clarke and a baseball player who prefers to remain anonymous — have the disease. In the past, tennis stars Billy Talbert and Ham Richardson, Notre Dame quarterback Coley O'Brien and Phillies' outfielder Bill 'Swish' Nicholson performed normally while afflicted.

Baseball star Jackie Robinson contracted diabetes after his retirement.

"They say it's hereditary, but I didn't get it until I was 15," Clarke explained. "It's not my fault and I'm certainly not ashamed of it."

Bob, a talented center from Flin Flon, Man., said his parents were not diabetics, but that the disease frequently skips a generation. "I think my grandfather's brother or uncle had it — but nobody ever knew," he said.

Because diabetics have an excess of sugar in their blood, they must inject themselves with insulin very morning. Then, as the day wears on, they burn up the sugar and sometimes have to gulp down a sweetened drink or candy bar to avoid a blackout.

"Clarke passed out twice at training camp in Quebec City," trainer Lewis said. "Both attacks followed early-morning workouts when he had skipped breakfast. The insulin tends to reduce your appetite and that's bad because a diabetic needs to eat a good solid breakfast."

Clarke said the Quebec City attacks were his first "in two or three years." He admitted his system was upset because he was a nervous rookie trying out for a major league hockey team. He had never played a pro game before.

"After that," Lewis said, "I told him he's gotta work closely with me all season. We've gotta be frank with each other. I

↑ **DIABETES DOESN'T SLOW HIM DOWN**
Bob Clarke overcomes his condition to win three Hart Trophies, lead the Philadelphia Flyers to two Stanley Cups and land in the Hall of Fame.

know how he feels about the disease and I try not to make a big project out of it when he needs something."

Lewis gives Clarke a Coke with two or three tablespoons of sugar before each game. Between periods, the rookie gets a half-glass of sweetened orange juice. After the game, he gets a full glass. "He doesn't like chocolate bars at game time because they make him thirsty," Lewis said. "But I have them in my training kit all the time. I also have a tube of 100 percent glucose which I'm supposed to force down his throat in case of emergency."

"As his career goes along, he'll be a source of inspiration to diabetics everywhere," Dr. Spoont said. "I'm really optimistic about this. We've got a tiger by the tail and we can control the tail, so to speak."

"We had the Mayo Clinic examine him and the report said the disease should not be a deterrent to his hockey career," Dr. Spoont said.

Diabetics are supposed to be highly susceptible to infection when cut, but Clarke hasn't been troubled yet.

"I've been carved up all over the face," he said. "Once I needed 15 stitches around my eye. I couldn't play the rest of the game because I couldn't see. But there was no infection."

Dr. Spoont says the healing process won't be slowed down until Clarke has been a diabetic for 20 or 30 years and his arteries harden. "We'll dress every wound and keep them clean," he said. "Bobby won't be rushing back on the ice after a cut."

Word of the Clarke story is spreading around the NHL and the Flyers already are receiving letters from patients.

"We have a boy here who's a peewee goalie," wrote someone from Children's Hospital in St. Louis. "He thought he could never play hockey again because of diabetes. But he heard about Clarke on television and his eyes lit up." THN

FACTS & STATS
from 1970-71

→ UNMASKED
Seven-time Vezina Trophy winner Jacques Plante teams with author Andy O'Brien on this book chronicling his life.

↓ STOPPER BECOMES SNIPER
In 1971, playing for the St. Louis Blues' Central League affiliate, Michel Plasse becomes the first pro netminder to score a goal. He's honored with this trophy and puck.

THE JACQUES PLANTE STORY
ANDY O'BRIEN
with Jacques Plante

Cup Winner
Montreal Canadiens

Leading Scorers
1. Phil Esposito, Bos, 152 points
2. Bobby Orr, Bos, 139 points
3. John Bucyk, Bos, 116 points

Rule Changes
Limit of curvature of hockey stick blade is set at half an inch.

Franchise News
Buffalo Sabres and Vancouver Canucks expand NHL to 14 teams. Oakland Seals change name to California Golden Seals.

Significant Records
Most assists by a defenseman, one season: Bobby Orr, Boston (102).
Most shots on goal, one season: Phil Esposito, Boston (550).

First Draft Pick, 1971
Guy Lafleur, RW, Montreal

HHOF Inductees
Busher Jackson
Gordon Roberts
Cooney Weiland
↓ Terry Sawchuk

Nickname of the Year
Wayne 'Swoop' Carleton

Worth Noting
Rookie goalie Ken Dryden goes 6-0 in the regular season before leading Montreal to the Cup.

Newsmakers & Top Headlines

1 Esposito and Orr lead Boston's record assault
The Boston Bruins set 37 NHL standards in a record-breaking season, including 57 wins, 121 points and 399 goals. Leading the way is center Phil Esposito, who collects his 59th goal and 127th point against the Los Angeles Kings March 11, surpassing the old NHL records in both categories. He finishes with 76 goals and 152 points. League MVP Bobby Orr becomes the first player to collect 100 assists (102). All three individual marks will stand for a decade.

2 Sabres and Canucks make NHL a 14-team league
A spin of the wheel gives Buffalo first pick in the amateur draft and Sabres coach-GM Punch Imlach grabs Montreal Jr. Canadiens phenom Gilbert Perreault.

Imlach vows the Sabres will be the first expansion team to win the Stanley Cup, but it's the Vancouver Canucks, the other first-year club, that makes a playoff run before fading in the second half of the season.

3 Rookie's dad killed in shootout over telecast
Roy Spencer, father of Toronto Maple Leafs rookie Brian Spencer, excitedly awaits the chance to see his son play against Buffalo on *Hockey Night In Canada* Dec. 12. When he tunes in and instead sees a Vancouver game, Spencer grabs his gun and drives 70 miles from his home in Fort James, B.C., to the CBC affiliate in Prince George, B.C. He enters the station and orders employees at gunpoint to switch to the Toronto game. Police arrive and Spencer is killed in the ensuing shootout.

1971-72 ‹

FACTS & STATS
from 1971-72

Cup Winner

Boston Bruins

Leading Scorers
1. Phil Esposito, Bos, 133 points
2. Bobby Orr, Bos, 117 points
3. Jean Ratelle, NYR, 109 points
4. Vic Hadfield, NYR, 106 points
5. Rod Gilbert, NYR, 97 points

Significant Records
Longest undefeated streak by a goaltender, one season: Gerry Cheevers, Boston (32 games)

First Draft Pick, 1972
Bill Harris, RW, NY Islanders

HHOF Inductees
Bernie Geoffrion
Hap Holmes
Gordie Howe
Hooley Smith
↓Jean Beliveau

Nickname of the Year
John 'Chief' Bucyk

Worth Noting
A 10-year-old, 70-pound center named Wayne Gretzky is an intermission guest on *Hockey Night in Canada* after a Toronto newspaper article chronicles his 378 goals in one season for his novice team in Brantford, Ont... Montreal goalie Ken Dryden wins the Calder Trophy as top rookie, one season after winning a Stanley Cup and Conn Smythe... Flyers goalie Bruce Gamble sustains a heart attack in a February game and is forced to retire.

↑ HOTTEST TICKET ON EARTH
Canada-Russia tilts were just as big of a deal across the Atlantic in 1972.

← ALTERNATIVE PROGRAMMING
Russia's cold, text-heavy program from the 1972 Summit Series adds to the then-unknown hockey nation's mystique, doesn't it?

Newsmakers & Top Headlines

1 Legends Howe and Beliveau retire
Two all-time greats are missing when training camps open in September. Gordie Howe, 44, the NHL's career leader in goals (786), assists (1,023) and points (1,809), retires after a record 25 seasons with the Red Wings. Howe finds his way back to the NHL eight years later. Meanwhile, Jean Beliveau, a 500-goal scorer and 1,000-point man who has hoisted the Stanley Cup five times as the Montreal captain, also retires.

2 Orr lands landmark contract
Bobby Orr becomes hockey's first million-dollar player when he signs a five-year contract Aug. 26 with the Bruins for $200,000 a year. "I'm very happy with the amount," Orr says. His agent, Alan Eagleson, goes one step further: "It's a safe assumption to say that Bobby's contract is the richest in NHL history." Orr proves he's worth it, winning the Hart Trophy for the third straight season — the last time a defenseman cops the honor until Chris Pronger wins it in 1999-2000.

3 Habs add Lafleur and Bowman
The NHL's June meetings could be described as the Montreal show. The Habs use the 1971 first pick overall, acquired the previous season from the California Golden Seals, to select junior star Guy Lafleur in the amateur draft. Winger John Ferguson joins Beliveau in retirement, then the defending champions complete their changes, naming St. Louis Blues' coach Scotty Bowman to replace Al MacNeil.

1972-73

OH, CANADA!

→ HARVEY DOESN'T TAKE THE BAIT

Not even the allure of this plaque and a Hall of Fame induction can stop Habs legend Doug Harvey from cancelling his fishing trip, which he claims is scheduled for the same day as his induction ceremony. His real reason for skipping out: he's upset over being previously snubbed by the Hall.

↓ TRAVELLING IN STYLE

One perk of playing for the Canadiens in the early '70s as they pile up Cups: classy, custom suitcases like this one belonging to Frank Mahovlich.

Cup Winner

Montreal Canadiens

Leading Scorers
1. Phil Esposito, Bos, 130 points
2. Bobby Clarke, Phi, 104 points
3. Bobby Orr, Bos, 101 points
4. Rick MacLeish, Phi, 100 points
5. Jacques Lemaire, Mtl, 95 pts

Rule Changes
Minimum width of stick blade is reduced to two inches from two-and-a-half.

Franchise News
Atlanta Flames and New York Islanders added, expanding NHL to 16 teams.

60 Moments
that changed the game
No. 6: Canada beats Soviet Union in eight-game Summit Series, but international hockey awareness is upon us.
No. 12: The rival World Hockey Association plays its first game and its 12-team league competes head-on for market share and player talent with the NHL.

First Draft Pick, 1973
Denis Potvin, D, NY Islanders

HHOF Inductees
Chuck Rayner
Tommy Smith
↓ Doug Harvey

Nickname of the Year
Eddie 'The Entertainer' Shack

Newsmakers & Top Headlines

1 Canada squeaks by Soviets in Summit Series
Experts predict an easy series win for Canada. But Soviet goalie Vladislav Tretiak, 20, is brilliant as his team stuns the Canadians 7-3 in Game 1 and takes a 3-1-1 lead after five games. Canada is in turmoil from day one. Stars Bobby Hull, Derek Sanderson, Gerry Cheevers and J-C Tremblay are dropped after jumping to the rival World Hockey Association and the injured Bobby Orr can't play. All looks lost until Paul Henderson scores two winning goals to tie the series. Henderson then becomes a national hero by scoring with 34 seconds left in Game 8 as Canada wins 6-5 to take the series.

2 Startup WHA steals stars from NHL
NHL moguls are not impressed by the World Hockey Association, which promises to be a major league rival. The laughing stops when Chicago superstar Bobby Hull signs a $1-million deal with the Winnipeg Jets. Cheevers, Sanderson, Bernie Parent and John McKenzie are other prominent NHLers to jump. The NHL's reserve clause, which ties a player to one team for life, is defeated in court by the WHA, opening the door to free agency.

3 Expansion Islanders set record for losses
As the league grows from 14 to 16 teams, the Atlanta Flames, coached by former Montreal star Bernie 'Boom Boom' Geoffrion, win 25 of 78 games and fare much better than their expansion cousins, the New York Islanders, who set an NHL record with 60 losses.

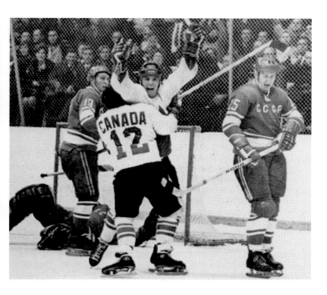

← SUMMITING
Yvan Cournoyer hugs Paul Henderson as he scores on Vladislav Tretiak to win the Summit Series in spectacular fashion.

↑ OFFICAL TEAM CANADA 1972
The official team photo of Team Canada 1972 taken on Aug. 29, 1972 at Maple Leaf Graden including Head coach Harry Sinden and Assistant coach John Ferguson. Team members (L-R): Red Berenson, Gary Bergman, Wayne Cashman, Bobby Clarke, Yvan Cournoyer, Marcel Dionne, Ron Ellis, Phil Esposito, Tony Esposito, Rod Gilbert, Brian Glennie, Don Awrey, Bill Goldsworthy, Joycelyn Guevremont, Vic Hadfield, Paul Henderson, Dennis Hull, Guy Lapointe, Frank Mahovlich, Pete Mahovlich, Rick Martin, Stan Mikita, Bobby Orr, Jean-Paul Parise, Brad Park, Gilbert Perreault, Jean Ratelle, Mickey Redmond, Serge Savard, Rod Seiling, Pat Stapleton, Dale Tallon, and Bill White.

>1973-74

BROAD STREET CUP

↑ **BACKSTOPPING THE BULLIES**
This Bernie Parent sweater swallows plenty of rubber during the Philadelphia Flyers' first successful Stanley Cup crusade.

← **POSITIVE REINFORCEMENT**
Just to erase any doubts the Flyers champion aggression in the 1970s: they reward anyone reaching 200 PIM in a season with a hard hat.

FACTS & STATS
from 1973-74

Cup Winner
Philadelphia Flyers

Leading Scorers
1. Phil Esposito, Bos, 145 pts
2. Bobby Orr, Bos, 122 points
3. Ken Hodge, Bos, 105 points
4. Wayne Cashman, Bos, 89 pts
5. Bobby Clarke, Phi, 87 points
6. Rick Martin, Buf, 86 points
7. Syl Apps Jr., Pit, 85 points
8. Darryl Sittler, Tor, 84 points
9. Lowell MacDonald, Pit, 82 pts
10. Brad Park, NYR, 82 points

60 Moments
that changed the game
No. 8: Borje Salming makes his debut with Toronto, opening a door for European acceptance in the NHL.
No. 38: Philadelphia Flyers use physical intimidation to win Stanley Cup, spurring a trend towards rough, brutal play.

First Draft Pick, 1974
Greg Joly, D, Washington

HHOF Inductees
Billy Burch
Art Coulter
Thomas Dunderdale
↓ Dickie Moore

Nickname of the Year
Lorne 'Gump' Worsley

Worth Noting
With owner Charles Finley unable to find a buyer, the NHL takes over operation of financially troubled California Golden Seals.

Newsmakers & Top Headlines

1 Flyers first expansion team to win title
Philadelphia's rugged Broad Street Bullies, who set an NHL penalty minutes record in 1972-73, become the first of the 1967 expansion teams to win the Stanley Cup. Billed as the team against the superstar, the Flyers, led by captain Bobby Clarke, defeat the Bruins in six games. "They had (Bobby) Orr and he can do an awful lot," says Flyers' coach Fred Shero. "But we've got 17 good hockey players and every one of them put out. It was 17 against one."

2 Howe teams with sons in WHA
One year after grabbing Bobby Hull, the WHA stages another coup, luring NHL career scoring leader Gordie Howe out of retirement. The Houston Aeros sign Howe, 45, to play on the same team with his sons Mark and Marty. Gordie leads the Aeros in scoring with 100 points after being away from the game two years. Howe finishes third in league scoring and is named the league's MVP. With the Howes in the lineup, Houston wins the Avco Cup title.

3 Horton killed in car accident
Buffalo GM Punch Imlach lures Tim Horton out of retirement with a signing bonus of an Italian-made Ford Pantera sports car. It turns out to be a fatal decision. The 44-year-old defenseman is driving the car from Toronto to Buffalo after a game Feb. 21 when he loses control and crashes near St. Catharines, Ont. Horton is killed instantly.

CUP CHAMPS BACK, BUT SOMETHING STILL MISSING

OCT. 5, 1973 BY CHRIS ZELKOVICH

MONTREAL, QUE. –

A telephone rang at Sam Pollock's hotel room in New York Sept. 13. The Montreal Canadiens' GM is now wishing he hadn't answered it. The man at the other end of the line was Vezina Trophy winner Ken Dryden and he wasn't calling Pollock to ask him about the weather. Dryden had called Sam to tell him he was retiring from hockey for one year to article in law in Toronto.

The reason? Money.

"This is the most difficult decision I've ever made," the 26-year-old netminder told newsmen at a press conference the following day. "But I feel it is a decision I have to make. But feeling that it is the right decision doesn't make it any easier."

Dryden's resolution to take a sabbatical from hockey in favor of articling with a Toronto law firm came after the Canadiens could not come to a satisfactory salary agreement with him.

Working on the second year of an $80,000, two-year contract, Dryden became dissatisfied when he saw others making more. He asked for a raise, but the Canadiens could not match his price, rumored to be $200,000.

"You look around the league and you see somebody else who you feel is making no more, no less a contribution to his team than you are," the articulate law graduate explained, "and when you see what salary he's making, it's very difficult to accept.

"Last year there were six goaltenders making more than I. There really is no reason for that. The Canadiens are not an impoverished organization, so there's no reason why they can't pay me the going rate."

Dryden signed his contract prior to the emergence of the World Hockey Association and missed out on the inflated salaries. The New York Rangers rewrote the contracts of several top players and Dryden felt he should get the same treatment. He didn't and decided to retire.

It wasn't a teary-eyed "retirement" like Joe Namath's or a jocular one like Vida Blue's. Dryden's retirement was a serious one.

What makes it even more serious for the Canadiens is that Ken admits he's been talking to the WHA Toronto Toros and that "They have offered me the going rate." It's been rumored that he has already signed with the WHA club, but Dryden denies that.

Hab management may have considered Dryden's retirement a bluff, but three days after the press conference, he started work with the law firm of Osler, Hoskins and Harcourt at $134 a week. With the man who led them to two Stanley Cups in his three-year career apparently serious about retirement, the Habs are faced with filling a gaping hole in the nets.

The three candidates for his job, Michel Plasse, Wayne Thomas and Michel Larocque, have an aggregate of two years NHL experience. Plasse and Thomas shared the Habs' backup chores last year while rookies, with Larocque spending his

↑ MAKING A 'FIRM' STAND

Habs' all-star stopper Ken Dryden seen here with his wife, leaves the team for a season in his prime to protest his mediocre salary. He goes to work for a law firm.

first pro season at Nova Scotia in the American League. All are confident of winning the number one job and Habs coach Scott Bowman also expressed confidence in their collective abilities.

"Thomas and Plasse did a great job with us last year," Bowman said. "I was expecting to start with three goaltenders this year, so it puts Larocque in the picture. All three are promising goaltenders."

Plasse, 25, fashioned a 2.58 average in 17 games last year and appears to be the heir apparent to Dryden.

Thomas, 26, actually has a lower goals-against average than Plasse (2.37 in 10 games) and could challenge him for the starting job. But Larocque, only 21, can't be counted out after his first season in pro hockey.

"You always come to camp trying to be number one," Larocque said. "You can't think you're not good enough to make it. It's a break for me with Dryden retiring, but even if it wasn't Dryden, it's just one less guy fighting for the job."

The loss of Dryden puts a slight dent in the Canadiens' depth chart, the key to repeating as Stanley Cup champions according to Bowman.

"The big question is whether or not we can count on the bench the way we did last year," Bowman said prior to training camp. "Last year we had 13 or 14 forwards we could count on. The year before, we didn't.

"If rookies, guys like (Yvon) Lambert, (Dave) Gardner, (Glenn) Goldup and (Bob) Gainey come through we'll do OK. When the injuries come, you've got to have replacements."

(Editor's Note: Dryden backed up his words by sitting out the entire 1973-74 season and working at the law firm. The Canadiens allowed 56 more goals that season and lost in the first round of the playoffs. Dryden and the Canadiens settled their differences the following summer and he resumed his Hall of Fame career.) **THN**

>1974-75

TOUGH GUYS NO. 1

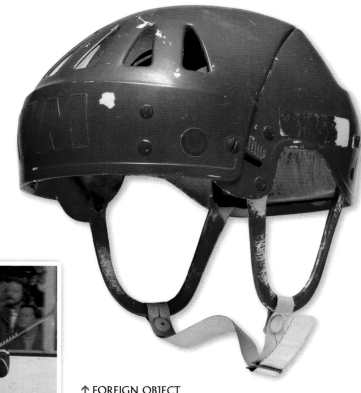

↑ FOREIGN OBJECT
Russia's Alexander Yakushev dons this helmet. NHLers experience his dominance in the 1972 Summit Series, but he never joins a North American pro league.

Newsmakers & Top Headlines

1 More expansion leads to realignment
Expansion franchises in Washington and Kansas City lead to the biggest changes in the NHL since 1967-68. The league moves to a four-division format, naming them after NHL icons Lester Patrick, Conn Smythe, Jim Norris and Jack Adams. Expansion teams win three of four divisions — Philadelphia (Patrick), Vancouver (Smythe) and Buffalo (Adams). The Capitals go 8-67-5 and set NHL records of 17 straight losses and the lowest winning percentage in history — .131.

2 Orr and Espo enjoy one last hurrah together
Boston teammates Bobby Orr and Phil Esposito put on another explosive scoring display. Little does anyone realize it's their swan song together. Orr pots a record 46 goals for a defenseman and wins his second Art Ross and eighth straight Norris Trophy. Esposito leads the league in goals for the sixth straight season with 61 and finishes behind Orr with 127 points. Neither reaches that output again. Esposito is traded next season while Orr, whose knees begin to go, never plays a full season again.

3 Islanders join '42 Leafs with miraculous comeback
The Islanders are down 3-0 in games to the Penguins in their quarterfinal, but when coach Al Arbour replaces goalie Billy Smith with rookie Glenn Resch, the tables turn. The Isles win four straight, including 1-0 in Game 7. They join the 1942 Toronto Maple Leafs as the only teams to rally from such a deficit.

CAPITALS SUBSTITUTE TRASH BASKET FOR CUP FOLLOWING ONLY ROAD VICTORY OF SEASON

APRIL 18, 1975 BY RUSS WHITE

WASHINGTON, D.C. –

The lovable Washington Capitals substituted a wastepaper basket for the Stanley Cup when they captured their first road victory after 37 consecutive failures.

Led by the inimitable Nelson Pyatt, the Capitals socked it to the California Golden Seals 5-3 in what could be hockey's zaniest victory of the season. The Capitals entered the game not only with their 0-37 road record, but with an NHL record 17 consecutive losses. Coach-GM Milt Schmidt was embarrassed to even talk about the pitiful streaks.

The victory in Oakland was fully appreciated by Schmidt and the players. He guzzled a Coors as if it were champagne from the Stanley Cup and the players held their waste-can high amid cheers of "Break up the Caps."

Pyatt, one of the new additions by Schmidt in a seven-trade spree in recent weeks, scored the winning goal at 6:31 of the third period and added the insurance goal into an empty net with only 16 seconds to play. It was the first empty-net goal in the amazing history of the Caps.

"It may be the end of the year," Pyatt said, "but finally it is a start."

In a game that was televised back to the Nation's Capital, the Capitals made an unprecedented quick start, scoring twice in the first four minutes. For those who tuned in late, expecting the Friday night TV chiller, "Weird Tales," there was some doubt as to if what was on were a movie or a game.

Veteran Doug Mohns scored the first Washington marker, his 249th career goal. Goaltender Ron Low, who was faced with only 20 shots, ripped off his mask and presented a smile that he had hidden for the closing minutes of the sweet Washington win. His teammates skated up to embrace Low and the group went off ice in glorious style.

"Sweeter than the Stanley Cup," Schmidt said.

The Caps returned home to play the Detroit Red Wings two nights after the Oakland victory and jumped to a 5-2 lead in this one with former Pittsburgh Penguin Ron Lalonde getting his team's first hat trick.

A flood of hats cluttered the ice at Capital Centre as the Washington fans acknowledged Lalonde's feat. The hats were cleared and the Caps were caught resting on their laurels as Detroit came back with six unanswered goals to win 8-5.

Schmidt was furious at the loose play as Marcel Dionne scored twice late in the second period. "By now these guys should know how important it is to play those closing minutes of any period. Our defense wasn't big league."

The Caps have yielded 424 goals, 77 over the record, and the count keeps going higher. Washington's amazing fans don't give a hoot, however, as there are few dropouts in season tickets for next year. The Capitals fans have a shindig planned next week and it's a sellout.

The Caps averaged more than 10,000 for the season, better than the Washington Bullets NBA team, a first place outfit.

↑ **FATHER OF TAYLOR AND TOM PYATT**
Nelson Pyatt scores two of his six goals on the season in the only road victory of the campaign for the hapless Washington Capitals.

AUG., 1975 BY DOUG McCONNELL

FIGHTING SAINTS MAKE FABULOUS OFFER IN BID TO LURE ORR AWAY FROM BRUINS. MINNESOTA WANTS KEON, TOO

ST. PAUL, MINN. – "We couldn't be more serious," said Minnesota GM Glen Sonmor, "and what's more, we think we've got a pretty good chance to getting him."

"Him," is Bobby Orr, the great defense star of the Boston Bruins to whom the Fighting Saints have made a multi-million dollar offer.

Bill Watters, an associate of Alan Eagleson (Orr's agent) calls the offer "obviously for three or four times more than Bobby Hull got for jumping to the Winnipeg Jets three years ago."

The signing bonus is $1 million.

Orr has one year remaining on his contract with the Bruins, which calls for about $250,000 a year.

"There is no way the Bruins can match the offer," Watters said.

"Can you imagine what that would do in this town?" Sonmor said.

"Wayne Belisle (club president) has been talking to Eagleson for some time about Orr," he added. "We've probably got more of Eagleson's clients than any team in hockey, including the National League. That should help in the negotiations, the fact that there is a mutual trust there from past dealings, and the fact that Orr and Mike Walton (the Saints' star center) are partners in a hockey school can't hurt."

The Saints also have hopes of landing former Toronto Maple Leaf star center Dave Keon and have already improved at center with the addition of Henry Boucha, who moves over from the NHL's Minnesota North Stars. Boucha missed part of the season with an eye injury sustained in an infamous stick-swinging run-in with Boston's Dave Forbes.

"We think we have a 50-50 chance of getting Keon," Sonmor said. **THN**

>1975-76

SITTLER'S BIG NIGHT

→ **WELL-TRAVELLED**
Ed Giacomin's pads take a trip in 1975-76. The Rangers waive their long-time stopper and Detroit claims him. He calls that day the toughest of his career.

Cup Winner
Montreal Canadiens

Leading Scorers
1. Guy Lafleur, Mtl, 125 points
2. Bobby Clarke, Phi, 119 pts
3. Gilbert Perreault, Buf, 113 pts
4. Bill Barber, Phi, 112 points
5. Pierre Larouche, Pit, 111 pts
6. J. Ratelle, Bos/NYR, 105 pts
7. Pete Mahovlich, Mtl, 105 pts
8. Jean Pronovost, Pit, 104 pts
9. Darryl Sittler, Tor, 100 points
10. Syl Apps Jr., Pit, 99 points

Significant Records
Most points, one game:
Darryl Sittler, Toronto (10).
Longest winning streak by a goaltender, one season:
Gilles Gilbert, Boston (17).

First Draft Pick, 1976
Rick Green, D, Washington

HHOF Inductees
Bill Quackenbush
↓Johnny Bower

Nickname of the Year
Claire 'The Milkman' Alexander

Worth Noting
Philadelphia's Reggie Leach sets an NHL record with 19 goals in the playoffs, after scoring 61 goals in the regular season. He wins the Conn Smythe Trophy as playoff MVP despite the fact his Flyers fall to Montreal...Toronto's Claire Alexander was a milkman before turning pro and making his NHL debut at 29.

Newsmakers & Top Headlines

1 **Bruins trade Esposito to Rangers**
In a move that would have been unthinkable when the two teams were on top of the NHL standings, the Bruins trade all-star Phil Esposito, Carol Vadnais and Joe Zanussi to the Rangers Nov. 7 for two other all-stars, Jean Ratelle and Brad Park. Esposito scores only 35 goals, 26 fewer than in 1974-75. "There should be a rule protecting veterans from trades after you've been with a team five or seven years," Esposito says.

2 **Ontario attorney general goes after NHL hooligans**
Following a brawl-filled playoff game in Toronto, Philadelphia's Mel Bridgman, Bob Kelly, Don Saleski and Joe Watson are charged with assault. It's part of Ontario attorney general Roy McMurtry's crackdown on hockey violence. Detroit's Dan Maloney also faces charges after an incident when he pounds the head of Toronto's Brian Glennie into the ice. Watson and Kelly plead guilty to common assault and are fined $750 and $200. The other players are cleared of all charges.

3 **Sittler's record night a perfect 10**
In an 11-4 win over Boston Feb. 7, Toronto's Darryl Sittler scores six times and adds four assists for an NHL-record 10 points. Then in Game 6 of a quarter-final series with Philadelphia, Sittler equals a Stanley Cup record with five goals. But he lists neither as his most memorable moment. "I figured I'd had my share of once-in-a-lifetime happenings back in 1971-72 when I had a perfect hand in cribbage."

→ KING OF LOS ANGELES
Marcel Dionne toiled in obscurity in
Southern California.

↑ IN A RUSH
Guy Lafleur 'The Flower' was known for
his end-to-end rushes, hair streaming back.

→ CRIBBAGE, ANYONE?
Darryl Sittler found a perfect cribbage
hand more exciting than scoring 10 points
in one game.

← **LABOR OF GLOVE**
Wearing these mitts, Jean Ratelle grips his stick oh-so tightly in the nail-biting Summit Series of 1972.

↓ GLOBAL GAME
Your eyes don't deceive you. Nations like
Laos, Mongolia and Belize have issued
Winter Olympic hockey stamps over the
years. Love for the sport extends beyond
the countries known for playing it well.

↑ WALL DECORATION
This jersey adorns legendary Russian goaltender Vladislav Tretiak and is a staple of his nation's battles with Canada throughout the 1970s.

← YOUTH FOUNDATION
These pads help an unknown kid named Tom Barrasso hone his puck-stopping skills. He dreams of playing in the NHL one day.

Newsmakers & Top Headlines

1 First Canada Cup stays home
For the first time, the world's top six hockey nations stage a true championship. The Canada Cup tournament ends when Canada sweeps a best-of-three final from Czechoslovakia, the only country to beat Canada in the opening round. The Soviet Union keeps eight of its greatest stars at home and finishes third. Skating virtually on one leg following a series of knee operations, Canada's Bobby Orr is named MVP. "This is the greatest hockey team in the world," proclaims Canada's Darryl Sittler, whose overtime winner decides it.

2 Orr leaves Beantown for Windy City
First, Phil Esposito is traded. Now Bobby Orr jumps ship — signing a $3-million free agent deal with the Black Hawks June 9 — leaving Boston minus its two icons. Bruins fans turn sour when they learn Boston didn't try to keep Orr. "We were offered the same deal as Chicago was," admits Boston president Paul Mooney. "We just didn't take it." Boston considers filing suit for compensation, but elects not to pursue the matter.

3 Cup-winning Habs win most games in NHL history
Perhaps the most dominant team in league history, the Canadiens roll to an NHL-record 60 victories and 132 points, then go 12-2 in the playoffs to win the Stanley Cup for the second straight season. The Canadiens are 33-1-6 at home and win a league-record 27 road games. Steve Shutt establishes a new mark for left wingers by scoring 60 goals to lead the league.

FACTS & STATS
from 1976-77

Cup Winner

Montreal Canadiens

Leading Scorers
1. Guy Lafleur, Mtl, 136 points
2. Marcel Dionne, LA, 122 points
3. Steve Shutt, Mtl, 105 points

Rule Changes
Rule dealing with fighting is amended to provide a major and game misconduct penalty for any player who is clearly the instigator of a bout.

Franchise News
California transfers to Cleveland to become the Barons. Kansas City transfers to Denver to become the Colorado Rockies.

60 Moments
that changed the game
No. 42: The Canada Cup ushers in an era of international best-versus-best hockey showcase.

Significant Records
Most goals by a defenseman, one game: Ian Turnbull, Toronto (5).

First Draft Pick, 1977
Dale McCourt, C, Detroit

HHOF Inductees
Alex Delvecchio
↓ Tim Horton

Nickname of the Year
Gilles 'Grattoony the Loony' Gratton

FACTS & STATS
from 1977-78

Cup Winner
Montreal Canadiens

Leading Scorers
1. Guy Lafleur, Mtl, 132 points
2. Bryan Trottier, NYI, 123 pts
3. Darryl Sittler, Tor, 117 points
4. Jacques Lemaire, Mtl, 97 pts
5. Denis Potvin, NYI, 94 points

60 Moments
that changed the game
No. 25: Ken Linseman, 19, wins a court battle allowing him to play pro hockey, marking a challenge to the 20-year-old draft.
No. 31: First-year coach Roger Neilson uses video footage to fine-tune his coaching strategies.

Significant Records
Most points by a defenseman, one game: Tom Bladon, Philadelphia (8).

First Draft Pick, 1978
Bobby Smith, C, Minnesota

HHOF Inductees
Andy Bathgate
Marcel Pronovost
↓Jacques Plante

Nickname of the Year
Yvan 'The Roadrunner' Cournoyer

Worth Noting
The Selke Trophy is introduced and awarded to the league's top defensive forward. Montreal's Bob Gainey wins it the first four seasons of its existence.

↑ THE TERRIFIC TENOR
Montreal's Roger Doucet is widely recognized as the greatest anthem singer in NHL history. With this microphone, the diminutive tenor stirs the Canadiens faithful into a lather in French and English during the 1970s.

Newsmakers & Top Headlines

1 Bossy shatters rookie goal record
Passed over until the 16th pick of the NHL amateur draft, right winger Mike Bossy from Laval of the Quebec League proves to be the find of the decade for the Islanders. Bossy's quick release allows him to score 53 goals, breaking the NHL rookie record of 44 set in 1971-72 by Buffalo's Rick Martin. Complacency isn't an issue for Bossy. The name over his dressing room stall remains written on masking tape with magic marker well into the season. "Maybe I'll get a nameplate like everyone else when they decide I can stay," Bossy says.

2 Linseman fights draft law and wins
Signed by the World Hockey Association's Birmingham Bulls, 19-year-old center Ken Linseman is re-fused permission to play by WHA president Howard Baldwin. The president is honoring an agreement with amateur hockey that the league will not sign or draft players under the age of 20. However, Linseman challenges the system in court and wins — opening the door to the drafting of underaged amateurs, a process which starts in the NHL in 1979.

3 Ziegler replaces Campbell as president
Clarence Campbell winds up his 31-season reign as president of the NHL, announcing his retirement prior to the campaign. John Ziegler, a lawyer employed as vice-president of the Red Wings, is recommended by Campbell and unanimously selected as his replacement by the 18 team owners.

1978-79

GOODBYE BOBBY / WHA

NEWS BULLETIN

CONTACT: John A. Hewig, Public Relations Director
OFFICE: 203-278-4240 • HOME: 203-651-8556 • TELEX: 966-485 WHA A HFD

STATEMENT RELEASED BY THE WORLD HOCKEY ASSOCIATION FRIDAY, MARCH 30, 1979

FOUR WHA TEAMS EXPAND INTO THE NHL

The National Hockey League expansion that will encompass four existing World Hockey Association teams (Edmonton, New England, Winnipeg and Quebec) for the 1979-80 season is not only in the best interests of both the WHA and the NHL, but, according to WHA President Howard Baldwin, it is also in the best interests of the sport of hockey.

"With major league hockey going back to one league, there in no question in my mind that this is an enormous step in solving many of the problems that have plagued this sport for the past seven years," said Baldwin when the expansion of the four WHA cities was announced Friday in New York.

"I have gone on record for years saying that I was a firm believer in the one league concept. It is evident to me that I am not alone in this opinion, and that the NHL expansion will improve our on ice product as well as make this sport a viable investment from the box office end.

This is John Ziegler's finest hour as President of the National Hockey League. I would like to personally thank him for his long tireless efforts, not only throughout these last two weeks of negotiations, but also over the many months that we have worked together on expansion.

"I must also offer my sincere appreciation to Donald Conrad, Exec. Vice President of Aetna, who has continually provided all those involved with his knowledgeable advice and recommendations.

I must also thank and congratulate the NHL Governors, particularly Bill and the WHA Trustees for their never ending patience and good judgment in expansion talks.

HOCKEY ASSOCIATION, SUITE 1700, ONE FINANCIAL PLAZA, HARTFORD, CONNECTICUT 06103

← THE POSITIVE SPIN
The press release announcing the NHL absorption of four teams from the floundering World Hockey Association reads more like an award acceptance speech from the WHA's behalf. In truth, financial problems and multiple years of contraction leave the WHA with no option other than to get swallowed by the NHL.

↓ 60-MINUTE PUCK
Hard to believe, but this puck lasts an entire 60-minute Los Angeles Kings' game. At left, Bernie Parent's final game-used stick with the Philadelphia Flyers.

Newsmakers & Top Headlines

1 **Gretzky stars in final WHA season**
In what will be its final season, the WHA stages a major coup when Indianapolis owner Nelson Skalbania signs Wayne Gretzky to a $1.75-million personal services contract. In November, the Racers sell his contract to Edmonton, where he places third in WHA scoring with 104 points. Then in March, the NHL votes 14-3 to adopt four WHA franchises — the Edmonton Oilers, Hartford Whalers, Quebec Nordiques and Winnipeg Jets — in 1979-80.

2 **Cherry bomb helps Habs win fourth straight title**
Leading Montreal 4-3 with 2:34 left in Game 7 of the semifinal, Boston blows its Stanley Cup chances with a careless too-many-men-on-the-ice penalty. Guy Lafleur scores, then Yvon Lambert wins it in OT and Boston coach Don Cherry is fired as a result. It's the fourth consecutive Cup for the powerhouse Canadiens and the fifth straight 50-goal season for Lafleur. Three prominent Habs — Yvan Cournoyer, Jacques Lemaire and Ken Dryden — retire at the end of the season.

3 **Bad knees end Orr's career**
The only thing that stops Bobby Orr is his health. Orr has knee surgery six times and retires Nov. 8 at the age of 30. He finishes his 12-year career with 270 goals and 915 points, both NHL records for defensemen at the time, as well as three Hart and eight Norris Trophies. Inducted into the Hall of Fame the next year, he's the youngest person to receive the honor.

FACTS & STATS
from 1978-79

Cup Winner

Montreal Canadiens

Leading Scorers
1. Bryan Trottier, NYI, 134 points
2. Marcel Dionne, LA, 130 points
3. Guy Lafleur, Mtl, 129 points
4. Mike Bossy, NYI, 126 points
5. Bob MacMillan, Atl, 108 points

Franchise News
Cleveland Baron and Minnesota North Stars merge to reduce league to 17 teams. Franchise will play in Minnesota.

60 Moments
that changed the game
No. 26: World Hockey Association announces it is merging four teams into the NHL the following season.
No. 40: Wayne Gretzky signs hockey's first personal services contract, sparking a trend.

Significant Records
Most points, one period: Bryan Trottier, NY Islanders (6).
Most penalty minutes, one game: Randy Holt, Los Angeles (67).

First Draft Pick, 1979
Rob Ramage, D, Colorado

HHOF Inductees
Harry Howell
Henri Richard
↓ Bobby Orr

Nickname of the Year
Larry 'Izzy' Goodenough

→ 50 X 9

Mike Bossy scored 50 goals in nine consecutive seasons. He holds the NHL record for most goals-per-game average of .762. He also scored consecutive Stanley Cup wining goals in 1982 and 1983.

→ ISLANDER DYNASTY

Led by the playmaking prowess of Bryan Trottier and Mike Bossy's snap shot, the New York Islanders won the Stanley Cup four years running.

BY ADAM PROTEAU

— 1979-1993 —

LIVE PUCK ERA

MORE MONEY, MORE TEAMS, MORE SCORING AND MORE BROKEN RECORDS. THAT WAS THE MANTRA OF THE GAME'S GLORIOUSLY GLUTTONOUS AGE

The point is, ladies and gentleman, that greed — for lack of a better word — is good. Greed is right. Greed works. Greed clarifies, cuts through and captures the essence of the evolutionary spirit. Greed, in all of its forms — greed for life, for money, for love, knowledge — has marked the upward surge of mankind." — Gordon Gekko (as played by Michael Douglas) in *Wall Street.*

Whether it was on the ice or in the boardroom, the NHL from 1979 through the early '90s was all about greed, pushing boundaries and excess. But the thirst for advancement at all costs wasn't only to be found in the sport's greatest league. It was everywhere.

In the United States, Americans went from single-term Democratic president Jimmy Carter's humanistic approach to two terms of Republican Ronald Reagan's business-first mentality. Canada took a little longer to follow that route, but sure enough, Canadians eschewed the bleeding heart Liberal party of legendary prime minister Pierre Trudeau in favor of the conservative, free-trade pushing mandate of Brian Mulroney.

And it was there in hockey. It was there in the NHL's victory over the rival World Hockey Association. For seven years beginning in 1972, the WHA competed with the NHL for star players (including all-time greats Gordie Howe and Bobby Hull, among others), but by 1979, it had folded and four of its teams — the Edmonton Oilers, New England/Hartford Whalers, Winnipeg Jets and Quebec Nordiques — were assimilated into what became now a 21-team NHL.

The late-70s expansion of the NHL brought with it a slew of WHA-raised talent, including Mark Messier and the immortal Wayne Gretzky, whose arrival heralded the start of a quicker, smarter, more thrilling style of hockey than ever had been seen before. Both those players were the ultimate team competitors, but both were also as driven — as greedy, you might say — to succeed as often as they could. And as members of the Oilers, they did just that, converting an incredible lineup (including future Hall of Famers Paul Coffey, Jari Kurri, Glenn Anderson and Grant Fuhr) into a dynasty.

That's another element of greed to be found in this era: this was the last of the true dynasties, of teams who weren't satisfied with a single Stanley Cup victory and instead racked up multiple championships. In fact, from 1979 (the year the Montreal Canadiens won the last of four consecutive Cups) to 1993, just five different teams won it all: Mike Bossy's New York Islanders won four straight (1980, '81, '82, '83); the Oilers won five of the next seven ('84, '85, '87, '88, '90); Montreal won again in '86 and '93; Pittsburgh won two in a row in '91 and '92; and Calgary was the lone one-time winner in '89.

That sense of always wanting more also carried over to the style of play that developed in this period of NHL history. Players were transitioning from a slower league where players often didn't get in shape until training camp began to a more modern entity where the pace was much closer to what you'd see at a racetrack and where athletes began treating their bodies as elite business machines to be maintained on a year-round basis.

The results of that evolution showed on the ice, as the league's goals-per-game average skyrocketed from 7.00 in 1978-79 to 7.69 in 1980-81 and a modern-day high of 8.03 the following season (the NHL had its all-time mark of 8.17 set in 1943-44). In fact, in 12 years of this 14-year stretch, the league's GPG average was above the 7.00 mark, but has never returned to that level since.

But that was the mentality of the time, said Anaheim Ducks right winger and future Hall of Famer Teemu Selanne, who set a still-standing NHL record of 76 goals as a rookie during his first season (1992-93) with the Winnipeg Jets. "The game was totally different when I started in the NHL," Selanne said. The biggest difference now is the attitude of the teams. Now, teams say, 'there's no way we're going to give up more than two or three goals a game.' But in my time, it was, 'whoever scores more goals wins.' The whole mindset was different and that's why there were so many high-scoring games back then."

See that? Whereas now, the NHL features defensive stinginess, variations of the trap and shot-blocking galore, the NHL from '79-93 was about piling up offense as best you could. The game hadn't yet been micromanaged and over-coached as it is today. It was all about getting yours and maximizing success wherever possible, whether you were a player or team owner.

For example, after the four WHA teams were brought into the fold, the

league realized there was more demand than ever for its product, so in 1990 it kicked off an era of unbridled expansion that would lead to the current 30-team setup: San Jose was the first new arrival in 1991, followed by Ottawa and Tampa Bay in 1992 and Anaheim and Florida in '93. This era also included the first NHL rink board advertising and the first on-ice ads.

Although many if not most of these business moves were met with widespread scorn by hockey diehards, it was clear the financial aspects of the game were overshadowing its humble roots and there was no turning back. The sports consumer world of satellite TV, sports talk radio and cable rights-holder deals was growing exponentially. Inroads made in merchandising and memorabilia were also funnelling more money into the pockets of owners and players.

Because of that collective sense of prideful avarice that Michael Douglas espoused as Gordon Gekko, NHLers began seeking better salaries. Hockey's top players averaged only a $200,000 payout in 1990, but that was the year the NHL Players' Association began publicly disclosing salaries in the hopes of — you guessed it — making the players more money.

Of course, the NHLPA and its constituents would be wildly successful in that regard, perfectly capping off the era where greed was not only a good thing, but the only thing. THN

↑ **HARDWARE HOARDER**
In hockey's greedy era, Wayne Gretzky's hunger for Stanley Cup rings and scoring records was insatiable. He dominated the game like no one since.

↑ **THERE IN A (FINNISH) FLASH**
Teemu Selanne assaulted the NHL with a record 76-goal rookie year in 1993. The strategy in his heyday was to score more goals, not allow fewer.

>1979-80

DO YOU BELIEVE?

Cup Winner
New York Islanders

Leading Scorers
1. Marcel Dionne, LA, 137 points
2. Wayne Gretzky, Edm, 137 pts
3. Guy Lafleur, Mtl, 125 points

Rule Changes
Helmets are made mandatory for players entering NHL.

Franchise News
Edmonton, Hartford, Quebec and Winnipeg transfer from WHA, making NHL a 21-team league.

60 Moments
that changed the game
No. 3: Wayne Gretzky debuts with the NHL's Edmonton Oilers and the live-puck era is on.
No. 10: The U.S. 'Miracle on Ice' team wins the Olympic gold medal led by coach Herb Brooks.
No. 20: Hockey helmets made mandatory for new players entering NHL.
No. 57: Trade deadline day gains prominence as Islanders acquire Butch Goring and win Cup.

First Draft Pick, 1980
Doug Wickenheiser, C, Montreal

HHOF Inductees
Harry Lumley
Lynn Patrick
↓Gump Worsley

Nickname of the Year
Marcel 'Little Beaver' Dionne

→ **MIRACLE MASK**
The art is simple — two stickers — but the design of this goalie mask is distinctively Jim Craig. The Boston University alum leads Team USA to unexpected glory at the 1980 Lake Placid Olympics.

Newsmakers & Top Headlines

1 'Miracle on Ice' ignites hockey interest in U.S
Mike Eruzione's third-period goal gives a spirited group of American collegians a stunning 4-3 upset victory over the Soviet Union at the 1980 Lake Placid Olympics. Team USA goes on to defeat Finland 4-2 Feb. 24 to win the gold medal. It's the first time since 1960, when the Americans also won at Squaw Valley, any nation other than the Soviet Union wins gold.

2 Four WHA refugees make NHL debuts
The NHL starts 1979-80 with four new teams, absorbing the Edmonton Oilers, Hartford Whalers, Quebec Nordiques and Winnipeg Jets from the WHA. This officially brings to an end a seven-year battle between the two leagues. Launched with 12 teams in 1972-73, the WHA peaks with 14 in 1974-75 and finishes in 1978-79 with six. The other two remaining franchises — the Cincinnati Stingers and Birmingham Bulls — are dissolved. At 51, Hartford's Gordie Howe scores 15 goals in his first NHL campaign since 1970-71. It's 'Mr. Hockey's' final NHL season.

3 Gretzky begins reign as NHL king
At 19, Wayne Gretzky becomes the youngest player to score 50 goals as well as win the Hart and Lady Byng Trophies. Although he ties Marcel Dionne with a league-high 137 points, Dionne wins the Art Ross Trophy because he has more goals (53 to 51). Gretzky is ruled ineligible for the Calder Trophy because of his WHA experience.

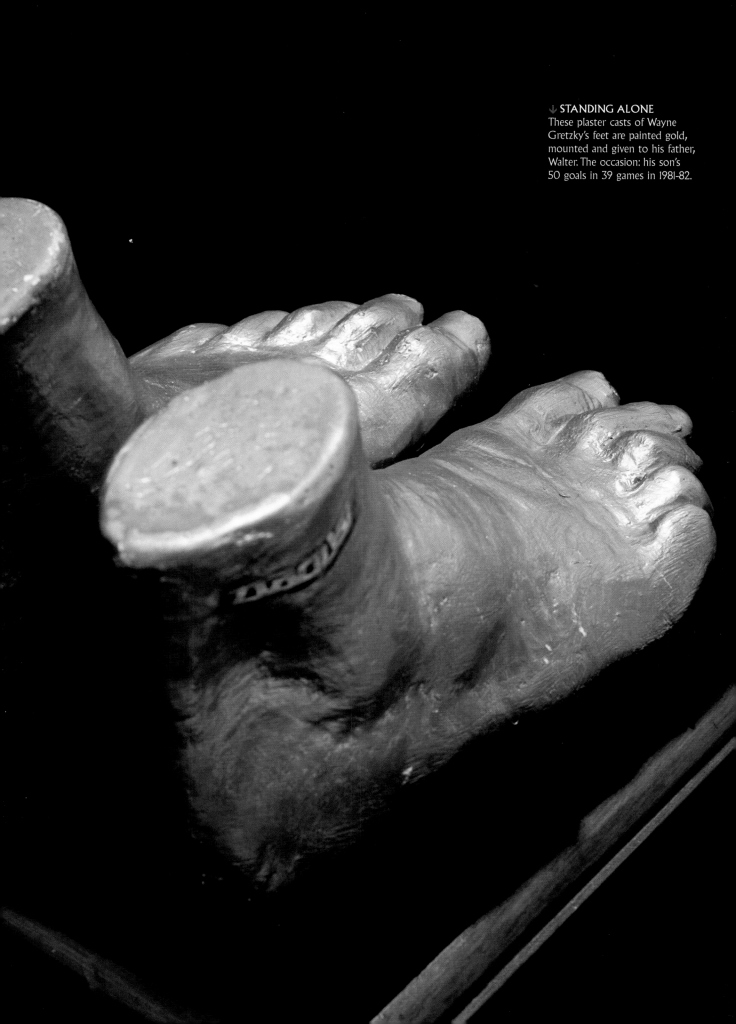

>1980-81

THE GREAT ONE

FACTS & STATS
from 1980-81

Cup Winner
New York Islanders

Leading Scorers
1. Wayne Gretzky, Edm, 164 pts
2. Marcel Dionne, LA, 135 points
3. Kent Nilsson, Cgy, 131 points
4. Mike Bossy, NYI, 119 points
5. Dave Taylor, LA, 112 points

Franchise News
Atlanta transfers to Calgary, retains Flames nickname.

60 Moments
that changed the game
No. 17: Peter and Anton Stastny defect from Czechoslovakia and sign to play with Quebec.

First Draft Pick, 1981
Dale Hawerchuk, C, Winnipeg

HHOF Inductees
John Bucyk
Frank Mahovlich
↓Allan Stanley

Nickname of the Year
Guy 'The Flower' Lafleur

Worth Noting
The Winnipeg Jets set an NHL record with a 30-game winless streak...Hartford's Mark Howe narrowly escapes a career-ending injury in which he crashes into the net. His buttock is punctured and the point inside the net frame just misses his spine. The net design changes to a straight bar across the back.

Newsmakers & Top Headlines

1 Gretzky breaks Esposito and Orr scoring marks
Wayne Gretzky has a record-breaking week that will become all too familiar. The Edmonton center records three assists March 30 at Pittsburgh, vaulting him past Phil Esposito's 10-year-old NHL record of 152 points. Two nights later, Gretzky collects his 103rd assist, breaking the NHL mark of 102 set by Esposito's teammate Bobby Orr in 1970-71. Gretzky finishes with 109 assists and 164 points and his 2.05 points-per-game average is the highest since Joe Malone's 2.40 in 1917-18.

2 Stastnys defect to play in Quebec
Stars of Czechoslovakia's national team, the Stastny brothers, Peter and Anton, defect and sign with the Nordiques. Peter garners a rookie-record 109 points and wins the Calder Trophy. Their defection leads to an agreement with the Czechoslovak federation allowing other talented players to leave the country legally to play in the NHL the next season. That includes Marian Stastny, who joins his brothers in Quebec.

3 Dionne king of Triple Crown line
Los Angeles center Marcel Dionne places second to Wayne Gretzky in the scoring race with 58 goals and 135 points. He leads the Kings' Triple Crown line, with wingers Dave Taylor and Charlie Simmer, to a banner season. The line produces 161 goals and 191 assists for 352 points. Dionne also records his 1,000th career point in only his 740th game, the fastest anyone has ever reached 1,000.

AN INTERESTING EXPERIMENT IN GARBAGE

OCT. 3, 1980 BY BILL LIBBY

↑ **ANYTHING BUT GARBAGE GOALS**
Vancouver's Thomas Gradin has magic hands around the net, scoring a career-high 37 goals and 86 points in 1981-82.

Most National Hockey League players have cabins by the countless lakes in Canada and spend their summers swimming, boating or fishing. Some play a lot of golf or tennis. Some run to stay in shape and a great many skate at hockey camps.

Thomas Gradin, the spectacular center of the Vancouver Canucks, spent this summer gathering garbage in his native Sweden. He got up at six o'clock every weekday morning to work as a garbage collector in a Stockholm suburb.

"I always hated weight training and running," he says, "so I thought this would be an interesting experiment. It's tough, but picking up 400 garbage sacks daily is good for your body."

Gradin turned 24 in February. At 5-foot-11 and 175 pounds he is a very durable player but he could stand some beefing up.

Like most Swedish players, Gradin was taught to skate, not check, and certainly not to fight. He has been tested by Canadians, who have roughed him up but found him to be fearless. He gets up and goes on. He missed four games with a broken bone in his left hand his first season. He didn't miss a game last season.

Gradin says the hardest thing he has learned to do is not only hit physically, but continue his checks until he has opponents pinned on the boards and out of the play.

"It is the way they play here so it is the way I have to play," he says. "Clean checking is good, but there is rough stuff here that takes away from the play.

"I am a skater and stick-handler. That is my game. I can shoot, but I'd just as soon pass. I like making a good play that gets my team a goal as well as I like scoring a goal myself."

Gradin has an easy, fluid style and explosive speed. He carries the puck skillfully, makes accurate passes, and is a quick, accurate shooter.

In Sweden, where he played just 35 games a year, Gradin notched 22 goals in his third season in the Swedish First Division while averaging 16 assists a season. In 1978-79, his first season in the NHL, Gradin scored 20 goals and 31 assists for 51 points. Last year he improved his stats to 30-45-75 while becoming the Canucks' second leading scorer in all departments (goals, assists and points).

When asked what the biggest differences are between the NHL and the hockey in Sweden, Gradin cites the length of the schedule as one big factor. "After 35 games here," he says, "I am not even halfway through the season. I have to build up my endurance."

While Gradin may be concerned about the adjustments he must make in his game to conform to the style in the NHL, Vancouver GM Jake Milford is not too worried about Gradin's progress. "He's been great," Milford says, "and he could become one of the greatest in the game. He has the un-

usual natural talent, works hard, and is serious about his sport. He could be more aggressive, but that is not unusual for a Scandinavian."

Gradin was born 24 years ago in Solleftea, a harbor town of 60,000 on the outskirts of Stockholm. His team, AIK, was named for the paper factory that provides employment to many of the townspeople.

His father, Kjell, drives a tractor and works in the mill. Tom's mother, Elsie, works at a day care clinic for crippled children.

Thomas attended university and graduated with a degree in Physical Education. He has worked as a gym teacher in the off-seasons. He has a home in Stockholm, where he and his wife, Lillibeth, spend their time after the season ends.

"Sometimes we miss our parents and friends back home during the winters, but we have by now made friends in Vancouver," he says. "At first here everything was a problem for us, but we have learned the language and the life. We like the life here, but our home is still Sweden."

Gradin can make more money in Vancouver and is gaining security for his future. Originally, he was drafted by Chicago back in 1976, but he did not like the kind of contract he was offered. "It was not so good," he smiles. Chicago traded the rights to him for a second-round draft choice in 1978, not one of the best trades Chicago GM Bob Pulford ever made. With the help of a Vancouver lawyer, Gradin got what he wanted from the Canucks. "It was good," he smiles.

All Gradin wants to do now is become an even better player than he already is, and he'll do anything to achieve that goal — including collecting garbage during the off season.

(Editor's Note: Gradin is still regarded as one of the best players in the history of the Canucks and as a scout convinced Vancouver to draft unheard-of Alexander Edler in the third round of the 2004 draft.) **THN**

200-POINT PLATEAU

FACTS & STATS
from 1981-82

Cup Winner
New York Islanders

Leading Scorers
1. Wayne Gretzky, Edm, 212 pts
2. Mike Bossy, NYI, 147 points
3. Peter Stastny, Que, 139 pts
4. Dennis Maruk, Wsh, 136 pts
5. Bryan Trottier, NYI, 129 points

60 Moments
that changed the game
No. 60: Advent of assistant coaches who devise defensive strategies to shut down the other team's offense.

Significant Records
Most goals, one season:
Wayne Gretzky, Edmonton (92).

First Draft Pick, 1982
Gord Kluzak, D, Boston

HHOF Inductees
Rod Gilbert
Norm Ullman
↓ Yvan Cournoyer

Nickname of the Year
Real 'Buddy' Cloutier

Worth Noting
Phil Esposito on Wayne Gretzky breaking his scoring records: "My father saw him play when he was 14 and told me, 'I've just watched the kid who's going to break all your records.' "...The Islanders set a league record winning 15 straight games – without the benefit of overtime.

→ THANK YOU. NO, THANK YOU

Not all unions make a bad impression on U.S. president Ronald Reagan. Hockey's biggest stars and NHL president John Ziegler and his staff exchange letters of thank-you after the league's first and only all-star break in Washington.

↓ BLOCKING BOOKENDS

The Flyers know they have a keeper when Swede Pelle Lindbergh makes his NHL debut. These pads protect him from pucks, but nothing can save him from a fatal car crash four years later.

THE WHITE HOUSE
WASHINGTON
April 2, 1982

Dear Mr. Ziegler:

I just want to thank you for your kind letter and to tell you what a pleasure it was for me to host that gathering prior to the 34th National Hockey League All-Star Game. I was delighted to join you, your fellow NHL officials, and so many fine athletes over lunch and to share my thoughts about this magnificent sport. Having time with such a distinguished group made February 8 a particularly memorable day for me, and I hope the same can be said for the captive audience that was forced to listen to reminiscences of my own hockey "career."

You also have my sincere gratitude for the thoughtful remembrances you presented to me. It was truly a great honor to receive the lettered All-Star jersey and the inscribed replica of the Stanley Cup. I have already expressed my thanks to you all, but I specifically wished you to know that these gifts will be most treasured for the friendship they represent.

With my best wishes to you and to all the officials and players in the NHL for many great seasons to come,

Sincerely,

Ronald Reagan

Mr. John A. Ziegler, Jr.
President
National Hockey League
14th Floor
1221 Sixth Avenue
New York, New York 10020

RECEIVED
APR 12 1982
NHL

Newsmakers & Top Headlines

1 Gretzky scores 92 goals and tops 200 points
Wayne Gretzky ravages the record book. He begins by scoring 50 goals in record time, hitting the magic mark in just 39 games — five fewer games than anyone else ever will. The 21-year-old finishes with 92 goals and shatters his own assists mark with 120. He becomes the first and only NHLer to top the 200-point plateau with 212, 48 more than his previous record. Gretzky helps Edmonton become the first team to score more than 400 goals in a season (417).

2 Soviets toy with Canada in Canada Cup blowout
For the second time in three seasons, the Soviet national team embarrasses some of the NHL's best, trouncing Canada 8-1 in the final of the Canada Cup tourney. Tournament organizer Alan Eagleson draws the champs' ire by refusing to allow them to take the trophy home. Canada defeats the Soviets 7-3 in round robin play and 3-2 in a pre-tourney test. "We didn't win the one that counts," says defenseman Brian Engblom.

3 Playoff realignment intensifies divisional rivalries
The NHL changes its format to emphasize divisional play in the post-season. Instead of seeding teams one to 16, each division plays down to a champion, followed by a conference final, with the conference champs meeting for the Stanley Cup. The change creates an imbalance. Only two teams in the Campbell Conference have winning records while all four playoff teams in the Adams Division are over .500.

1982-83 ‹

Cup Winner

New York Islanders

Leading Scorers
1. Wayne Gretzky, Edm, 196 pts
2. Peter Stastny, Que, 124 pts
3. Denis Savard, Chi, 121 pts
4. Mike Bossy, NYI, 118 points
5. Marcel Dionne, LA, 107 pts
6. Barry Pederson, Bos, 107 pts
7. Mark Messier, Edm, 106 pts
8. Michel Goulet, Que, 105 pts
9. G. Anderson, Edm, 104 pts
10. Kent Nilsson, Cgy, 104 pts

Franchise News
Colorado transfers to New Jersey to become the Devils.

First Draft Pick, 1983
Brian Lawton, C, Minnesota

HHOF Inductees
Bobby Hull
Stan Mikita
↓Ken Dryden

Nickname of the Year
Don 'Murder' Murdoch

Worth Noting
Wayne Gretzky not only sets a new high for assists (125), he matches Bill Cowley's 1940-41 record of earning more assists than anyone has points… Boston's Pete Peeters wins the Vezina on the strength of eight shutouts. No other goalie tops four…The three remaining players from the Original Six era retire – Carol Vadnais, Serge Savard and Wayne Cashman.

← THE BRIGHTEST STARS
Nothing like a bit of Campbell Conference orange to wake up the retinas. Vancouver coach Roger Neilson guides his all-stars to a 9-3 victory over Al Arbour's Wales Conference all-stars on Long Island.

Newsmakers & Top Headlines

1 Islander Cup dynasty hits four years
The Islanders make it look easy, sweeping the upstart Oilers in a four-game final and holding scoring champion Wayne Gretzky goal-less, to join the Canadiens as the only NHL teams to win four straight Stanley Cups. Immediately, talk begins of the Canadiens' record of five consecutive Cups (1956-60). "Our guys are never satisfied," says Islanders' GM Bill Torrey. "Who knows how long they'll keep it up?"

2 Brain hemorrhage ends Leveille's career
In a tragic end to a brief career, Boston forward Normand Leveille, 19, collapses Oct. 23 during the first intermission in Vancouver. He's rushed to hospital and found to have suffered a brain hemorrhage. The 1981 first round draft pick is left partially paralyzed and his career is over after just 75 games. Almost 13 years later at the Boston Garden closing ceremony, Leveille receives a standing ovation as he skates on to the ice with the help of Ray Bourque and Terry O'Reilly.

3 Draft day blues for St. Louis
The Blues seem destined to relocate to Saskatoon, Sask., in the Canadian prairies. When NHL governors vote 15-3 to reject the sale, team owner Ralston Purina begins the process of liquidating the franchise and the Blues don't participate in the NHL entry draft. The league assumes control of the team and sells it to Harry Ornest in July for the bargain-basement price of $3 million.

FACTS & STATS
from 1983-84

Cup Winner
Edmonton Oilers

Leading Scorers
1. W. Gretzky, Edm, 205 pts
2. Paul Coffey, Edm, 126 points
3. Michel Goulet, Que, 121 pts
4. Peter Stastny, Que, 119 pts
5. Mike Bossy, NYI, 118 points
6. B. Pederson, Bos, 116 pts
7. Jari Kurri, Edm, 113 points
8. Bryan Trottier, NYI, 111 pts
9. Bernie Federko, StL, 107 pts
10. Rick Middleton, Bos, 105 pts

Rule Changes
Five-minute overtime introduced for regular season tied games.

60 Moments
that changed the game
No. 43: OT in regular season.

Significant Records
Most assists, one period: Dale Hawerchuk, Winnipeg (5). Most points by a goalie, one season: Grant Fuhr, Edmonton (14). Longest point scoring streak: Wayne Gretzky, Edmonton (51 games, 153 points).

First Draft Pick, 1984
Mario Lemieux, C, Pittsburgh

HHOF Inductees
Jacques Lemaire
Bernie Parent
↓Phil Esposito

↑ NO KEYPAD ISSUES
Legendary hockey writer Elmer Ferguson bangs out some masterpieces on this travel-friendly Smith-Corona. He works in the industry for more than 60 years and is honored in 1984 when the Hockey Hall of Fame creates an award in his name.

Nickname of the Year
Brad 'Motor City Smitty' Smith

Newsmakers & Top Headlines

1 Edmonton strikes oil to win first Stanley Cup
The Oilers continue to rewrite the record book. Wayne Gretzky sets NHL records for goals per game (1.18), assists per game (1.59) and points per game (2.77) and runs up a record 51-game scoring streak. Teammates Jari Kurri and Glenn Anderson join him in the 50-goal club, while four others score 40 as Edmonton finishes with a record 446 goals. Art Ross runner-up Paul Coffey scores the most points (126) for a defenseman since Bobby Orr, but finishes a record 79 points behind Gretzky (205). The Mark Messier-led Oilers continue the assault in the playoffs, ending the Islanders' dynasty, to bring the Stanley Cup to Edmonton for the first time, winning the series in five games and outscoring New York 21-12.

2 NHL works overtime back into regular season
After a 41-year hiatus, overtime is reintroduced to NHL regular season games with a five-minute sudden-death period. Although 54 of 140 games are decided in the extra session, not everyone is a fan of the brief period. "Five minutes of overtime is like 15 seconds of sex," says Islanders' GM Bill Torrey. "If we're going to have overtime, then let's play to a finish."

3 Rookie Barrasso raises bar in Buffalo
Jumping from Acton-Boxboro high school in Massachusetts, Buffalo goalie Tom Barrasso, 18, surprises with a 26-12-3 record and 2.84 goals-against average, earning first all-star status and winning both the Calder and Vezina Trophies.

MESSIER HAS ONE MIND-BOGGLING VACATION

OCT. 14, 1983 BY DICK CHUBEY

EDMONTON, ALTA. –

The video machine in the coaches' office was serving another painful reminder of the Stanley Cup final...

"This team has more character than any other in professional sport," announced New York Islanders' coach Al Arbour following a not-so-instant replay of Game Four.

A perturbed Mark Messier, a member of the losing opposition back in May when the action was live, quickly peeled down to nothing but a frown. The Edmonton Oilers' left winger whipped a towel from around his waist and snapped it in the direction of the television screen.

"Little does he know!" snorted Messier, storming away.

Yes, the Oilers' other first-team all-star has not lost any of his youthful abrasiveness over the summer.

While Wayne Gretzky spent the off-season rubbing shoulders with the Hollywood set, Messier hung in with the peasants and Buddhists in the Far East for six weeks.

"I like playing hockey and I enjoy the fringe benefits, but eight months is long enough," said the 22-year-old, beginning a somewhat unique how-I-spent-my-summer-holidays report. "I have to get far away from it during the off-season. Maybe not mileage-wise, but certainly in my mind.

"I think it took a month for my shoulder (partial separation suffered in Chicago) to heal and two months for my mind to get back to normal. There are so many little mind games played throughout the season, you don't know what has to be in better shape – your body or your mind."

Was Thailand far enough removed from the maddening hockey crowd?

"Was it ever wild," Messier said of a tour in the company of fellow bachelors Darryl Morrow, Vince Magnan, along with his older brother Paul. "We rode bikes everywhere we went – to beaches where the sand is as white as the paper you're writing on.

"Every day was a hair-raising experience. The four of us, we kind of cruise together. We've pretty well got the whole world covered now, but Bangkok has got to be the wildest place I've been."

How wild?

"I think I'll leave that to the peoples' imagination," Messier said. "Put it this way: You could see the most beautiful temples in the world to the poorest slum areas to the most outrageous sexual fantasies imaginable. That pretty well covers the whole infield right there."

Ahem, indeed.

The Eastern front didn't solely present a devil-may-care sort of scene for Messier. He's been virtually conformed into a born-again Buddhist. "It's a wild religion," Messier said. "Not that I'm a totally faithful Monk, but I have read books on it and find it interesting."

Holed up on a junk somewhere in a Far Eastern harbor,

↑ HAIR-RAISING EXPERIENCE
Prairie boy Mark Messier discovers his spiritual side during a memorable summer vacation with peasants and Buddhists in the Far East.

Messier missed his second consecutive all-star nomination. He admits he was pleasantly surprised when he finally received the news. After all, Michel Goulet outdistanced him in goals (57-to-48) and Messier only managed one more point (106-to-105) than the Quebec Nordiques' left winger.

A training-camp holdout four years ago after coming off a 47-game World Hockey Association stint in which he scored but one goal, Messier has developed into the most sought-after left winger in the NHL. Agent Art Kaminsky lumps him in with Gretzky and Mike Bossy as the only players who could "run past compensation" where free agency is concerned.

"That's a pretty high compliment...I don't know if it's true or not," shrugged Messier, who is entering his option season. His agent, Norm Caplan, is involved in negotiations with coach-GM Glen Sather, but Messier refuses to discuss figures. "One thing I want to do is keep it out of the paper or try."

He isn't about to argue with a statement by Sather that if and when the Oilers win a Stanley Cup, then he's more apt to comply with demands for large salaries.

"It's not such an unfair statement, because I feel we are going to win the Cup," Messier said. "We've got no excuses."

As far as comparisons to Gretzky's salary, which is approaching $1 million annually, Messier draws an analogy: "I talked to a guy who is involved in a $20,000 hockey pool, with $12,000 going to the winner. Gretz has been ruled ineligible. His salary is the same thing. He sells hockey. Probably all of the GMs in the league would throw in 50 grand each to keep him around."

Besides, each has his own standards to live up to and the cost of rice in Thailand is considerably lower than the price of caviar among the Hollywood tinsel set.

Some guys dig Dom Perignon, others enjoy sake. THN

→ HUMBLE BEGINNINGS
Grant Fuhr is a key stopper during Edmonton's dynasty run in the 1980s. In the 1970s, Fuhr was flashing these leather mitts in Spruce Grove, Alta., youth hockey.

Newsmakers & Top Headlines

1 Lemieux brings magic to Pittsburgh
After scoring 282 points in his last junior season at Laval, Mario Lemieux, the most heralded draft prospect since Guy Lafleur, goes to the Penguins first overall in the entry draft. Lemieux declines to go to the podium when his name is called. "I didn't want to shake the hand of (Penguins' GM) Eddie Johnston if he does not want to give me a good contract," says Lemieux, who later signs a three-year, $600,000 deal. He scores on his first NHL shift and finishes with 100 points to win the Calder Trophy.

2 Coffey saves Team Canada's bacon
Canada is on the ropes when Soviet players Vladimir Kovin and Alexander Skvortsov get a 2-on-1 break in overtime of the Canada Cup semifinal. But Paul Coffey makes a game-saving block on Kovin's pass. Seconds later, fans at the Calgary Saddledome go wild when Coffey's shot deflects in off Mike Bossy to give Canada a 3-2 triumph. Canada goes on to beat Sweden in straight games in an anti-climactic best-of-three final, reclaiming world hockey supremacy after its Canada Cup loss in 1981.

3 Superstars Lafleur, Clarke retire
Frustrated over reduced playing time under coach and former linemate Jacques Lemaire, Guy Lafleur, 34, retires Nov. 26. Philadelphia Flyers' star Bobby Clarke, 35, becomes Flyers' GM after retiring in the summer of 1984. He guides Philly to the Cup final.

TALKING HELPS MACTAVISH COPE WITH PAIN

DEC. 7, 1984 BY JIM KERNAGHAN

It's only about 30 minutes from center ice at Boston Garden to the Lawrence Alternatives Correctional Centre. For Craig MacTavish, though, there are light years between the venerable Garden and the turn-of-the-century reform facility. The distance is immeasurable. They're worlds apart.

This is not really his world. His world is Lowell University some 15 minutes west, where he established school records while on a hockey scholarship. His world is to the south, in the midst of mercantile and maritime Boston, at the Garden, where he cracked the Bruins' lineup two seasons ago.

It is difficult for MacTavish, the Bruin left winger, to verbalize the sweep of emotions and the depth of remorse that has enveloped him since last Jan. 26. That was the fateful evening after a few beers with the boys that left many lives altered forevermore.

It was on that evening MacTavish, travelling home for dinner, struck the rear bumper of a car driven by Kim Radley of West Newfield, Mass. Her car went out of control and she was critically injured. Shortly afterward, she died. MacTavish was charged with vehicular homicide and decided to plead guilty and pay whatever the courts exacted from him. He was sentenced to a year in jail without the prospect of parole.

He is halfway through that sentence. He will be freed May 13. He is in superb condition, but will begin skating immediately to prepare for his return to hockey. Somewhere. He will not forget.

"It's something you just can't explain," he said of bearing responsibility for someone else's death. "You have to live with it yourself to realize how it feels. You just can't imagine it. You try to rationalize it, but you can't. It's something that will always be there and you just have to accept it."

MacTavish wants no sympathy from anyone. He accepts his responsibility, wants to pay his debt and get on with his life. He wants no publicity, but realizes his experiences could be of benefit to somebody else.

MacTavish arises each day at 4:50 a.m. and prepares breakfast for the 60 or so inmates. He is finished at 8 a.m. and spends the remainder of the day in the gym, jogging or studying toward his business degree at Lowell.

He undergoes a grilling himself, too, at local schools where he speaks to classes about the costs of alcohol abuse. He doesn't like it much and while he is not a spellbinding speaker ("Captive, not captivating"), he gets through to the kids.

"I'm not naive enough to think I can help every kid," he said. "I remember what I was like at that age. But it could help some. In ways, it has helped me, too. I'm not afraid of anything people might ask."

But that therapeutic approach has its limits. Once he is free, MacTavish realizes reporters will want to know about his experiences. He will stick to anything concerning hockey and that's it. He said the support of his parents and family, of his friends and of the Bruins has been of inestimable help.

"Boston has a reputation of standing behind its players in

↑ RIDING A HIGH BEFORE A LOW
Craig MacTavish is the last NHL player to skate without a helmet, but did wear a bucket for a brief stretch earlier in his checkered career.

all kids of adversity and the players too, have a reputation for being a close-knit group," MacTavish said. "The guys have really been terrific."

Most of the Bruins have visited him. MacTavish recalls Gord Kluzak suffered a knee injury that will sideline him for the balance of the season. MacTavish's teammates are candid about the episode.

"He accepted responsibility for his actions and I have a great deal of respect for (that)," said captain Terry O'Reilly. "Some people might have tried to wriggle out of it, but he pleaded guilty. You hate to see an example set, but a young lady was killed. If it can save others down the road…"

The first part of his sentence was spent at Salem, a state pen, where the slamming of a metal door behind him the first time was a devastating counterpoint to the judge's gavel when he was sentenced. He had no trouble with the hardened convicts, finding that many wanted to talk hockey. After a couple of months, he was removed to the less stringent Lawrence center.

"I'm in the best shape of my life," he said. "I'm running, cycling, working out. It isn't hockey shape, but as soon as I get out, I'll be on skates."

He is a free agent without compensation. He wants to return to the Bruins, although there is some speculation within management that the fans might react unfavorably.

His lawyer, Bob Murray, has had discussions with other teams. Whatever happens, MacTavish wants to play hockey.

His life isn't grim. When a teammate brought in a VCR, a fellow inmate broke him up by saying, "That's what I'm here for, stealing 14 of those."

Despite the relative freedom, urinalysis checks are taken at random for possible substance abuse. Break any of the rules and you will land back in a state slammer.

So it goes with Craig MacTavish, who longs for the day he will be out and skating, when his only penance will be his own personal one. **THN**

>1985-86 FAMOUS OWN-GOAL

FACTS & STATS
from 1985-86

Cup Winner
Montreal Canadiens

Leading Scorers
1. Wayne Gretzky, Edm, 215 pts
2. Mario Lemieux, Pit, 141 pts
3. Paul Coffey, Edm, 138 points
4. Jari Kurri, Edm, 131 points
5. Mike Bossy, NYI, 123 points
6. Peter Stastny, Que, 122 pts
7. Denis Savard, Chi, 116 points
8. Mats Naslund, Mtl, 110 pts
9. D. Hawerchuk, Wpg, 105 pts
10. Neal Broten, Min, 105 points

60 Moments
that changed the game
No. 41: New rule aimed at Edmonton's high-flying Oilers states play remains 5-on-5 after coincidental minor penalties.

Significant Records
Most points, one season: Wayne Gretzky, Edmonton (215).
Most power play goals, one season: Tim Kerr, Philadelphia (34).
Goals by defenseman, one season: Paul Coffey, Edmonton (48).
Longest point scoring streak by a defenseman: Paul Coffey, Edmonton (28 games, 55 points).

First Draft Pick, 1986
Joe Murphy, C, Detroit

HHOF Inductees
Leo Boivin
Dave Keon
↓ Serge Savard

→ **BEHIND THE MASK**
Richard Brodeur faces a lot of rubber throughout his seven-plus seasons in Vancouver, including 1985-86, when he plays a career-high 64 games for the Canucks.

Newsmakers & Top Headlines

1 Smith gaffe ends Oilers' Cup streak
In a bid to slow down the high-flying Oilers, the NHL changes its rule to allow for substitutions during off-setting penalties — effectively limiting 4-on-4 manpower situations. Still, the Oilers roar to their fifth straight Smythe Division title. But they lose in the division final, blowing a 2-0 third-period lead in Game 7 against the Flames. Defenseman Steve Smith's clearing attempt bounces into the Edmonton net off goalie Grant Fuhr and Calgary wins 3-2, ending Edmonton's two-year Cup reign.

2 Coffey breaks Orr's goal record
It's a mark that looks unbeatable, but Edmonton's Paul Coffey surpasses Bobby Orr's 1974-75 defenseman record of 46 goals when he scores his 46th and 47th April 2 against the Canucks. Coffey finishes with 48 and his 138 points are one shy of Orr's record for points (1970-71). Coffey, who wins his second straight Norris Trophy, also has an eight-point outing in a March 14 win over the Red Wings, tying Tom Bladon's 1977-78 record.

3 Lindbergh killed in car accident
After celebrating the club's 10th straight victory with a night on the town, 26-year-old Flyers' goalie Pelle Lindbergh dies after crashing his Porsche into a concrete wall. It's determined he was driving 60 miles per hour in a 35 mph zone. His blood-alcohol level is measured at .24, twice the legal limit.

Nickname of the Year
Barry 'Bubba' Beck

OILERS LINKED TO COCAINE

MAY 23, 1986 BY STAN FISCHLER

NEW YORK, NY —

The NHL, which has enjoyed unique, virtually drug-free status among the major professional sports, has been socked in the gut with allegations to the contrary.

Edmonton's dethroned champion Oilers are spotlighted in a *Sports Illustrated* expose, dated May 12, that raises questions about the off-ice behavior of Glen Sather's club.

Among the charges leveled by anonymous sources are:

• At least five Edmonton players have had "substantial" cocaine problems.

• No fewer than three sources said they had seen Oilers use cocaine or marijuana at parties in Edmonton and other NHL cities.

• An NHL player (not an Oiler) told of having used cocaine with three members of the Oilers during the past season.

• An agent for one of the Edmonton players said the player told him, "Every time we go into New York City, it's a real blizzard (as in cocaine) and I'm not talking about the weather."

• The chief of the RCMP's Edmonton drug squad is quoted as saying, "… we have information that there are users on the club."

Perhaps even more noteworthy is the assertion by *SI's* managing editor Mark Mulvoy that the story authored by Donald Ramsay and Armen Keteyian only touched the tip of the drug-use iceberg.

"We were able to print only half (of the material) of what we had," Mulvoy says. "Because of the legal ramifications there were stories that required triple and quadruple verification and we simply couldn't get that. So, we were allowed to print only so much. If there were not lawyers involved, it would have been a completely different story."

Although the *SI* story had been rumored in the works for several weeks, many hockey people were stunned by its appearance.

Reaction from NHL headquarters was mixed. When originally informed the article was about to hit the stands, league president John Ziegler expressed surprise and said he had expected it to be out a week later.

"I won't have time to read it tomorrow," Ziegler commented off-handedly. "Someone will have to read it to me."

When phoned a day later, Ziegler offered no comment but said in a prepared statement: "We do not have and have not had any evidence of drug use by any player. If professional investigators on the scene in Edmonton haven't sufficient evidence to bring a charge, then why should the NHL?"

An NHL spokesman chided *SI* for emphasizing specifics about some Oilers' financial problems — in particular Grant Fuhr's — without naming names in terms of drug abuse.

"The story in *SI* read more like *The Financial Times* than High Times," says NHL public relations director John Halligan.

NHL Players' Association executive director Alan Eagleson says he was "disturbed" by *SI's* liberal use of unnamed sources, unnamed players and an unnamed agent.

↑ **WALKING THE LINE**
Oilers coach-GM Glen Sather says a *Sports Illustrated* story that accuses some of his players of having cocaine problems is "absolute innuendo."

"All it does," Eagleson said, "is raise a blanket of suspicion. There's not enough evidence. Not that I blame *Sports Illustrated.* They've gone after every major sport and now it's hockey. But if what they printed is all they've got on hockey, then I'm the happiest guy in the world."

Eagleson adds that he's aware NHL players are in a position to be exposed to drugs. "I'm not naïve enough to think that there isn't a player out there who has smoked marijuana or tried cocaine but I'm sure it's not rampant. I spoke to Kevin Lowe (the Oilers' player representative) and he told me that nobody on the team ever missed a practice or a game because of any of those problems. He said if there's a problem on the club, he sure hasn't seen it and he's right there."

Although some players have criticized the NHL and NHLPA for failure to take a more aggressive approach to drug abuse, Eagleson insists "there's been no indication of a problem at the players' level."

Bryan Trottier, president of the NHLPA, had this to say:

"The fact is not enough has been done in terms of alcohol and drug abuse to find out who the users are and the NHL has no avenue for rehabilitation. The policy has been we don't take action until the actual charges have been made for possession. And then they sit back and wait until a guy is proven guilty."

Oilers president-GM-coach Sather, though widely quoted in the article, seemed shocked by the article's appearance.

"I'm surprised *Sports Illustrated* would print something like this," said Sather, who planned no retaliatory legal action. "Maybe they're trying to become the new *National Enquirer.* It is absolute innuendo. Any time I confronted a player about anything, they denied it."

What the magazine states is that "the Oilers have been the subject of rampant drug-use rumors," a fact that has been well-known in the hockey-writing community. **THN**

↑ HABS HALVE IT
Brian Hayward, with his bleu, blanc et rouge pads, splits time with Patrick Roy all season, but takes over in the playoffs before losing in the conference final.

Newsmakers & Top Headlines

1 Junior players die in bus crash
Travelling to Regina for a Dec. 30 Western League game, the bus carrying the Swift Current Broncos careens out of control on a curve, flips over and slams to the ground on its right side. Four players — Scott Kruger, 19, Trent Kresse, 20, Chris Mantyka, 19 and Jason Ruff, 16 — are killed. Among the survivors are future NHLers Joe Sakic and Sheldon Kennedy. The Broncos regroup from the tragedy, finish the season and, in 1989, win the Memorial Cup.

2 Rendez-vous '87 masterpiece on ice
For the second time, the All-Star Game takes on an NHL vs. Soviet Union format as the league's stars and Soviets' best clash in an exciting two-game series in Quebec City. The NHL and the USSR split, 4-3 for the NHL and 5-3 for the Soviets. Twenty-year-old Soviet star Valeri Kamensky sparkles in the second game, scoring two brilliant second-period goals to give his team a 3-1 lead.

3 Junior tournament punch-up ends in darkness
Leading the Soviets 4-2 on the last day of the World Junior Championship in Piestany, Czechoslovakia, Canada will take the gold medal if it wins by five goals. But a vicious, bench-clearing brawl erupts in the second period. Referee Hans Ronning of Norway leaves the ice with his linesmen and the lights are turned out. In the aftermath, both teams are disqualified and Finland is awarded its first gold medal at the event.

FACTS & STATS
from 1986-87

Cup Winner
Edmonton Oilers

Leading Scorers
1. Wayne Gretzky, Edm, 183 pts
2. Jari Kurri, Edm, 108 points
3. Mario Lemieux, Pit, 107 pts
4. Mark Messier, Edm, 107 pts
5. Doug Gilmour, StL, 105 pts
6. Dino Ciccarelli, Min, 103 pts
7. D. Hawerchuk, Wpg, 100 pts
8. Michel Goulet, Que, 96 pts
9. Tim Kerr, Phi, 95 points
10. Ray Bourque, Bos, 95 points

Rule Changes
Delayed offside is no longer in effect once the players of the offending team have cleared the opponents' defensive zone.

First Draft Pick, 1987
Pierre Turgeon, C, Buffalo

HHOF Inductees
Ed Giacomin
Jacques Laperriere
↓ Bobby Clarke

Nickname of the Year
Rick 'Nifty' Middleton

Worth Noting
After playing 11-plus seasons without missing a game. Hartford's Doug Jarvis breaks Garry Unger's ironman record of 914 straight games Dec. 26. Jarvis extends the streak to 964 games... Toronto's Borje Salming is cut in the face by a skate blade. He requires surgery and more than 200 stitches to close the wound.

→ **PICTURE OF CONFIDENCE**
The logo on this 1987 Mario
Lemieux Canada Cup jersey is
modelled after the Canada Cup
itself. A little presumptuous,
perhaps, but Lemieux and his
countrymen back it up with a
victory for the ages.

FACTS & STATS
from 1987-88

Cup Winner
Edmonton Oilers

Leading Scorers
1. Mario Lemieux, Pit, 168 pts
2. Wayne Gretzky, Edm, 149 pts
3. Denis Savard, Chi, 131 pts
4. D. Hawerchuk, Wpg, 121 pts
5. Luc Robitaille, LA, 111 points
6. Peter Stastny, Que, 111 pts
7. Mark Messier, Edm, 111 pts
8. Jimmy Carson, LA, 107 pts
9. Hakan Loob, Cgy, 106 points
10. Michel Goulet, Que, 106 pts

60 Moments
that changed the game
No. 58: Goalie Rox Hextall shoots and scores, ushering in an era of goalies taking charge with loose pucks.

First Draft Pick, 1988
Mike Modano, C, Minnesota

HHOF Inductees
Tony Esposito
Buddy O'Connor
Brad Park
↓ Guy Lafleur

Nickname of the Year
Larry 'Big Bird' Robinson

Worth Noting
St. Louis and Boston combine to score two goals in two seconds in a regular season game. Ken Linseman brings the Bruins to within a goal with 10 seconds remaining before Doug Gilmour of the Blues scores off a faceoff into an empty net.

Mrs. Robert Jones
requests the pleasure of your company
at the marriage of her daughter
Janet Marie
to
Wayne Douglas
son of Mr. & Mrs. Walter Gretzky
on Saturday, July the sixteenth
nineteen hundred and eighty-eight
at four o'clock
St. Joseph's Basilica
10044 - 113 Street
Edmonton, Alberta

Reception: 5:30 p.m.
Westin Hotel
10135 - 100 Street
Edmonton

← FIRST GLORY, THEN FAME
After winning his fourth Cup, Wayne Gretzky weds model/actress Janet Jones. This invitation goes to Craig Simpson. A few weeks later, hockey's power couple is Hollywood-bound.

Newsmakers & Top Headlines

1 Lemieux and Gretzky Canada's dynamic duo
Three exciting 6-5 games decide the Canada Cup final between Canada and the Soviets, with the teams splitting two overtime verdicts. The score is tied 5-5 late in Game 3 when Canada's Wayne Gretzky, Mario Lemieux and Larry Murphy get a 3-on-1 break. Gretzky feeds Lemieux a perfect pass and Super Mario blasts the puck past Sergei Mylnikov at 18:34, sending fans at Hamilton's Copps Coliseum into hysteria. It's a coming-of-age party for Lemieux, who scores the deciding goal in both Canadian wins.

2 Donutgate leaves NHL in hole
Angry following a 6-1 loss to the Boston Bruins in Game 3 of the Wales Conference final, New Jersey Devils' coach Jim Schoenfeld confronts referee Don Koharski, calling him a "fat pig" and suggesting he "have another doughnut." Schoenfeld is suspended by the NHL, but gets a court injunction and is back for Game 4. NHL officials refuse to work the game and amateurs are used in their place as the league endures one of its most embarrassing moments ever. NHL president John Ziegler can't be found to help resolve the issue.

3 Penguins brew up Coffey deal
Edmonton GM Glen Sather makes the first move in the undoing of the Oilers' dynasty. Demanding to re-negotiate his contract, two-time Norris Trophy-winning defenseman Paul Coffey holds out and is shipped Nov. 24 to Pittsburgh in a seven-player deal.

SPENCER 'STILL NAIVE' IN DEATH AT 38

JUNE/JULY, 1988 BY JEFF HALE

Brian Spencer, a man accustomed to violence on the ice and accused of it off the ice, ultimately became a victim of violence.

Spencer, 38, was pronounced dead June 3 from a gunshot wound that pierced his heart shortly after friend Greg Cook completed a drug deal in Riviera Beach, Fla., late on the night of June 2.

"He was outgoing, gregarious and never believed anybody wouldn't tell the truth and nobody could be a bad person," said girlfriend Monica Jarboe.

Yet Spencer was caught up in a lifelong maelstrom of violence and tragedy. In his 10-year NHL career, he accumulated 634 penalty minutes and 223 points. His father, Roy, was shot and killed after a stand-off with the Royal Canadian Mounted Police. Spencer himself was acquitted last October of first-degree murder charges following a 10-month trial.

During his NHL career, Spencer played for Toronto, the Islanders, Buffalo and Pittsburgh. He broke in with the Leafs in 1969-70. His last NHL season was with Pittsburgh in 1978-79. In 553 games, he earned 80 goals and 143 assists. His best season was 1974-75 with Buffalo when he earned 41 points in 73 games. His highest penalty minute total was 115, in 1970-71.

It was during that season, on Dec. 12, 1970, Spencer's father was shot and killed by the RCMP at the age of 57. Brian had told his parents he would be a second-period intermission guest during Hockey Night in Canada's telecast of the Leaf game against Chicago.

But when his father discovered the CBC affiliate near the family's Fort St. James, B.C., home was carrying the Vancouver-California game instead, he became enraged. He drove two hours to Prince George television station CKPG, produced a pistol, held the employees hostage and forced them to cut transmission power. A shootout with the RCMP followed.

Jarboe said Spencer talked "off and on" about his father's death. "He wouldn't dwell on it," she said. "I know it still hurt him, especially after he got into hockey... it was his father's dream. He could have used his advice."

The father's son would share a fate equally violent.

"He was still naive about a lot of things," said Jarboe. "Whether it was good or not-so-good, Brian would go along with the group because he wouldn't know any better."

When Greg Cook came to the Palm Beach Gardens apartment Spencer shared with Jarboe on June 2 to ask Spencer to help him repair a friend's car, Spencer went along. Jarboe said Spencer would not have been involved in the drug buy.

"Like, Brian doing drugs... that was ridiculous. They weren't a big factor in Brian's life. They weren't any factor in Brian's life. He hadn't even been drinking. He hadn't had one drink since last November. We'd been doing real good. Now, I hear he did have a couple beers at a bar (the night of the shooting). Greg should have known never to take Brian to a bar.

"It (drug buy) was just a spontaneous thing on Greg's part," added Jarboe, who talked with Cook a few days after

↑ **HOCKEY TRAGEDY**
After former NHL journeyman Brian Spencer's NHL career ended, his life ended too -- in a tragic shooting that may have been revenge.

the shooting. "I never saw Greg do any drugs. Brian told me everything and he didn't tell me he was doing drugs.

"Greg was his friend. Greg wouldn't have set him up. Something might have been done unwittingly. Somebody might have hired two crazy guys a long time ago. It's not like somebody was waiting for him to show up."

Former Leaf defenseman Jim McKenny, a friend of Spencer's, said, "He walked down a lot of avenues people have never been. He experienced a lot of things people never have."

In February, a disillusioned Spencer visited McKenny, a Toronto sportscaster. "He thought he was the only bad person in the NHL," said McKenny. "He felt he was the only person who failed. But I told him there were 200 other guys who messed up worse than he thought he had.

"I told him he shouldn't feel guilty. It's really tough to re-establish yourself after hockey. He was all alone. When he came here he was amazed at the interest of people. He was surprised people still cared about him."

McKenny said movie companies inquired about making a film on Spencer's life. Since the conclusion of his murder trial, Spencer's notoriety was on the upswing. Toronto author Martin O'Malley, published *Gross Misconduct: The Life of Spinner Spencer* in 2012.

"Everything was fine," said Jarboe. "We were getting ready to move to a better apartment. He was so happy about that. He had everything to live for."

Former Toronto sportscaster Peter Gross joined McKenny and Spencer on a ski trip during the latter's Toronto visit.

"He was quite thrilled to be out of jail," said Gross. "He was quite gregarious about it. We'd get on the (ski) lift and he was quite aware going up on a ski lift on a sunny day was better than being in jail. He was very energetic, childish, very happy.

"I said to him, 'Regardless of your guilt or innocence... I'd be concerned about revenge.' He said, 'I guess so.' " THN

FACTS & STATS
from 1988-89

→ 'KILLER' DUDS

These pants fit Doug Gilmour just fine. He wins his only Stanley Cup in his first season with Calgary after being traded from St. Louis.

Cup Winner

Calgary Flames

Leading Scorers
1. Mario Lemieux, Pit, 199 points
2. Wayne Gretzky, LA, 168 pts
3. Steve Yzerman, Det, 155 pts
4. Bernie Nicholls, LA, 150 pts
5. Rob Brown, Pit, 115 points

60 Moments
that changed the game
No. 5: Wayne Gretzky is traded to Los Angeles and growth of the game in the U.S. takes off.
No. 39: Detroit Red Wings select three Europeans in the 1989 draft, opening up a new region for intense scouting.

Significant Records
Most shorthanded goals, one season: Mario Lemieux, Pittsburgh (13).

First Draft Pick, 1989
Mats Sundin, C, Quebec

HHOF Inductees
Herbie Lewis
Darryl Sittler
↓ Vladislav Tretiak

Nickname of the Year
Borje 'King' Salming

Worth Noting
Minnesota North Stars right winger Dino Ciccarelli serves a day in jail and is fined $1,000 for hitting Toronto's Luke Richardson with his stick Jan. 19.

Newsmakers & Top Headlines

1 Gretzky says goodbye to Edmonton
It was rumored for days, but even after it happens people can't believe it — the Oilers trade Wayne Gretzky. On Aug. 9, 1988, the seven-time scoring champ and eight-time Hart Trophy winner goes to the Kings with Mike Krushelnyski and Marty McSorley for Jimmy Carson and Martin Gelinas, three first round picks and $15 million. The media says Oilers' owner Peter Pocklington needs the cash, but 'Peter Puck' claims it was Gretzky's idea.

2 Lemieux within one of 200 points
At 23, Lemieux scores 85 goals and wins his second straight scoring title. His assists (114) and points (199) are the most in NHL history for any player other than Wayne Gretzky. His most impressive effort comes New Year's Eve against the Devils. He scores for the cycle — five goals in five different situations — at even strength, on the power play, shorthanded, on a penalty shot and into an empty net.

3 Soviets irate after Mogilny defection
Unheralded Soviet Sergei Priakhin, 25, debuts with the Flames March 31 with his federation's blessing, but when the talented Alexander Mogilny, 20, defects May 4 and signs with the Sabres, Soviet officials cry foul. After the World Championship in Sweden, Mogilny surreptitiously leaves his hotel and flies to the U.S. with Buffalo GM Gerry Meehan and player development director Don Luce. The Soviets call him a traitor.

FACTS & STATS
from 1989-90

Cup Winner

Edmonton Oilers

Leading Scorers
1. Wayne Gretzky, LA, 142 pts
2. Mark Messier, Edm, 129 pts
3. Steve Yzerman, Det, 127 pts

60 Moments
that changed the game
No. 18: NHLPA hires Bob Goodenow to replace Alan Eagleson, ushering in an era of escalating player costs and work stoppages.
No. 21: Soviet Ice Hockey Federation releases five of its veteran star players to join NHL teams, opening another vein of talent.
No. 30: Outgoing NHLPA boss Alan Eagleson announces the union will release salary disclosure for the first time, causing a spike in wages.

First Draft Pick, 1990
Owen Nolan, RW, Quebec

HHOF Inductees
Bill Barber
Fernie Flaman
↓ Gilbert Perreault

Nickname of the Year
Ken 'The Rat' Linseman

Worth Noting
Experienced international star Sergei Makarov wins the Calder Trophy at 31. The NHL rules going forward that players who start a rookie season 26 or older are ineligible for the award.

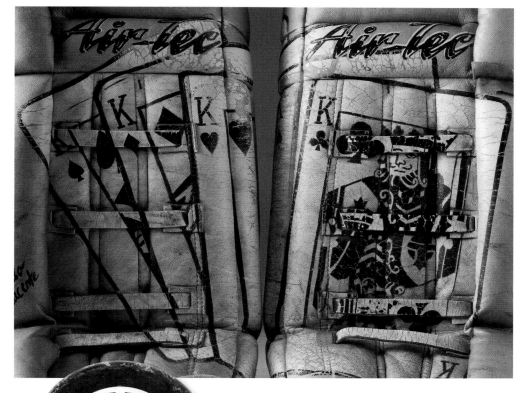

↑ STAUBER'S STOPPERS
Los Angeles is fashion central as Robb Stauber becomes the first NHL goalie to incorporate a design on his pads.

← RECORD-BREAKING REVENGE
Almost 30 years after Gordie Howe became the NHL's leading scorer, Wayne Gretzky passes him with point No. 1,851 — a goal against his old team, the Oilers.

Newsmakers & Top Headlines

1 Soviet invasion begins in NHL
Following years of negotiations, the Soviet Ice Hockey Federation agrees to release veterans to the NHL. Center Igor Larionov, 28, and left winger Vladimir Krutov, 29, sign with the Canucks. Defensemen Viacheslav Fetisov, 31, and Sergei Starikov, 30, join the Devils and right winger Sergei Makarov, 31, goes to the Flames.

2 'The Great One' passes 'Mr. Hockey'
Kings' megastar Wayne Gretzky treats his Oiler fans when he overtakes Gordie Howe as the NHL career scoring leader in a 5-4 victory in Edmonton Oct. 15. He records a first-period assist to tie Howe's 1,850 points and, with 53 seconds left to play, sets the record by beating Edmonton goalie Bill Ranford to send the game into overtime. The crowd gives the former Oiler a five-minute standing ovation. Gretzky adds the overtime winner.

3 Eagleson on the way out as NHLPA leader
Three major events combine to change the course of events in NHL Players' Association history. First, executive director Alan Eagleson loses the players' support and agrees to step down, effective Dec. 31, 1991. Second, at the 1990 All-Star Game in Pittsburgh, the players name hard-nosed Detroit lawyer Bob Goodenow to succeed Eagleson. And third, the players agree to salary disclosure, a primary catalyst for salary escalation. Players release a salary survey for the first time in February.

FACTS & STATS
from 1990-91

Cup Winner
Pittsburgh Penguins

Leading Scorers
1. Wayne Gretzky, LA, 163 pts
2. Brett Hull, StL, 131 points
3. Adam Oates, StL, 115 points
4. Mark Recchi, Pit, 113 points
5. John Cullen, Pit/Hfd, 110 pts
6. Joe Sakic, Que, 109 points
7. Steve Yzerman, Det, 108 pts
8. Theo Fleury, Cgy, 104 points
9. Al MacInnis, Cgy, 103 points
10. Steve Larmer, Chi, 101 pts

Significant Records
Most shorthanded goals, one game: Theo Fleury, Calgary (3). Most goals by a right winger, one season, Brett Hull: St. Louis (86). Longest consecutive assist streak: Wayne Gretzky, Los Angeles (23 games, 48 assists). Most penalties, one game: Chris Nilan, Boston (10).

First Draft Pick, 1991
Eric Lindros, C, Quebec

HHOF Inductees
Denis Potvin
Bob Pulford
Clint Smith
↓ Mike Bossy

Nickname of the Year
Bernie 'The Pumpernickel Kid' Nicholls

Worth Noting
Brett Hull joins Bobby Hull to form the only father-son tandem to win the Hart Trophy.

↓ **FLAMING OUT**
The 1990-91 season with the Boston Bruins is Reggie Lemelin's last as a bona fide NHL netminder. He plays just 18 games over the next two seasons, then retires. Lemelin's busiest years come prior to Beantown, using these pads as the No. 1 goalie for the Calgary Flames before being usurped by Mike Vernon.

Newsmakers & Top Headlines

1 Lemieux backs Pens to first Stanley Cup
Pittsburgh captain Mario Lemieux misses the first 50 games with a back injury, but the club keeps battling under new coach Bob Johnson to win the Patrick Division, a franchise first. Aided by new arrivals Ron Francis and Ulf Samuelsson, Pittsburgh wins its first Cup, ousting Minnesota in six games in the final. Lemieux wins the Conn Smythe Trophy with 44 points in 23 games.

2 North Stars find way to San Jose
The first franchise split in NHL history is arranged: it's revealed the North Stars will be divided into two teams after 1990-91, with the Gund brothers selling the team in exchange for a new franchise in San Jose. The roster will be split to stock the teams and an expansion draft held for both clubs. Bobby Clarke, fired as Philadelphia GM, takes over in Minnesota and hires Bob Gainey as coach. Meanwhile, the league grants new franchises to Ottawa and Tampa Bay for 1992-93.

3 Stevens signing causes outrage
Sparks fly when St. Louis signs restricted free agent defenseman Scott Stevens to a four-year, $5.1-million contract, surrendering five first round draft picks as compensation. "It scares the hell out of me," says Vancouver GM Pat Quinn of how the deal might affect the NHL salary structure. Stevens' stay in St. Louis doesn't last long. One season later, he's awarded as compensation to New Jersey after St. Louis signs another free agent — Brendan Shanahan.

FACTS & STATS
from 1991-92

Cup Winner
Pittsburgh Penguins

Leading Scorers
1. Mario Lemieux, Pit, 131 pts
2. Kevin Stevens, Pit, 123 pts
3. Wayne Gretzky, LA, 121 pts
4. Brett Hull, StL, 109 points
5. Luc Robitaille, LA, 107 pts
6. Mark Messier, NYR, 107 pts
7. Jeremy Roenick, Chi, 103 pts
8. Steve Yzerman, Det, 103 pts
9. Brian Leetch, NYR, 102 pts
10. A. Oates, StL/Bos, 99 pts

Rule Changes
Video replays are employed to assist referees in judging goal/no goal situations.

Franchise News
San Jose Sharks added, expanding NHL to 22 teams.

60 Moments
that changed the game
No. 36: NHL board of governors approves use of video replay to assist on-ice officials in goal/no goal situations.

First Draft Pick, 1992
Roman Hamrlik, D, Tampa Bay

HHOF Inductees
Marcel Dionne
Woody Dumart
Bob Gainey
↓Lanny McDonald

Nickname of the Year
Stan 'Steamer' Smyl

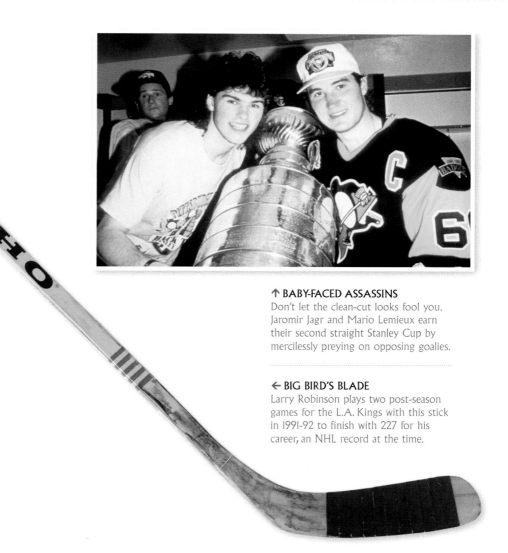

↑ BABY-FACED ASSASSINS
Don't let the clean-cut looks fool you. Jaromir Jagr and Mario Lemieux earn their second straight Stanley Cup by mercilessly preying on opposing goalies.

← BIG BIRD'S BLADE
Larry Robinson plays two post-season games for the L.A. Kings with this stick in 1991-92 to finish with 227 for his career, an NHL record at the time.

Newsmakers & Top Headlines

1 Stanley Cup threatened by 10-day walkout
It's no April Fool's joke when players walk off the job for the first time April 1. With the playoffs in jeopardy, the league and Players' Association reach an agreement April 10, saving the NHL's 75th season. The NHL makes concessions in card-licensing monies and free agency, grants a 15 percent raise in the minimum salary and guarantees no salary cap will be installed.

2 Penguins rally after 'Badger' Bob's death
On the eve of the 1991 Canada Cup, U.S. coach 'Badger' Bob Johnson of Stanley Cup-champion Pittsburgh is diagnosed with a brain tumor, an illness which claims his life Nov. 26. The American team tries desperately to win the tourney for him, but loses to Canada in the final. "His will was contagious and I think his spirit will be contagious for a long time," says Penguins' center Bryan Trottier. Player development director Scotty Bowman, the NHL's winningest coach, takes over and, after a rough start, leads Pittsburgh to a second straight Cup.

3 Record deal brings Gilmour to Toronto
Doug Gilmour is the big prize in a 10-player trade, the largest in NHL history. Calgary sends Gilmour, Jamie Macoun, Rick Wamsley, Ric Nattress and Kent Manderville to Toronto Jan 2. for Gary Leeman, Alexander Godynyuk, Jeff Reese, Michel Petit and Craig Berube. Gilmour brings respectability back to the Leafs, leading Toronto to the semifinal the next two seasons.

LEMIEUX VS. CANCER

Cup Winner
Montreal Canadiens

Leading Scorers
1. Mario Lemieux, Pit, 160 points
2. Pat LaFontaine, Buf, 148 pts
3. Adam Oates, Bos, 142 points

Rule Changes
The NHL adopts an instigator rule to reduce fighting.

Franchise News
Tampa Bay and Ottawa added as expansion teams.

60 Moments
that changed the game
No. 52: In an effort to curtail frequent fighting, the NHL adopts an instigator rule.

Significant Records
Most assists by a left winger, one season: Joe Juneau, Boston (70). Most points by a left winger, one season: Luc Robitaille, L.A. (125). Most goals by a rookie, one season: Teemu Selanne, Wpg (76).

First Draft Pick, 1993
Alexandre Daigle, C, Ottawa

HHOF Inductees
Billy Smith
Steve Shutt
Edgar Laprade
↓Guy Lapointe

↑ **LEGACE BEGINS LEGACY**
Nineteen-year-old Manny Legace lets his gear get beat up as he backstops Canada's world junior team to its first of five straight gold medals.

← **MAKING HER MARK**
Manon Rheaume's jersey from one of two World Championship golds she wins in the early 1990s. In '92, she makes a pre-season start for Tampa Bay, becoming the first woman to play in the NHL.

Newsmakers & Top Headlines

1 Lemieux makes incredible recovery from cancer
A superhuman player faces a very human ordeal as Pittsburgh superstar Mario Lemieux is, on Jan. 11, diagnosed with Hodgkin's disease — cancer of the lymph nodes. "It's scary when you hear that word 'cancer'," Lemieux says. He makes an amazing recovery following surgery and radiation treatments, returning March 2 against the Flyers. He scores a goal and an assist after having a radiation treatment in the morning. He leads the Penguins to the longest winning streak in NHL history — 17 games from March 9 to April 10. Lemieux scores 56 points in his final 20 games to overtake Buffalo's Pat LaFontaine for the Art Ross Trophy, despite playing 24 fewer games. Lemieux is also awarded the Hart and Masterton at season's end.

2 Bettman named NHL commissioner
On Dec. 11, Gary Bettman, vice-president of the NBA, is named the NHL's first commissioner. He starts his job Feb. 1, taking over from Gil Stein, who has served as interim president since John Ziegler resigned in June. "I believe the opportunities that face this league are virtually limitless," Bettman says.

3 NHL homes get warmer and warmer
Two new teams, the Ottawa Senators and Tampa Bay Lightning, begin play, while two other cities — Miami (Florida Panthers) and Anaheim (the Mighty Ducks) are awarded franchises Dec. 10 to begin play in 1993-94. At the end of the season, the Minnesota North Stars announce they are relocating to Dallas.

Nickname of the Year
'Missing' Link Gaetz

→ **INTENSITY**
Mario Lemieux carried the Penguins on his bad back to two Stanley Cup championships.

↓ **COFFEE TIME**
Paul Coffey advises Jaromir Jagr on the finer points of the game.

→ GOALTENDING EXELLENCE
Patrick Roy (Right) and Martin Brodeur (below) took turns setting new records for shutouts, wins, goals against average, and Stanley Cup victories. They each won the Conn Smythe Trophy.

NO ADMISSION: STEIN OUT

SEPT. 3, 1993 BY MICHAEL ULMER

Gil Stein's final grab for hockey immortality has landed him a place of infamy.

The former NHL president orchestrated his March 30, 1993 election to the Hockey Hall of Fame, according to an independent report unveiled Aug. 17 in Toronto. It concludes Stein abused his position as NHL president, right down to surreptitiously writing his own nomination letter. The final words of that communication, under which NHL board of governors chairman Bruce McNall's signature appears, read:

"Throughout his long and distinguished career in the league, Mr. Stein has been the epitome of a team player, achieving many honors for his team, not himself. It is time for his team to honor him."

Instead, there is only shame for Stein.

The 65-year-old league executive informed commissioner Gary Bettman of his intention to withdraw from the Hall before the report was tabled by two of North America's most prominent lawyers, Yves Fortier of Montreal and Arnold Burns of New York City.

Stein refused all interview requests on the subject, but issued a brief press release. He said the four-month investigation showed he broke no league or Hall of Fame rules. He also pointed out the report confirmed his election to the Hall was not part of a negotiated severance package and rejected the independent lawyers' contention he rigged his own election.

The report found Stein bullied his way into the Hall, in part, by orchestrating two changes to voting procedure. The board of directors, which votes on enshrinement for builders and on-ice officials, abandoned the traditional secret ballot in favor of an open vote and lowered the necessary majority for induction from 75 to 51 percent.

More significant, though, was board adoption of a motion proposed by former Canadian Prime Minister John Turner, one of Stein's five NHL appointees. Turner recommended the board take the unprecedented step of voting on all four 1993 nominees – Vancouver Canucks' owner Frank Griffiths, Buffalo Sabres' president Seymour Knox and longtime Canadian Amateur Hockey Association official Fred Page were the others – as a slate.

That linked the Hall of Fame fates of all four men.

"A vote against the slate," said Hall chairman Scotty Morrison," was also a vote against Frank Griffiths, Fred Page and Seymour Knox, all deserving candidates."

The group passed the motion, but the exact vote isn't known because there are no minutes from the meeting.

Mario Gentile, a board member representing the municipality of Metro Toronto, said it was pointless to debate the issue when Turner moved the entire slate to be elected.

"When a former prime minister, with more knowledge and experience in government and professional life than you have, makes a motion and that person is appointed by the NHL, you figure they should know," Gentile said.

Stein's election to the Hall became an issue when Canadian

↑ FROM FAME TO SHAME
Former NHL president Gil Stein withdraws from the Hall of Fame after he's accused of orchestrating his own election. He denies any wrongdoing.

Amateur Hockey Association president Murray Costello resigned his seat on the board of directors after participating in the balloting.

"(The vote) was not a pleasant scene," Costello said, "and I did not want to be a part of it."

Costello did not attend a meeting the morning of March 30 when Stein hinted the NHL appointees would lose their seats if support for his initiatives was not forthcoming.

Other NHL appointees were Toronto lawyer Larry Bertuzzi, NHL vice-president of operations Jim Gregory, Washington lawyer Lawrence Mayer and Philadelphia businessman Leslie Kaplan.

Stein also pushed through a change calling for a "cooling-off period" that prevents board members from being elected to the Hall for two years.

That change had the desired effect of making Brian O'Neill, a former NHL vice-president and Hall of Fame nominee, ineligible for consideration. He had recently been replaced on the board of directors.

Stein and O'Neill both served under former NHL president John Ziegler, but were more rivals than colleagues. "There was never that much love lost between us," O'Neill said.

Although Stein viewed current or recent directors as facing a conflict of interest, he did not consider himself in the same situation. Others feared, however, that would be the public perception and urged him to step aside.

Bettman asked Stein to decline the nomination three times before a public outcry and NHL internal unrest led to the investigation. Fortier, former Canadian ambassador to the United Nations and Burns, one-time deputy U.S. attorney general, were commissioned by Bettman to probe allegations Stein manipulated the process and was offered Hall membership as part of a severance package with the NHL. Among the report's eight recommendations was for Stein not to be inducted "at this time."

Unknown to the authors was Stein had already withdrawn his name, becoming the first of 871 inductees to North American professional baseball, football, basketball and hockey to turn down their sport's highest honor. THN

— 1993-2004 —

DEAD PUCK ERA

THE HIGH-OCTANE '80S GOT STUCK IN NEUTRAL WHEN THE TRAP ARRIVED, SMOTHERING SCORING TO DEATH AND USHERING IN DEFENSE-FIRST PLAY

There's a reason why your high school history teacher skipped over the Middle Ages. Civilization plateaued for roughly a thousand years from the fall of Rome to the Renaissance and none today would much care if that millennium fell from memory, nerdy medievalists notwithstanding.

Ask puck fans about the Dark Ages of the NHL and you'll likely get a similar response and a close consensus on the most forgettable flat-line in hockey history — the aptly named Dead Puck Era, when clutching and grabbing, masked Michelin Men in goal and the dreaded neutral-zone trap all contributed to a death-drop in goal-scoring. After the fast-paced, high-flying, firewagon hockey of the 1980s and early '90s came a lumbering, plodding, trudging, low-scoring game, in which defense-first and counterattack offense philosophies that fans rued ruled the day.

Someone has to hang for the sins of the Dead Puck Era and it might as well be David Volek. From 1976 to 1990, three teams — the Montreal Canadiens, New York Islanders and Edmonton Oilers — won all but one Stanley Cup (Calgary Flames 1989) and the Pittsburgh Penguins were well on their way to being crowned the next dynasty after winning back-to-back titles in '91 and '92 and expecting to make it three in '93. But in skated Volek, who inaugurated the Dead Puck Decade when he scored the Game 7 overtime winner in Round 2 for the underdog Islanders, punting the heavily favored Penguins from the playoffs. It was emblematic of the coming era in the NHL: a goal scored on the counterattack after a turnover at the defensive blueline, with a bottom-six grunt in Volek being chased by the league's superstar, Mario Lemieux.

The next season, offense dropped nearly a goal a game from 7.25 to 6.48, the largest single-season decline since 1944-45. By the end of 2003-04, it had dropped to 5.14, the lowest since 1955-56. Gone forever were seven-plus goals per game, along with the four straight Stanley Cups of the Canadiens and Islanders, and four in five years for the Oilers. Offense went AWOL, but the dynasty wasn't entirely dead — just redefined. In came a similar stretch of domination by a select group of clubs. From 1995 to 2003, three

teams took all the titles save for one (Dallas Stars in 1999) — the New Jersey Devils and Detroit Red Wings won three Cups apiece and the Colorado Avalanche won two.

Of the three, the Devils are the team that defines the Dead Puck Era (the name derives from the Dead Ball Era in Major League Baseball in the early 20th century). Franchise greatness is achieved by championships, but influence is measured by impact on the way the game is played. And New Jersey brought about a paradigm shift in the NHL that is still felt today.

The Devils made defensive systems sacrosanct. They had the top such systematizer in coach Jacques Lemaire and copycat teams sought out others to mimic him. They hired assistant coaches (previously a rarity), brought in specialty coaches and broadened their cadre of scouts. The game became more about defensive orchestration than offensive improvisation and it's easy to see why the Devils did this.

It's simple math, really. From 1991-92 to 2000-01, the NHL added nine teams, topping at 30, and gradually expanded the player pool by 43 percent. The league filled much of that with third- and fourth-liners, bottom-pair defensemen and perennial backups. More teams meant more jobs, which were filled by lower-skilled players, which required defensive schemes to organize them, which led to fewer goals. Expansion meant contraction.

The dramatic disappearance of goal scoring is the lowlight of the Dead Puck Era, but perhaps the most lamentable alteration of the game came on the fashion front. Baggy, blow-your-mind bad, what-were-they-thinking third jerseys were major fashion flubs (see Anaheim's 'Super Duck,' circa 1995-96). This revenue-generating gaffe made bellbottoms and acid wash look like classic fashion. Fortunately, tampering with tradition was restricted as the NHL's pseudo-fashionistas of the time were limited to non-Original Six teams. And thankfully, this trend has gone out of style.

Now, before you go thinking fans should just pretend the Dead Puck Era didn't happen, consider this: although many view it as the dreariest decade in hockey history, this point in the evolution of the game still threw up some of the all-time best offensive talents.

Take Peter Forsberg, for example, who had 885 points in his career. Impressive, though good for only 102nd all-time. But 'Foppa' did that in just 708 games. That puts his point-per-game pace at 1.25 — eighth all-time and better than Phil Esposito, Guy Lafleur, Gordie Howe, Steve Yzerman and Joe Sakic.

Pavel Bure was similarly dominant in goal scoring. The 'Russian Rocket' had 437 career goals. Not bad, but good for just 63rd all-time. But Bure did that in just 702 games. That puts his goals-per-game pace at 0.623 — fifth all-time and ahead of Wayne Gretzky, Brett Hull, Bobby Hull, Maurice Richard and Cam Neely. Imagine if injuries hadn't cut their careers short. Imagine if they had played in a different decade.

While the strategy of the game underwent a wholesale alteration, so too did the demographics of the NHL's player personnel. And the league is much better for it today. The Russians had already been coming before the Dead Puck Era began, but from 1993-94 to 2003-04 the number of European players in the NHL from Sweden, Czech Republic, Finland and Slovakia rose significantly. Swedes (117 percent), Czechs (161 percent), Finns and Slovaks (280 percent each) increased, while the number of Americans (one percent) and Russians (two percent) barely rose and Canadians actually decreased (three percent). Several players from the European invasion thrived when offense was at its most awful — Nicklas Lidstrom, Jaromir Jagr, Teemu Selanne and Peter Bondra.

Whether the game evolved or devolved is debatable and ultimately a matter of taste. If you like soccer-style scores, then the Dead Puck Era was a dynamite decade. After all, it gave us three of the game's greatest goalies in their primes: Patrick Roy, Martin Brodeur and Dominik Hasek. If offense is your preference, then doomsday couldn't have come at a better time when the lockout struck in 2004-05.

By the time the Apocalypse had cleared, the NHL's medieval times were as forgotten as friars and feudalism. Sidney Crosby and Alex Ovechkin, shootouts and plenty of power plays were on the horizon and the next chapter in the history of the greatest game had begun. **THN**

↑ GOALIES DOMINATE
Virtually unbeatable stoppers such as Dominik Hasek were a big reason for all the 2-1 and 1-0 games of the late 1990s and early 2000s.

↑ EXCELLENT EXCEPTION
Peter Forsberg was a rare player who fought through the hooks and holds to produce points at a throwback rate during the Dead Puck Era.

›1993-94 BROADWAY SMASH

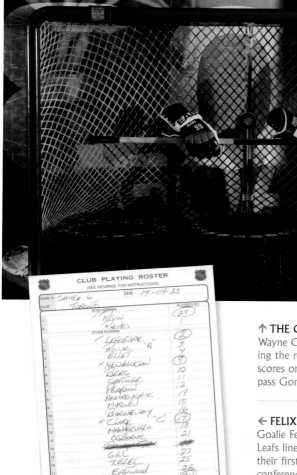

Cup Winner
New York Rangers

Leading Scorers
1. Wayne Gretzky, LA, 130 pts
2. Sergei Fedorov, Det, 120 pts
3. Adam Oates, Bos, 112 pts
4. Doug Gilmour, Tor, 111 pts
5. Pavel Bure, Van, 107 points
6. Mark Recchi, Phi, 107 points
7. Jeremy Roenick, Chi, 107 pts
8. B. Shanahan, StL, 102 points
9. Dave Andreychuk, Tor, 99 pts
10. Jaromir Jagr, Pit, 99 points

Franchise News
Florida Panthers and Mighty Ducks of Anaheim join as expansion teams, growing NHL to 26 franchises. The Minnesota North Stars are transferred to Dallas to become the Stars.

First Draft Pick, 1994
Ed Jovanovski, D, Florida

HHOF Inductees
Harry Watson
↓Lionel Conacher

Nickname of the Year
Andre 'Red Light' Racicot

Worth Noting
Mark Messier of the Rangers creates sports lore when he guarantees a playoff win in Game 6 of the conference final against the Devils, then delivers a decisive third-period natural hat trick... There are 99 regular season shutouts, a mark that destroys the record of 85 set in 1974-75.

↑ THE GREAT ONE ALONE AT THE TOP
Wayne Gretzky's gear and 802 pucks, including the record-breaking one — all in the net he scores on in Los Angeles March 23, 1994 — to pass Gordie Howe on the all-time NHL goals list.

← FELIX 'THE CAT' CLEANS UP
Goalie Felix Potvin, who's first on this Maple Leafs lineup sheet, shuts out Chicago 1-0 to win their first round series. Toronto makes it to the conference final for the second straight season.

Newsmakers & Top Headlines

1 Rangers end 54-year Stanley Cup jinx
The endless chants of "1940" stop at Madison Square Garden as the Rangers score a seven-game Stanley Cup final win over Vancouver, their first title since 1939-40. Mike Keenan coaches his first Cup winner, but the party's barely over when he signs as coach-GM of St. Louis. The Rangers charge Keenan with breach of contract. The NHL fines the Blues and Red Wings — who also negotiate with him — for tampering. Keenan is suspended 60 days and Petr Nedved of St. Louis is awarded to the Rangers in exchange for Esa Tikkanen and Doug Lidster as part of a compensation package.

2 Gretzky shoots past Howe's goal mark
In his last truly great season, the Kings' Wayne Gretzky becomes the top goal-scorer in NHL history. His goal March 23 is No. 802, surpassing Gordie Howe's career mark. Gretzky had previously overtaken Howe for the all-time assists and points leads. The Great One wins his 10th and last Art Ross Trophy with 130 points, but he misses the playoffs for the first time.

3 Sweden's Olympic win gets stamp of approval
Peter Forsberg becomes a hero in Sweden, scoring a spectacular goal in the shootout of the final game to give his country its first Olympic gold medal. Forsberg's incredible one-handed backhand goal on Canada's Corey Hirsch is commemorated on a Swedish stamp, but Hirsch refuses permission to have his image on it.

FACTS & STATS
from 1994-95

FACTS & STATS
from 1994-95

Cup Winner
New Jersey Devils

Leading Scorers
1. Jaromir Jagr, Pit, 70 points
2. Eric Lindros, Phi, 70 points
3. Alex Zhamnov, Wpg, 65 points
4. Joe Sakic, Que, 62 points
5. Ron Francis, Pit, 59 points

60 Moments
that changed the game
No. 11: New Jersey Devils sweep Detroit in Stanley Cup, ushering in era of trap-defense hockey.
No. 27: The NHL's first lockout ends when owners capitulate on demand to have a salary cap.
No. 48: The NHL and IIHF agree to allow NHL participants in the 1998 Winter Olympics.

First Draft Pick, 1995
Bryan Berard, D, Ottawa

HHOF Inductees
Bun Cook
↓ Larry Robinson

Nickname of the Year
John 'Beezer' Vanbiesbrouck

Worth Noting
Chicago's Chris Chelios during lockout: "If I was Gary Bettman, I'd be worried about my family. Some crazed fan or player might figure if they get him out of the way, this might get settled." Chelios later apologizes. Paul Coffey cracks top 10 in league scoring; no D-man does again until Erik Karlsson (T-10) in 2011-12.

↑ **SUNSHINE ON ICE**
After winning silver medals with Team USA at the World Championship in 1990, '92 and '94, Kelly Dyer takes her glove hand, and the rest of her goalie gear, to the play with men in the Sunshine Hockey League for a few seasons.

← **DEMONS DO THE DEED**
Conn Smythe winner Claude Lemieux (center) and the Devils finish fifth in the Eastern Conference, then dispatch the heavily favored Detroit Red Wings to become the first team lower than a top-four seed to win the Cup.

Newsmakers & Top Headlines

1 Lockout knocks out season until New Year
Hockey fans get worried when NHL owners lock out the players Sept. 30 because there is no collective bargaining agreement in place. Owners give commissioner Gary Bettman approval Dec. 12 to shut down the season. It looks like the season will be axed when both sides reject each other's "final offers" Jan. 7. But four days later, the NHL Players' Association negotiating committee switches gears and endorses the owner's offer and an agreement is reached six days later, ending a 103-day lockout. A 48-game season begins Jan. 20.

2 Former players win pension suit
Former NHLers, led by a group including Carl Brewer and Brad Park, win their lawsuit that contends the NHL skimmed money from the pension fund when the Supreme Court of Canada dismisses the league's appeal July 28, 1994. In 1992, an Ontario court ruled the NHL contravened bylaws set in 1949. The league is estimated to owe $40 million to retired players.

3 Super Mario sits out season
The only thing that can stop Mario Lemieux is his health. The four-time scoring champion, limited to 22 games in 1993-94, announces he'll sit out the 1994-95 season. "There's a strong possibility I will be able to come back," says Lemieux, who acknowledges after the season he will return for 1995-96. The Penguins still finish third overall, thanks mainly to Jaromir Jagr, who wins his first Art Ross Trophy with 70 points.

1995-96

CUP FLIES MILE-HIGH

↑ ROY'S ROPE
Patrick Roy wins his 300th career game despite letting five Edmonton shots hit this mesh. His Colorado Avalanche go on to win the franchise's first Stanley Cup a year after leaving Quebec.

← RAT ATTACK IN PANTHERS PUSH
After Scott Mellanby slapshots a dressing room rodent, Cats fans start throwing plastic rats on the ice whenever Florida scores at home. The Panthers and their plastic pals later make their first and only Stanley Cup final appearance.

Newsmakers & Top Headlines

1 Old Nordiques make smashing debut as Avalanche
After years of last-place finishes, Quebec Nordiques' fans miss the rewards when the club is bought May 25 by COMSAT and moved to Denver as the Colorado Avalanche. The Avs shine in their first season, sweeping Florida in the final to become the only NHL team to win the Stanley Cup in its first season in a new city. Quebec isn't the only Canadian city to receive bad news. The NHL approves the sale and transfer of the Winnipeg Jets to Phoenix Jan. 19, where they begin play as the Coyotes in 1996-97.

2 Wings soar to record heights
It's a winning season for captain Steve Yzerman's Detroit Red Wings. They finish with an NHL-record 62-13-7 slate, bettering Montreal's 60-win campaign of 1976-77. The Wings also equal Philadelphia's record for home wins with 36. It's a personal triumph for coach Scotty Bowman, who also guided the 1976-77 Habs. He moves past Al Arbour (1,606) into first spot on the all-time list of games coached, finishing with 1,654. But the Wings lose to Colorado in the conference final.

3 NHL stars to play in Olympics
At an Oct. 2 meeting involving the NHL, NHLPA and IIHF, the Canada Cup is renamed the World Cup. More importantly, plans are unveiled to include NHL stars in the 1998 Olympic tournament in Nagano, Japan. The league will take a 17-day break in the middle of the season to let the players participate.

FACTS & STATS
from 1995-96

Cup Winner
Colorado Avalanche

Leading Scorers
1. Mario Lemieux, Pit, 161 pts
2. Jaromir Jagr, Pit, 149 points
3. Joe Sakic, Col, 120 points
4. Ron Francis, Pit, 119 points
5. Peter Forsberg, Col, 116 pts
6. Eric Lindros, Phi, 115 points
7. Paul Kariya, Ana, 108 points
8. T. Selanne, Wpg/Ana, 108 pts
9. A. Mogilny, Van, 107 points
10. Sergei Fedorov, Det, 107 pts

Franchise News
Quebec transferred to Denver to become Colorado Avalanche.

60 Moments
that changed the game
No. 44: Quebec Nordiques are sold, move to Denver, sparking Canadian team relocation talk.

Significant Records
Most assists by a right winger, one season: Jaromir Jagr, Pit (87). Most points by a right winger, one season: Jaromir Jagr, Pit (149). Most appearances by a goalie, one season: Grant Fuhr, StL (79).

First Draft Pick, 1996
Chris Phillips, D, Ottawa

HHOF Inductees
Bobby Bauer
↓ Borje Salming

Nickname of the Year
Stu 'The Grim Reaper' Grimson

1996-97 ‹

FACTS & STATS
from 1996-97

Cup Winner

Detroit Red Wings

Leading Scorer
1. Mario Lemieux, Pit, 122 points
2. Teemu Selanne, Ana, 109 pts
3. Paul Kariya, Ana, 99 points

Rule Changes
Players must clear attacking zone prior to puck being shot into that zone. Opportunity to tag up and return to the zone is removed.

Franchise News
Winnipeg transfers to Phoenix to become Coyotes

60 Moments
that changed the game
No. 49: Goalie Garth Snow's oversized equipment blamed as tipping point in scoring reduction. No. 56: Seeds of complaint against obstruction planted when Mario Lemieux retires at 31.

Significant Records
Longest undefeated streak by a goaltender from start of career: Patrick Lalime, Pit (16 games).

First Draft Pick, 1997
Joe Thornton, C, Boston

HHOF Inductees
Bryan Trottier
↓ Mario Lemieux

Nickname of the Year
Pat 'Little Ball of Hate' Verbeek

↑ CRAZY LIKE A FOX
The 'FoxTrax' puck is cut in half and wired to emit a glow onscreen during telecasts, making the biscuit easier to follow. The network experiments with it from 1996-1998 before scrapping it.

Newsmakers & Top Headlines

1 Junior coach James guilty of sexual assualt
The hockey world is shocked when Graham James, coach of the Western League's Swift Current Broncos, is convicted on charges of sexually assaulting two players. Boston right winger Sheldon Kennedy and another player, who chooses not to give his name, provide police with details. James is sentenced to three-and-a-half years in federal prison; a statement of facts says James committed about 350 offenses against the two players.

2 Triumph and tragedy in Hockeytown
Detroit sweeps Philadelphia to win the Stanley Cup for the first time since 1954-55. The joy is short-lived. Six days after the final game, a limousine transporting Detroit defensemen Vladimir Konstantinov and Viacheslav Fetisov, with team masseur Sergei Mnatsakanov, crashes into a tree in a Detroit suburb. Mnatsakanov, 43, and Konstantinov, 30, a second-team all-star in 1995-96, suffer debilitating brain injuries ending their careers. Fetisov, 39, has minor injuries, but will play one more season and win another Cup.

3 Lemieux retires with 11 records
Mario Lemieux can boast he went out on top. The Pittsburgh center scores 50 goals and wins his sixth Art Ross Trophy with 122 points, then retires after 12 seasons. Hampered during his career by Hodgkin's disease and serious back problems, Lemieux, 31, leaves with 11 league marks. After three years in retirement, he returns in 2000-01 to play parts of five more seasons.

>1997-98

CZECH MATE

→ **MITTS OF A MAGIC MAN**
Jari Kurri gets an early Christmas gift, scoring his 600th goal, Dec. 23, 1997, with these gloves, as a member of the Colorado Avalanche. He adds one more that season, then calls it career.

Newsmakers & Top Headlines

1 Hasek leads Czechs to Olympic gold
In a battle of NHL dream teams, the Czech Republic blanks Russia 1-0 to win the Olympic gold medal in Japan behind the spectacular goaltending of Dominik Hasek. The Czechs reach the final after shocking Canada in the semifinal. Tied 1-1 after a scoreless 10-minute overtime, the Czechs win in a shootout when Hasek stones all five Canadians and Robert Reichel beats Patrick Roy. Finland upsets Canada 3-2 for the bronze, while the U.S. goes home in shame, trashing rooms in the Olympic Village after losing in the quarterfinal.

2 Eagleson sent to sin bin
Facing more than 30 charges of racketeering, fraud, obstruction of justice, embezzlement and accepting kickbacks, hockey czar Alan Eagleson pleads guilty to three counts of fraud Jan. 6 in a Boston court. He does the same the next day in a Toronto courtroom and is sentenced to 18 months in a minimum-security correctional center and fined $1 million.

3 NHL shooters caught in trap
Pittsburgh Penguins star Jaromir Jagr is the NHL's only 100-point scorer. His 102 points are the lowest Art Ross-winning total in a full season since 1967-68 as teams employ the neutral zone trap and scoring drops to a 40-year low of 5.28 goals per game. Player crease violations become a major issue; a total of 304 reviews conducted by video goal judges result in 110 goals being disallowed.

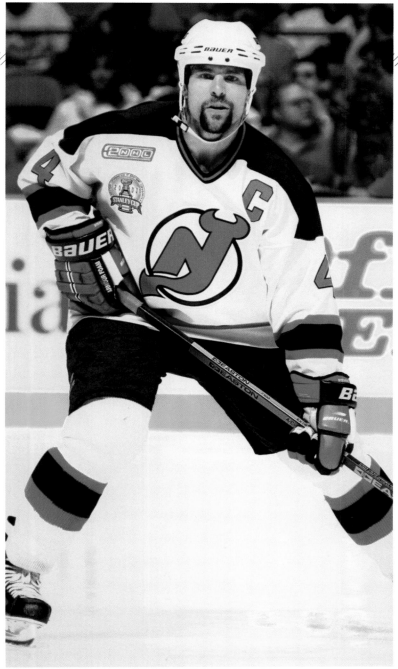

→ KEEP YOUR HEAD UP
Scott Stevens created a reputation for delivering the most lethal bodychecks in the NHL.

↓ THE RUSSIAN CONNECTION
Stars of Russian hockey like Sergei Fedorov and Igor Larionov merged with Steve Yzerman to lead the Detroit Red Wings to their first Stanley Cup since the 1950s.

→ SON OF BOBBY
Brett Hull powers the Dallas Stars to
their first (and only) Stanley Cup victory,
blasting shots like his father.

↓ FOOT IN OR FOOT OUT...
That is the question that Buffalo Sabres
fans are still debating about Brett Hull's
overtime Cup-winning goal.

1997-98 ‹

Forgotten Tales
from The Hockey News Crypt

TITANIC STRUGGLE FOR EX-SABRE

JULY 3, 1998 BY BRIAN COSTELLO

He sees his name in newspapers daily. It's on marquees everywhere, getting higher billing than even Leonardo DiCaprio.

Critics have been raving for months. It was a virtual clean sweep at the Oscars celebration of excellence.

His name is unforgettable. It conjures an image of flawed invincibility. It rolls off the tongue with a chill.

He's Titanic. Morris Titanic.

In a year when *Titanic* is the talk of the entertainment industry, Morris Titanic walks through downtown Buffalo in obscurity.

He's a 45-year-old salesman for a large commercial printing company, but there was a time when Titanic left dock christened to be a future star for the Buffalo Sabres.

Titanic was a 20-year-old scoring port sider for the Ontario League's Sudbury Wolves when the Sabres selected him 12th overall in the 1973 draft. The Toronto native was expected to be another piece of a growing puzzle assembled by Sabres GM Punch Imlach.

Buffalo's first pick the previous year was Jim Schoenfeld. Richard Martin was the Sabres first rounder in 1971, Gilbert Perreault in 1970.

"There are big expectations from a first-rounder," Titanic said. "Especially when (Buffalo's) past first rounder made such huge contributions."

Titanic played 17 games in his rookie season of 1974-75. Back problems curtailed his second season and complications following surgery all but ended his pro career. A spinal fusion operation forced him to go through two years of rehabilitation. He never played in the NHL again.

Titanic's zero-filled NHL statistical line looks eerily like a bunch of icebergs bobbing side-by-side in the Atlantic Ocean: 19 games played, zero goals, zero assists, zero points, zero penalty minutes.

After a few seasons in the minor leagues, Titanic tore up his knee and his playing career was over at 27. He dabbled in coaching at the Jr. B level before putting on a business suit in 1985.

Titanic's only connection to the most successful motion picture ever is he went to go see it one night in April. Imagine the symbolism that went unnoticed in the theatre when, while taking a sip of soda, Titanic slammed his mouth shut on an incoming piece of ice.

"It was a great movie, I loved it," Titanic said. "I'd love to have a cut of that pie."

Unfortunately, Titanic is not due any royalties. That doesn't stop the sideways glances Titanic gets when he introduces himself or when cashiers process his credit card.

"Some people think it's a joke at first," he said. "It's good for a chuckle."

The name is Ukrainian. Titanic's father emigrated to Toronto with his parents as a child.

"There aren't many Titanics out there," Morris said. "I saw a list once. There were maybe 12 in all of North America."

↑ SIDE-SWIPED BY INJURIES
Like the big ship by the same name, projections and expectations are sky-high for Morris Titanic. Sadly, his ship never comes in.

MAY 8, 1998 BY BRIAN COSTELLO

HOCKEY AGENT MARRIES MINOR LEAGUER

Hockey super agents Michael Barnett, Don Meehan and Don Baizley couldn't pull this one off if they worked on it together.

Certified player agent Paige Tatters negotiated the longest contract ever entered into by a pro player. The lifetime contract is a hockey first because it's a marriage contract and her client is also her husband.

Tatters, a 26-year-old agent certified by the NHL Players' Association last May, married her client, 22-year-old Miloslav Cermak of the West Coast League's Tucson Gila Monsters, in an on-ice ceremony Feb. 27 in Tucson, Ariz. Terms of the contract weren't disclosed, but it's believed Cermak signed a long, long, long-term contract. In return, Tatters said she'll waive her standard three percent agent fee and promise to keep in touch with her client daily. "I don't plan on doing this with all my (27) clients," joked Tatters.

The Pittsburgh-based Tatters was a model travelling in France a year ago when she met some players eager to pursue hockey in North America. Attempts to get them agents were fruitless, so she took the steps to become an agent.

The ceremony took place 20 minutes before Tucson's Feb. 27 game against the Fresno Fighting Falcons. Cermak wore full equipment and a dark away sweater to set him apart from teammates. Tatters wore a white dress and skates. "I took my helmet off," said Cermak. "How would it look if I kissed her with my visor in the way?"

What happened after the ceremony? "I hadn't missed a game all year," Cermak said. "I couldn't miss this game, either."

Tatters understood. What's best for the player is best for the agent. **THN**

1998-99

99's CURTAIN CALL

↓ **BLESSED BAGGAGE**
Wayne Gretzky bids farewell to an epic career, leading the NHL in assists in two of his last three seasons with the New York Rangers.

FACTS & STATS
from 1998-99

Cup Winner
Dallas Stars

Leading Scorers
1. Jaromir Jagr, Pit, 127 points
2. Teemu Selanne, Ana, 107 pts
3. Paul Kariya, Ana, 101 points
4. Peter Forsberg, Col, 97 points
5. Joe Sakic, Col, 96 points

Rule Changes
The league institutes a two-referee system with each team to play 20 regular season games with two referees and a pair of linesmen.

Franchise News
Nashville Predators added to make NHL a 27-team league.

First Draft Pick, 1999
Patrik Stefan, C, Atlanta

HHOF Inductees
↓ Wayne Gretzky

Nickname of the Year
Wayne 'The Great One' Gretzky

Worth Noting
It's fitting Jaromir Jagr scores the winning goal in Wayne Gretzky's final game. "Everyone always talks about passing torches," Gretzky says. "He caught it."... Jagr wins his first Hart Trophy and third Art Ross with 127 points. He figures in 52.5 per cent of Pittsburgh's 242 goals, a percentage Gretzky never matched in his career.

Newsmakers & Top Headlines

1 The Great One Says good-bye
Following weeks of speculation, Wayne Gretzky acknowledges April 16 he's retiring. Two days later, he plays his final game for the Rangers at Madison Square Garden in New York. Before the puck is dropped, NHL commissioner Gary Bettman declares No. 99 will be retired across the league. Gretzky picks up one final point — an assist on Brian Leetch's goal in a 2-1 overtime loss to Pittsburgh. New York Rangers' coach John Muckler calls timeout in the final minute of regulation and the crowd has one last chance to salute The Great One. "That's when it really hit me that I'm done," Gretzky says. He finishes his amazing career with 894 goals and 1,963 assists for 2,857 points, just three of the 61 NHL records he holds or shares.

2 Stars Hull home Cup amidst video dispute
The Stanley Cup heads to the Lone Star State for the first time as the Stars defeat the Sabres. Controversy erupts when cameras show Brett Hull's foot in the crease on his Cup-winning goal in triple overtime. The NHL says it reviewed the goal and Hull had control of the puck, making it legal. Two days later, the league returns crease violation calls to on-ice officials.

3 Chiasson killed in car crash
Losing control of his truck following a season-ending party, Carolina defenseman Steve Chiasson is killed May 3. Chiasson, 32, has a blood-alcohol count three times the legal limit, isn't wearing a seatbelt and is speeding at the time of the accident.

IT'S ALL WRITE FOR AL SMITH

SEPT. 4, 1998 BY MARK BRENDER

I t's 7:45 on a Saturday night in downtown Toronto, 15 minutes to show-time. You can't help but think how three decades and 30 pounds ago, this must have been a time Al Smith cherished. But standing outside the Alumnae Theatre, you're just perplexed. The front door is locked, the sidewalk bare and the prospects for a performance dimming with each passing moment.

After a minute or so, alerted by pounding, a man peeks out the window and rushes down the stairs. As the door swings outward, he offers apologies as he grabs a stand-up wood placard and places it on the sidewalk: "Confessions to Anne Sexton, by Al Smith, 8:00." Sheepishly, he says he thought someone else would have opened up by now.

Up the stairs, the lobby is bare and quiet save for a ticket-seller behind the counter. No one else, it seems, has come to see this play penned by a 52-year-old cab driver and struggling artist in his own hometown. The novelty, in a country where hockey is the greatest art form imaginable, is that this particular cab driver spent 15 years as an NHL and WHA goalie.

In Canada, hitting Broadway doesn't get much bigger than that. The legacy eats away at him, fuels his frustration. The promotions people who convinced Smith to put a goalie mask on the ads which he soon regretted doing, the media which portray his work as sorry offshoot to a once-successful career, they won't let him get on with his life.

"We're finished at 34 years old," he asks with exasperation. "Thirty-four! Come on, be fair, you a—holes!"

The stage and 140 unfilled seats are undisturbed behind another set of closed doors. Five minutes to showtime, the playwright sits alone in a long, narrow corridor behind the theatre balcony. He's leaning back on the rear legs of his chair, feet crossed on the window sill in front of him.

After greeting a visitor, the former goalie asks if anyone else is waiting in the lobby. He accepts the answer as a confirmation of his thoughts, much like a student's reaction on finding out he received an 'F' on the test he didn't bother to study for. But there is a melodramatic fatalism to his speech and every so often the disappointment comes to the fore.

"I've never played on a team like this," he says wistfully. "I can't think of a rink this empty, I really can't."

Smith has put some bulk on since his days in the nets — he retired from the Colorado Rockies, his eighth team, in 1981 — but driving a cab for 13 years will do that to anyone. He says he has been in the car all day just to scrape enough money together to pay the four actors. He's spent his "Carl Brewer money" from the NHL pension settlement — $34,862 — to finance the project.

The young director of the play appears at the end of the hallway. Smith tells him this night's performance will be cancelled, but the matinee show tomorrow afternoon will go on and that will be the end of it. The actors go through their

↑ DRIVEN TO WRITING SUCCESS
Former NHL stopper Al Smith turns to driving cabs and writing plays in his retirement years. The audience isn't as accepting.

lines for the final time on June 21, their anticipated four-week run already cut down to three, whether anyone shows or not. Then Al Smith will go back to writing when he can, driving his cab because he must. In another 13 years, perhaps he'll have the money to do it all again.

"It's an awful thing," Smith says of his aspiration, his compulsion to write. It broke up his marriage years ago. "And if you're not good at it…" and here he pauses and laughs. "There's a lot of oldtimer hockey out there, but I couldn't bear to watch."

"Confessions" is Smith's second self-financed play. The first one two years ago played to an empty house for two nights before Smith tore the set down. A review in the Toronto *Globe and Mail* described the play as "an interior monologue in several voices, written in allusive, repetitive, strenuously poetic language." Smith says it's a play about the middle-aged problems of two middle-aged men, one of whom happens to be an ex-hockey player.

"It's a good, left play. You know, John Kennedy and all that stuff, Jane Fonda. It was a good play. It was a good play to squander on this type of situation. There are a few hippies out there and the hippies came an enjoyed it. There just aren't as many as I thought."

He feels awful for the actors. The real stars in the play, he says, are in the audience; Brewer, writer Alan Abel, Florida Panthers scout and friend Paul

Henry, Skip Stanowski, "an old hippie from Cornell" and son of former NHLer Wally Stanowski; two of his three children, including a daughter who helped him.

Opening night provided the biggest draw: 17 people including his mother. Overall there were 21 shows, six shutouts. A good performance was a show when the people who did come stayed. These were the real theatre people, Smith says. The ones who heard a familiar name from a generation ago and came looking for some sort of hockey epiphany walked out at intermission, he says. It happened more than once.

His definition of success: "To have all these a—holes you call the culture of this country to finally accept the fact that I'm a writer. Whenever they do that, I'll be satisfied." THN

>1999-00
MCSORE LOSER

→ NO 'O' FOR DANEYKO

Ken Daneyko is all elbows when it comes to goal-scoring. He goes goal-less in three straight seasons, beginning in 1999-00, before finally breaking out with a pair in 2002-03 when he wins his third Stanley Cup. He then retires, as do his pads.

Newsmakers & Top Headlines

1 McSorley attacks Brashear with stick

Marty McSorley's reputation is forever stained Feb. 21, 2000. Playing for the Bruins, McSorley loses a tussle with Vancouver Canuck Donald Brashear, the NHL's heavyweight champion enforcer. Brashear dusts off his hands following the bout and taunts the Bruins throughout the game. A seething McSorley wants revenge. With seconds left in the contest, he swings his stick at Brashear's head and knocks him to the ice, concussing him severely. McSorley insists he was aiming for the shoulder and trying to start another fight, but can't escape an indefinite suspension — or criminal charges. He is found guilty of assault with a weapon and never plays another NHL game, finishing 39 games shy of 1,000 for his 17-season career.

2 Bruins trade Bourque to Colorado at deadline

Nearing the end of a legendary career, Ray Bourque still hasn't won a Cup and his team, Boston, isn't good enough to do so any time soon. In a stunning deal March 6, 2000, the Bruins give Bourque a shot at glory, shipping him to contender Colorado along with Dave Andreychuk for Brian Rolston, Samuel Pahlsson, Martin Grenier and a first round pick. Bourque doesn't win the Cup that spring, but does in 2001.

3 Pronger wins a momentous Hart Trophy

On the strength of a 62-point campaign with St. Louis, Chris Pronger becomes the first defenseman since Bobby Orr to win the league's MVP award. Needless to say, at plus-52, he also takes the Norris.

FACTS & STATS
from 1999-00

Cup Winner
New Jersey Devils

Leading Scorers
1. Jaromir Jagr, Pit, 96 points
2. Pavel Bure, Fla 94 points
3. Mark Recchi, Phi, 91 points
4. Paul Kariya, Ana, 86 points
5. Teemu Selanne, Ana, 85 pts
6. Tony Amonte, Chi, 84 points
7. Owen Nolan, SJ, 84 points
8. Joe Sakic, Col, 81 points
9. Mike Modano, Dal, 81 points
10. Steve Yzerman, Det, 79 pts

Rule Changes
Introduction of 4-on-4 overtime with the winning team in the five-minute session getting two points and the OT loser one.

Franchise News
Atlanta Thrashers added to make NHL a 28-team league.

First Draft Pick, 2000
Rick DiPietro, G, NY Islanders

HHOF Inductees
Joe Mullen
↓ Denis Savard

Nickname of the Year
Dominik 'The Dominator' Hasek

Worth Noting
The Roger Crozier Saving Grace Award is introduced and given to the goaltender with the best save percentage. Ed Belfour of Dallas is the inaugural winner with a .919 mark.

COACH SMUGGLES IN PLAYER

MARCH 17, 2000 BY BOB McKENZIE & JIM CRESSMAN

The Ontario League ordered one of its highest-profile coaches stripped of his GM duties after an 18-year-old Ukrainian player was twice smuggled across the Canada-U.S. border in the lower baggage compartment of the Barrie Colts team bus.

The Hockey News has learned Bill Stewart was demoted from coach-GM to coach after an OHL investigation in mid-January confirmed the former NHL player and coach was responsible for hiding defenseman Vladimir Chernenko amongst team equipment bags during two border crossings.

Chernenko, who was without the necessary paperwork to enter the U.S., made the illegal entries on Oct. 16 for a game at Plymouth, Mich., and Dec. 4 for a game in Erie, Pa.

In addition to Stewart's demotion and the commensurate loss in pay — $25,000 over three years — the Colts' organization was ordered by the league to bear the costs of a league-wide immigration education program and policy, to be instituted at a later date.

"It was concluded that Bill Stewart acted inappropriately," said OHL commissioner David Branch, who conducted a formal disciplinary hearing with Stewart on Jan. 28. "He exercised poor judgment."

Branch said he chose not to make the incidents or punishments public because "there was a sensitivity towards the ramifications on a number of individuals, notably the player involved. We felt we had an obligation and responsibility to handle this in a decisive fashion and we felt we did that." We didn't feel we were obliged to make public the punishments." Our solicitors made contact with immigration authorities to see what our obligation was. We feel we satisfied that obligation with how we handled the situation."

Stewart, who was interim coach of the New York Islanders last season and then signed a three-year contract to be coach-GM of the Colts, issued the following statement to THN and the London (Ont.) *Free Press:* "The situation has been dealt with by the league and by the Barrie Colts and both parties have put this matter behind them."

Whether U.S. immigration authorities — after first hearing of the incidents from THN and the *Free Press* — will choose to do the same is unclear.

"Based on what you have told me, we have what we consider to be an alien smuggling," said Winston Barrus, acting district director for the United States Immigration and Naturalization Service in Buffalo.

Barrus said any alien who aids, abets or encourages any other alien to enter the U.S. illegally could be banned from entering the country. He said a ban is lifetime "unless the law changes." A person can apply for a waiver and it may be lifted if it's determined the person is rehabilitated and won't engage in the same act again.

"They're very lucky no harm came to this person," Barrus said. "It was an act of stupidity. It was a very foolish thing to do without thinking through the ramifications."

↑ DEALING WITH HIS BAGGAGE
Barrie coach Bill Stewart is demoted and banned from entering the United States for twice smuggling a Ukrainian player over the border.

Chernenko, since traded from Barrie to the Owen Sound Platers and then to the Sudbury Wolves, has a visa that allows him to live and play junior hockey in Canada. In order to enter the U.S. to play a game there — the 20-team OHL has two U.S.-based franchises — the Ukraine national needs a multi-entry visa. Generally, it can be obtained in three to four days by visiting any U.S. consulate and paying a fee of $195.

U.S. immigration authorities said they have no interest in pursuing or sanctioning any alien if he's no longer in the U.S., though Canadian immigration authorities said they could review the status of any individual who's in the country on a visa and makes an illegal border crossing to the U.S.

Chernenko is represented by Calgary-based player agent Vlad Shushkovsky of AKT Sports Management. Shushkovsky was not available for comment, but AKT Sports president Anton Thun of Toronto said Chernenko would not comment on the incidents.

"What we have here is a nice kid and he's just a kid with limited English, who doesn't understand the system, the ins and outs of immigration and travel between Canada and the United States," Thun told THN.

"He's just a hockey player and hockey players, especially those from Vlad's background, have been taught to do what their coaches and teams tell them to do. Vlad just wants to play hockey."

No details of the two illegal crossings were available. Just when Chernenko was placed in the lower baggage compartment and for how long is unknown. A spokesman for the London (Ont.) Police Dept. said the Highway Traffic Act of Ontario doesn't specifically prohibit a person being transported in such a manner.

Barrus said he cannot stress enough the perils associated with smuggling a human being across the border, especially in a baggage compartment. He said besides the legal ramifications, there is a variety of related physical dangers, including carbon monoxide poisoning and the possibility of a collision, shifting of the load or bay door opening. "This was an incredible, irresponsible act," Barrus said. **THN**

>2000-01 BACK IN BLACK

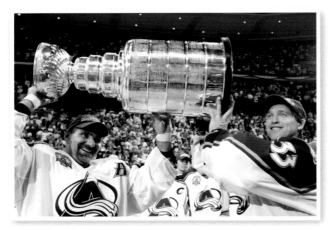

↑ DUCKS FEET A GOOD FIT
J-S Giguere has his best seasons with these skates in Anaheim. He shares duties with Guy Hebert in 2000-01 before taking over the following season.

← ONE LEGEND TO ANOTHER
Patrick Roy (right) enjoys his fourth Stanley Cup victory as Ray Bourque soaks in his first. Bourque goes out on top by retiring, while Roy plays two more seasons before packing it in. Both go on to the Hall of Fame.

Newsmakers & Top Headlines

1 Mario makes magnificent return
The NHL thought it had seen the last of Mario Lemieux when he retired in 1997, but in 2000, he returns to the team he owns. At 35, he rejoins the Pittsburgh Penguins lineup Dec. 27 against the Toronto Maple Leafs. Lemieux wastes no time, notching an assist 33 seconds in and ending the night with a goal and three points. In a remarkable partial season, he finishes with 76 points in 43 games, leading the league in points per game. He guides the Penguins to a conference final berth.

2 Roy passes Sawchuk to become NHL's wins leader
It was only a matter of time until Patrick Roy became the NHL's winningest all-time goalie. On Oct. 17,

2000, Roy stops 27 Washington Capitals shots as his Colorado Avalanche win 4-3 in overtime. The victory is Roy's 448th, breaking Terry Sawchuk's historic mark. Roy holds the wins crown until Martin Brodeur takes it from him in 2009.

3 Bourque finally raises the Cup
Star defenseman Ray Bourque and the Colorado Avalanche fell short of fulfilling his Cup dream in 1999-2000, but the following spring is one to remember. After he notches 59 points as a 40-year-old, he's a crucial playoff contributor as the Avalanche defeat the Devils in seven games. It's Colorado's second Cup and, of course, Bourque's first, capping a 22-year career that stands among the best ever for an NHL blueliner.

FACTS & STATS
from 2000-01

Cup Winner
Colorado Avalanche

Leading Scorers
1. Jaromir Jagr, Pit, 121 points
2. Joe Sakic, Col, 118 points
3. Patrik Elias, NJ, 96 points
4. Alex Kovalev, Pit, 95 points
5. Jason Allison, Bos, 95 points
6. Martin Straka, Pit, 95 points
7. Pavel Bure, Fla, 92 points
8. Doug Weight, Edm, 90 points
9. Ziggy Palffy, LA, 89 points
10. Peter Forsberg, Col, 89 pts

Rule Changes
NHL institutes the two referee system for all games.

Franchise News
Columbus Blue Jackets and Minnesota Wild added, expanding the NHL to its current 30-team structure.

60 Moments
that changed the game
No. 33: Experimental two-referee system incorporated full-time in NHL action.

First Draft Pick, 2001
Ilya Kovalchuk, LW, Atlanta

HHOF Inductees
Viacheslav Fetisov
Dale Hawerchuk
Jari Kurri
↓ Mike Gartner

Nickname of the Year
Mario 'The Magnificent' Lemieux

FACTS & STATS
from 2001-02

Cup Winner
Detroit Red Wings

Leading Scorers
1. Jarome Iginla, Cgy, 96 points
2. Markus Naslund, Van, 90 pts
3. Todd Bertuzzi, Van, 85 points
4. Mats Sundin, Tor, 80 points
5. Jaromir Jagr, Wsh, 79 points
6. Joe Sakic, Col, 79 points
7. Pavol Demitra, StL, 78 points
8. Adam Oates, Wsh/Phi, 78 pts
9. Ron Francis, Car, 77 points
10. Mike Modano, Dal, 77 points

First Draft Pick, 2002
Rick Nash, LW, Columbus

HHOF Inductees
Rod Langway
Bernie Federko
↓ Clark Gillies

Nickname of the Year
Curtis 'Cujo' Joseph

Worth Noting
Brittanie Cecil, a 13-year-old Columbus fan, dies two days after getting hit in the head with a deflected puck at a Blue Jackets game, marking the first fan fatality in the 85-year history of the league…Scotty Bowman, the NHL's most accomplished coach of all time, bids farewell the best way possible: with a Stanley Cup. His Red Wings defeat the Hurricanes in five games to cement Bowman's record ninth championship and third with Detroit. He retires immediately afterward, holding the regular season wins record with 1,244.

← SWEET VICTORY IN SALT LAKE
Canada's Jayna Hefford uses this stick to score the game-winner with one second left in the second period to beat the U.S. at the '02 Olympics.

↓ DOMINATOR'S DUFF STUFF
Dominik Hasek sits on this sacred dressing room stool in Detroit, where he captures his first of two Stanley Cups. His second follows in 2008.

Newsmakers & Top Headlines

1 Gold rush for Canada after 50-year wait
After flopping in 1998, Team Canada is hungry for gold in Salt Lake City, Utah. Led by Joe Sakic and Jarome Iginla, each of whom scores twice in the clinching victory over the U.S., Canada captures the gold medal for the first time in 50 years. The deciding factor might be the 'Lucky Loonie' buried under the playing surface.

2 Kings scouts killed in terrorist attacks
Los Angeles Kings pro scouts Garnet 'Ace' Bailey and Mark Bavis are casualties of the Sept. 11, 2001, terrorist attack on New York as their United Airlines flight 175 is commandeered and crashed into one of the World Trade Center towers. Bailey, 53, won a Stanley Cup during a 10-year NHL career.

3 Jagr trade starts Dark Age in Pittsburgh
Even after Mario Lemieux's comeback season, the Penguins remain in dire financial straits. With key contributors Martin Straka, Alex Kovalev and Robert Lang hitting free agency, the Pens know they must do something drastic to retain them. The solution: trading superstar Jaromir Jagr, rumored to be disgruntled and struggling to share the spotlight with Mario, though he says he wants to help save the team. On July 11, 2001, Pittsburgh ships Jagr and Frantisek Kucera to Washington for Kris Beech, Ross Lupaschuk, Michal Sivek and future considerations. The trade ends up among the most lopsided in league history, as the Penguins' package of prospects doesn't pan out. They tank in the standings.

>2002-03 MONEY MATTERS

MONEY MATTERS

↑ A GOAL-SCORER'S GLOVES
Richard Zednik uses these mitts to lead the
Montreal Canadiens with a career-high 31
goals for an offense-challenged club, but
his Habs still fail to make the playoffs.

Newsmakers & Top Headlines

1 Bankruptcy plagues multiple NHL franchises
Several teams find themselves knocking on financial
death's door. One is the Ottawa Senators, who, despite
enjoying a stellar season, are so strapped for cash that
they can't pay their players at one point. They file for
bankruptcy Jan. 9, 2003. The NHL bails them out tem-
porarily before Eugene Melnyk swoops in to buy them
in the summer. Also struggling to make ends meet: the
Buffalo Sabres, who file for bankruptcy protection. The
Pittsburgh Penguins continue to unload stars, such as
Alex Kovalev, to avoid declaring bankruptcy again.

2 Death of Columbus fan prompts change
The death of 13-year-old Columbus fan Brittanie
Cecil during the 2001-02 season spurs the NHL to

implement mandatory netting at either end of the
rink in every arena to start 2002-03. The white mesh,
which protects spectators from stray pucks, is met with
mixed reviews and evolves into black mesh at most
NHL facilities. Cecil died two days after getting hit in
the temple off an Espen Knutsen shot.

3 Burns finally wins the big one
Coaching some highly competitive Montreal and
Toronto teams got Pat Burns close to glory, but he
finally achieves the Stanley Cup dream in 2003 with
the New Jersey Devils, who outlast the Mighty Ducks
of Anaheim in seven games. He only coaches one more
season before he begins a lengthy battle with cancer
that will claim his life at 58 in 2010.

FACTS & STATS
from 2002-03

Cup Winner
New Jersey Devils

Leading Scorers
1. Peter Forsberg, Col, 106 pts
2. Markus Naslund, Van, 104 pts
3. Joe Thornton, Bos, 101 pts
4. Milan Hejduk, Col, 98 points
5. Todd Bertuzzi, Van, 97 points
6. Pavol Demitra, StL, 93 points
7. Glen Murray, Bos, 92 points
8. Mario Lemieux, Pit, 91 points
9. Dany Heatley, Atl, 89 points
10. Ziggy Palffy, LA, 85 points

Rule Changes
Hurry-up faceoff and line-change
rules are implemented.

Significant Records
Fastest two goals from start of
game: Mike Knuble, Boston (0:27)

First Draft Pick, 2003
Marc-Andre Fleury, G, Pittsburgh

HHOF Inductees
Pat LaFontaine
↓ Grant Fuhr

Nickname of the Year
Pavel 'The Russian Rocket' Bure

Worth Noting
Jean-Sebastien Giguere wins the
Conn Smythe Trophy in a losing
effort – the first to do so since
Ron Hextall in 1987 – after posting a 1.62 goals-against average,
.945 save percentage and five
shutouts in 21 games. His Ducks
fall to the Devils.

FACTS & STATS
from 2003-04

FACTS & STATS
from 2003-04

Cup Winner

Tampa Bay Lightning

Leading Scorers
1. Martin St-Louis, TB, 94 pts
2. Ilya Kovalchuk, Atl, 87 points
3. Joe Sakic, Col, 87 points
4. Markus Naslund, Van, 84 pts
5. Marian Hossa, Ott, 82 points
6. Patrik Elias, NJ, 81 points
7. Cory Stillman, TB, 80 points
8. Daniel Alfredsson, Ott, 80 pts
9. Robert Lang, Wsh/Det, 79 pts
10. Brad Richards, TB, 79 points
11. Alex Tanguay, Col, 79 points
12. Mats Sundin, Tor, 75 points
13. Milan Hejduk, Col, 75 points
14. Mark Recchi, Phi, 75 points
15. J. Jagr, Wsh/NYR, 74 points

First Draft Pick, 2004
Alex Ovechkin, LW, Washington

HHOF Inductees
Paul Coffey
Larry Murphy
↓ Raymond Bourque

Nickname of the Year
Olaf 'Godzilla' Kolzig

Worth Noting
Ilya Kovalchuk, Jarome Iginla and Rick Nash share the Rocket Richard Trophy. Each scores 41 goals, the lowest league-leading total in a full season since Gordie Howe scored 38 in 1962-63. In lockout-shortened 1994-95, leader Peter Bondra had 34 goals…Mark Messier plays his final NHL game. His 1,756 games are 11 behind Howe for the league's all-time lead.

→ **BEAT THE CHILL**
Jose Theodore dons this toque over his helmet during the first Heritage Classic between his Montreal Canadiens and the Oilers in Edmonton. He makes 34 stops in the Habs' 4-3 win.

Newsmakers & Top Headlines

1 Danton arrested in murder-for-hire plot
In April 2004, St. Louis' Mike Danton is arrested and charged with conspiracy to commit murder. His suspected target: agent David Frost. Danton pleads guilty to attempting to hire a hitman to murder Frost and is sentenced to seven-and-a-half years in prison. Both Danton and Frost later deny Frost was the actual target; Danton later states his father, Steve Jefferson, was the real target. He goes on to serve 62 months.

2 Bertuzzi's attack ends Moore's career
On March 8, 2004, Canucks superstar Todd Bertuzzi stalks Colorado's Steve Moore, anxious to avenge a controversial hit Moore delivered to Vancouver captain Markus Naslund Feb. 16. Bertuzzi attacks Moore with a sucker punch from behind and crashes to the ice on top of him. Moore, 25, sustains a concussion and multiple fractured vertebrae. He never plays again. The NHL suspends Bertuzzi indefinitely; he misses the rest of the season and playoffs.

3 Snyder killed, Heatley injured in car crash
On Sept. 29, 2003, Atlanta winger Dany Heatley loses control of his Ferrari while driving with teammate Dan Snyder. The car strikes a wall and ejects Snyder. Snyder sustains severe head trauma and dies in hospital six days. later. Heatley sustains multiple injuries, but survives. He pleads guilty to second-degree vehicular homicide. He admits he drank alcohol before the crash, but his blood alcohol content was below the legal limit.

>2004-05

THE LOST SEASON

↑ **STUPID SABBATICAL**
The NHL's dumbest day gets the appropriate treatment with our black and white cover announcing the cancellation of the 2004-05 season.

Newsmakers & Top Headlines

1 Lockout lasts entire NHL season
The NHL and NHL Players' Association fail to finalize a new collective bargaining agreement by the start of 2004-05. Heated, hostile talks occur between the league, headed by commissioner Gary Bettman, and the union, headed by Bob Goodenow. The main sticking point: the owners demand a salary cap. The players refuse to budge on the issue, rejecting the idea of a cap wholeheartedly and heading overseas by the dozen to find other hockey employment. In the New Year, talks heat up and by February the union counter-offers the owners' proposed cap number. In the end, no deal occurs before Bettman cancels the season Feb. 16, 2005. The NHL is the only North American pro league to lose a full season due to labor issues.

2 AHL experiments with major rule changes
While the NHL awaits a season, it uses the American League as a testing ground for significant rule changes, including: a major crackdown on hooking, holding and all obstruction-related infractions; deploying no-touch icing; and using shootouts to decide regular season games tied after five minutes of overtime.

3 Zholtok dies after collapsing during game
Still wanting to play during the NHL lockout, Nashville Predators center Sergei Zholtok returns to his native Lativa. On Nov. 3, 2004, while playing in Belarus, he excuses himself mid-game. He heads to the dressing room, collapses and dies. The autopsy reveals heart failure as the cause of death.

FACTS & STATS
from 2004-05

Cup Winner
None; season cancelled

60 Moments
that changed the game
No. 2: An entire season of hockey is lost when the NHL locks out its players due to a labor dispute.
No. 28: Detroit left winger Brendan Shanahan holds a two-day think tank of hockey minds to discuss recommendations to improve the game.

First Draft Pick, 2005
Sidney Crosby, C, Pittsburgh

HHOF Inductees
Valeri Kharlamov
↓Cam Neely

Nickname of the Year
'Lucky' Luc Robitaille

Worth Noting
During the lockout, NHLers still want to play, so some take their talents to Europe. A total of 388 players join leagues across the big pond, some leading their new teams to championships… Niklas Hagman, Rick Nash and Joe Thornton lead Swiss club HC Davos to the league title… Daniel Alfredsson, P.J. Axelsson, Sami Salo, Samuel Pahlsson and Christian Backman help bring the Swedish League title to Frolunda…Canadian Governor General Adrienne Clarkson proposes awarding the Stanley Cup to the best women's hockey team, but the idea fizzles.

BY MATT LARKIN

— 2005-PRESENT —

POST-LOCKOUT ERA

THE NEW NHL BROUGHT US SPEED, A SALARY CAP AND SUPERSTARS. TODAY'S GAME IS DANGEROUS AND FLAWED, BUT BEAUTIFUL. TIME TO EMBRACE IT

It's Nov. 10, 2005. Every last person at Mellon Arena stands with baited breath, eyes glued to the bright, white sheet of ice, clean except for one skater and one goalie.

In a blur of black and yellow, the skater takes off toward Montreal's Jose Theodore. We all remember what happens next. He feints, kicking his right foot back in the air, stacks three more dekes on top of dekes, moves to his backhand and...POP! Off flies the water bottle at impossible speed as the puck bulges the twine.

It was rookie Sidney Crosby's first shootout winner. It was fast, furious and spectacular. And, to me, it signalled everything that was the 'New NHL.' There was no turning back.

In a year, hockey went from free-market spending to salary cap. From clutch-and-grab to unleashed offense and power plays galore. From standard definition TV to bright, brilliant HD. From ties to shootouts.

This wasn't your granddaddy's NHL, nor was it even your daddy's. And the arrival of Crosby and Alex Ovechkin, this generation's answer to Wayne Gretzky and Mario Lemieux, represented not just the sport's modern incarnation, but a paradigm shift in the way we think. Gretzky stood for incredible smarts and timing. Lemieux was unbelievable grace and finesse. But 'Sid the Kid' and 'Alexander the GR8' mixed those skills with the speed and power of a fancy sportscar.

These new stars are tailored to what we want. We live in the world of now. We slam our keyboards in frustration if our web browsers take more than three seconds to load. We want — no, we *need* — Internet access on our phones, in our cars, on airplanes, for cryin' out loud. We announce our statuses via social media. We know exactly where each other is, who just got engaged, who drank too much green beer on St. Patrick's Day. And we want our mega-hyped stars to deliver immediately, just like Crosby, Ovechkin, Steven Stamkos and Patrick Kane did as teenagers in the post-lockout era.

The unstoppable freight train that was the New NHL showed us unprecedented athleticism and league parity. And it also left some old souls in

its wake. We said goodbye to the goon, the Stu Grimson or Troy Crowder, the guy who had the worst hands on the team and made his living solely by clenching those hands into fists and pummelling anyone who stood in his way. The game was simply too fast and employing him meant putting your team at a disadvantage with an archaic strategy. If you want to fight in today's NHL, you better be able to skate your tail off, too.

Players also lost their ability to keep their heads down and hide from media. This is the era of camera phones and YouTube and the 24-hour news cycle. Every John Tortorella quote is an endlessly replayed sound bite. We know all about Mike Fisher and Carrie Underwood, Mike Comrie and Hilary Duff and Sean Avery's sloppy seconds. Every dirty hit goes viral. We don't gather around the water cooler to discuss Raffi Torres; we gather around the computer and watch the hit over and over, playing armchair Brendan Shanahan. Under a bigger microscope than ever, players feel greater pressure to succeed than ever. Is it any wonder no Canadian team has won a Stanley Cup in 20 years? Media and fans obsess over them, smother them, track their trade deadline activity and July free agent frenzy around the clock. The New NHL and its coverage operate just as frenetically off the ice as on it.

And like that aforementioned sportscar, sometimes it feels the game itself is a bit too fast, a bit out of control, a bit dangerous. Hockey was already the fastest game on Earth and new rules, not to mention human evolution, make it faster still. Bodychecks aren't just collisions that shake the momentum of a game anymore. They're explosions of unstoppable-force-meets-immovable-object, train wrecks that, sadly, produce casualties at an alarming rate. Concussions and their terrifying after-effects are at the forefront of hockey's greatest debates today.

To acknowledge the darker side of the modern game is not to condemn it, but simply to understand it. We can't hide from the fact head injuries are a serious problem to address. We must face the fact fighting is no longer a staple of the sport and may be gone from the game in a decade or two. And we should accept it's only a matter of time before someone comes

↑ MOMENTUM
Patrick Kane, Duncan Keith and Jonathan Toews helped build the momentum that led to a Stanley Cup victory in 2010 and again in 2013.

out of the closet as the league's first openly gay player.

Accepting change doesn't mean disrespecting the past and being a bleeding heart. There was a place for fisticuffs in the sport for a long time, just as helmetless skaters and maskless goalies were once kosher. But "because that's how it's always been" doesn't fly as an argument. Guess what? The world was once perceived as flat and women couldn't always vote. Our thinking evolved and will continue to evolve.

Those who don't get with the times, who believe the game has gone soft, who turn their backs on the New NHL, miss out on a whole lot of good. The game has never been played at a higher pace and skill level and people are noticing. Don't believe me? Look no further than HBO's amazing *24/7* series, the NHL's record-breaking revenue of $3.3 billion in 2011-12 and rising TV ratings. The sport of hockey is in good hands, even if the labor politics behind it aren't, and should only keep improving.

The New NHL is here to stay, at least until the 'New New NHL' comes along. The more we embrace the game for its strengths and weaknesses, the better we can make it.

Bob Dylan put it best: "You better start swimmin' or you'll sink like a stone, for the times, they are a-changin'" THN

↑ INSTANT RETURNS
Players face immense pressure today. Elite prospects are expected to be impact performers before their teen years are up, just ask Steven Stamkos.

> 2005-06 NEW AND IMPROVED

FACTS & STATS
from 2005-06

Cup Winner
Carolina Hurricanes

Leading Scorers
1. Joe Thornton Bos/SJ, 125 pts
2. Jaromir Jagr, NYR, 123 points
3. Alex Ovechkin, Wsh, 106 pts

Rule Changes
Tag-up offside rule reinstituted. Goalies not permitted to play puck outside designated trapezoid-shaped area behind net. A team that ices the puck is not permitted to make player substitutions prior to the faceoff. The size of goaltender equipment is reduced. If a game remains tied after five minutes of overtime, the winner will be decided by a shootout.

60 Moments
that changed the game
No. 7: Salary cap instituted, assuring the NHL and teams a more cost-certain structure. No. 22: Center red line removed (and two-line pass abolished) in an effort to create more offense. No. 34: Shootout added to decide games tied after five minutes of 4-on-4 overtime.

First Draft Pick, 2006
Erik Johnson, D, St. Louis

HHOF Inductees
Dick Duff
↓ Patrick Roy

Nickname of the Year
Ed 'The Eagle' Belfour

↑ **FORECAST FOR FLEURY**
Marc-Andre Fleury, 2003's No. 1 overall draft pick, sticks as Pittsburgh's full-time starter in 2005-06, using a festive yellow trapper and blocker. He becomes an integral part of a Cup-winning foundation.

← **STACKED IN A SHOOTOUT**
Breakaways don't faze Fleury, who dons these pads early in his career. His 36 shootout wins are third all-time.

Newsmakers & Top Headlines

1 Lockout ends, gives birth to 'New NHL'
After the 2004-05 season is cancelled, The NHL and NHL Players' Association tentatively reach a new collective bargaining agreement July 13, 2005. The deal is ratified July 21 with 87 percent of players voting in favor. The new CBA includes a $39-million salary cap and guaranteed player contracts. The 2005-06 season starts on time and with several new rules implemented, including an obstruction crackdown and the introduction of shootouts. League-wide scoring jumps above six goals per game for the first time since 1995-96.

2 Crosby, Ovechkin take league by storm
Alex Ovechkin and Sidney Crosby are drafted first overall in consecutive years, but debut at the same time because of the league's year-long hiatus. Ovechkin is a Capital and Crosby becomes a Penguin after the 2005 first overall pick is awarded via lottery. They waste no time becoming the sport's premier draw, each eclipsing the 100-point barrier as rookies. Ovechkin edges Crosby for the Calder Trophy as the league's top freshman.

3 Thornton trade rocks power balance
On Nov. 30, 2005, the Bruins deal Joe Thornton to the Sharks for Brad Stuart, Marco Sturm and Wayne Primeau. Thornton goes on a tear upon arriving in California, recording 92 points in his final 58 games, winning the league's scoring crown and capturing the Hart Trophy as league MVP. Thornton goes on to become San Jose's all-time assists leader.

THE KID IS KING

FACTS & STATS
from 2006-07

Cup Winner

Anaheim Ducks

Leading Scorers
1. Sidney Crosby, Pit, 120 points
2. Joe Thornton, SJ, 114 points
3. V. Lecavalier, TB, 108 points
4. Dany Heatley, Ott, 105 points
5. Martin St-Louis, TB, 102 pts

Significant Records
Longest consecutive point streak by a rookie: Paul Stastny, Colorado (20 games, 29 points). Most minutes played by a goaltender, one season: Martin Brodeur, New Jersey (4,697.) Most wins by a goaltender, one season: Martin Brodeur, New Jersey (48).

First Draft Pick, 2007
Patrick Kane, RW, Chicago

HHOF Inductees
Ron Francis
Al MacInnis
Scott Stevens
↓ Mark Messier

Nickname of the Year
Nikolai 'The Bulin Wall' Khabibulin

Worth Noting
For the first time in the history of the NHL, neither of the previous season's Stanley Cup finalists qualifies for the post-season. The Edmonton Oilers and the defending Cup-champion Carolina Hurricanes finish outside the top eight in their conferences.

↑ RING BLING
This collection of Cup rings includes Anaheim's in 2007. GM Brian Burke ensures Ducks staffers get theirs, too.

← LONG TIME COMING
In his second stint with Anaheim, Teemu Selanne finally captures that elusive Stanley Cup after a season in which the 36-year-old scores 48 goals.

Newsmakers & Top Headlines

1 Crosby becomes youngest NHL scoring champ
Sidney Crosby's legend rapidly grows in his second NHL season. Notching 120 points as a 19-year-old, he becomes the youngest player ever to win a league scoring title. Crosby also helps the Pittsburgh Penguins reach the playoffs for the first time since 2000-01.

2 Pronger, Selanne get rings as Ducks win first Cup
The Anaheim Ducks capture their first Stanley Cup in franchise history thanks to a unique team personality and some aggressive off-season moves. Under coach Randy Carlyle and GM Brian Burke, both of whom champion team toughness, the Ducks lead the league in fighting majors by a huge margin. The NHL's meanest team also becomes the most difficult to penetrate as Burke creates a superstar 'D' pairing when he signs Scott Niedermayer away from New Jersey and acquires Chris Pronger from Edmonton. Ageless wonder Teemu Selanne, playoff specialist goalie Jean-Sebastien Giguere and rising stars Corey Perry and Ryan Getzlaf lead a Ducks team that loses just five times through the 2007 playoffs, ousting Ottawa in five games in the final.

3 Flyers take stunning plunge in standings
Following a 101-point campaign in 2005-06, the Flyers endure their worst season in their 40-year history, setting franchise full-season lows for losses (60 including overtime and shootouts) and points (56). Known for being one of the scariest teams to face on the road, the Flyers win just 10 of 41 home games.

2007-08
CAT HAS NINE LIVES

← **NICK KNOCKS SOCKS OFF**
Nicklas Lidstrom wears these during the regular season and playoffs as his Red Wings rack up the Presidents' Trophy and the Stanley Cup in dominant fashion. For his play, Lidstrom wins his sixth Norris Trophy.

Newsmakers & Top Headlines

1 Zednik survives gruesome throat injury
Florida Panthers winger Richard Zednik suffers a terrifying throat injury calling to mind goaltender Clint Malarchuk's misfortune almost two decades earlier. During a Feb. 10 game against Buffalo, Zednik's teammate, Olli Jokinen, is upended by Clarke MacArthur. As Jokinen lands head-first, his skate kicks up and slashes Zednik's throat, almost completely severing his carotid artery. Zednik rushes off the ice and is loaded into an ambulance. Doctors stop the bleeding and perform emergency surgery in time to repair Zednik's artery. He suffers no brain damage and doctors go on to say his life was never in jeopardy despite the injury's gruesome nature. He returns to game action with Florida the following season.

2 'Ovie' soars to new heights
'Alexander the GR8' indeed. Alex Ovechkin's 65 goals are the most by any player since 1995-96. His 112 points win him the Art Ross Trophy and he captures the Hart Trophy as league MVP. He leads a resurgent Capitals team to seven straight wins to close out the regular season and squeak into the playoffs.

3 Winter Classic debuts
The NHL tested the waters with the 2003 Heritage Classic, but the annual outdoor game as we know it debuts as the Winter Classic Jan. 1, 2008 when Buffalo hosts Pittsburgh at Ralph Wilson stadium. League poster boy Sidney Crosby — who else? — wins the game for the Pens, beating Ryan Miller in a shootout.

FACTS & STATS
from 2007-08

Cup Winner
Detroit Red Wings

Leading Scorers
1. Alex Ovechkin, Wsh, 112 pts
2. Evgeni Malkin, Pit, 106 points
3. Jarome Iginla, Cgy, 98 points
4. Pavel Datsyuk, Det, 97 points
5. Joe Thornton, SJ, 96 points
6. Vincent Lecavalier, TB, 92 points
7. Jason Spezza, Ott, 92 points
8. Henrik Zetterberg, Det, 92 pts
9. Daniel Alfredsson, Ott, 89 pts
10. Ilya Kovalchuk, Atl, 87 points

Significant Records
Most goals by a left winger, one season: Alex Ovechkin, Washington (65).
Best shootout save percentage, one season: Mathieu Garon, Edmonton (.938).

First Draft Pick, 2008
Steven Stamkos, C, Tampa Bay

HHOF Inductees
Glenn Anderson
↓ Igor Larionov

Nickname of the Year
Johan 'The Mule' Franzen

Worth Noting
After an astounding career spanning 16 seasons with four teams, Dominik Hasek retires on top, as his Red Wings capture their fourth Cup in 11 seasons. Hasek finishes with 389 wins, 81 shutouts, six Vezina Trophies and two Hart Trophies. THN names him the No. 5 goalie of all-time.

THREE MINUTES OF GOALIE GLORY

JAN. 8, 2008 BY COREY ERDMAN

"Back then I thought, 'Well, there'll be other days.' I didn't realize that that was the only day." — 'Moonlight' Graham in 1989 film Field of Dreams

Meet Robbie Irons, the 'Moonlight' Graham of the NHL. Kevin Costner's epic *Field of Dreams* immortalized ballplayer Archibald 'Moonlight' Graham, who appeared in one inning of Major League Baseball play. Irons, similarly, has the dubious honor — along with former Blackhawks netminder Christian Soucy — of the shortest NHL career in history: Three minutes.

He takes this moment of fame light-heartedly and, these days, describes himself as "the same old Robbie Irons."

While playing Jr. B hockey in the Toronto suburb of Etobicoke, Irons was noticed by New York Rangers scout Louis Passador. In 1967, Irons led the New York-sponsored Kitchener Rangers to a first-place finish.

A broken arm from an off-season baseball game prevented Irons from reporting to the Omaha Knights of the International League. But an agreement was made with Fort Wayne, a city he would become a legend in, and Irons began his professional career as a Komet.

"It was what you'd call a 'bus league,' but that meant you'd have some fierce rivalries," Irons said. "All the teams were in the Midwest states and some of the teams, like Toledo, Columbus, Dayton…it was as if they were playing against their neighbor every night. You learned a lot, though, guys like Lenny Thornson (who played 12 seasons with the Komets) taught me a great deal. You learned how to compete, most of all."

After appearing in 43 games and leading the Komets to the post-season in his first full pro season in 1967-68, Irons was traded to the St. Louis Blues and sent to the Kansas City Blues of the American League.

The Blues were stocking up on goaltending, despite having two legends in Glenn Hall and Jacques Plante. It was a plan only the winningest coach of all-time could have drawn up.

"One day I got a call from Scotty Bowman and he said I was coming up with the big club so they could have a look at me and after two months they'd send me back to Kansas City," Irons said.

He was now standing in the shadows of legends.

"I couldn't believe it," he said. "One week I'm at (the IHL) level and the next thing you know, I'm sitting across the room from Jacques Plante and Glenn Hall, two of my heroes."

Bowman employed an innovative three-goalie system that allowed his two Hall of Fame goaltenders to be fully rested.

On Nov. 13, 1968, Robbie Irons finally got his chance.

"I remember Plante had taken the late plane from Boston, where we were for the previous game," said Terry Crisp, Irons' old teammate and a former NHL coach. After a Glenn Hall misconduct penalty, Irons skated onto NHL ice for the first and only time.

↑ **A BRIEF CUP OF COFFEE**
Blink and you miss the NHL career of International League all-star goaltender Robbie Irons. It lasts just 180 seconds.

"I think he bumped the ref or something," Irons remarked of his often quirky goalie partner. "Glenn was probably upset about the long trip or the curved sticks. Scotty told me to go in, but he was creating a delay. I thought I was all set to finish (the game) off. This was my shot and I'd either make it or I wouldn't."

What Irons didn't know was that Plante had arrived and the delay Bowman was creating was to give him time to suit up.

After three minutes and a whistle, Plante emerged from the dressing room to replace Irons — never to be seen in the NHL again.

"It was an experience I wish had gone on a lot longer, but one I will never forget," Irons said.

Added Crisp: "He was the victim of a snipe hunt. The same thing happened to Teddy Ouimet (whose lone 60 minutes of NHL play also came with St. Louis the same season)."

Following his brief NHL moment, Irons returned to Fort Wayne and won the Turner Cup in 1974, as well as a spot on the IHL all-star team during his final campaign in 1980-81. "To be an all-star in your final season is phenomenal," said Steve Janaszak, Irons' goalie partner during his final season.

Janaszak knows about being unheralded, having been stuck behind Chico Resch, Don Beaupre and Gilles Meloche at various points in his career — and of course, Jim Craig during Team USA's 'Miracle on Ice' run in 1980.

"You sit there and scratch your head…you have a highly regarded goaltender, great discipline, loved the game and you wonder, how does he keep doing it every day? Just a phenomenal human being," Janaszak said.

Irons didn't walk away from the NHL without learning a thing or two. During his stint with the Blues, he provided commentary alongside Dan Kelly for two games in 1968. Today, Irons is doing the same for the Fort Wayne Komets.

His NHL career was fleeting, but to the people of Fort Wayne, he is not only a hero, but one of them — the same old Robbie Irons. **THN**

DEVIL OF A GOALIE

FACTS & STATS
from 2008-09

Cup Winner
Pittsburgh Penguins

Leading Scorers
1. Evgeni Malkin, Pit, 113 points
2. Alex Ovechkin, Wsh, 110 pts
3. Sidney Crosby, Pit, 103 pts
4. Pavel Datsyuk, Det, 97 points
5. Zach Parise, NJ, 94 points
6. Ryan Getzlaf, Ana, 91 points
7. Ilya Kovalchuk, Atl, 91 points
8. Jarome Iginla, Cgy, 89 points
9. N. Backstrom, Wsh, 88 pts
10. Marc Savard, Bos, 88 points

First Draft Pick, 2009
John Tavares, C, NY Islanders

HHOF Inductees
Brett Hull
Brian Leetch
Steve Yzerman
↓ Luc Robitaille

Nickname of the Year
Sidney 'Sid the Kid' Crosby

Worth Noting
The Cup final features a rematch of the previous season for the first time since 1984…The Columbus Blue Jackets reach their first-ever playoffs…In a Nov. 3 game, the Islanders' Chris Campoli scores twice in one overtime. He beats Columbus goaltender Fredrik Norrena, but the puck goes through the net undetected. He subsequently pots the winner…Dallas' Sean Avery is suspended six games for criticizing and demeaning Dion Phaneuf's girlfriend, actress Elisha Cuthbert, who is Avery's ex.

↑ BIG IMPACT
These shoulder pads provide enough protection for Dustin Byfuglien's 6-foot-5, 265-pound frame. 'Big Buff' and the upstart Blackhawks get to the final four, then make it all the way the following season, capturing their first Cup since 1961.

Newsmakers & Top Headlines

1 Brodeur passes Roy for all-time wins mark
"Thank-you Mar-ty!" chants echo through New Jersey's Prudential Center March 17, 2009 as the final seconds of Martin Brodeur's 552nd NHL victory tick away against the Chicago Blackhawks. The 3-2 win breaks a deadlock with Patrick Roy, placing Brodeur alone atop the league's all-time wins list among goaltenders. Next in Brodeur's crosshairs: Terry Sawchuk's shutout record.

2 Sanderson dies after on-ice fight
The fight debates rage to a boil when on-ice fisticuffs claim a life. On Dec. 14, 2008 during a fight, Ontario senior AAA player Don Sanderson's helmet falls off. He and his opponent crash to the ice and Sanderson's unprotected head bears the brunt of the impact. He loses consciousness. He briefly comes to, then slips into a coma. He dies Jan. 2, 2009.

3 Crosby hoists first Cup as Penguins avenge loss
A year after falling to the Detroit Red Wings in the Stanley Cup final, the Pittsburgh Penguins get their revenge, defeating the Red Wings in seven games. Marc-Andre Fleury robs Nicklas Lidstrom with a legendary save in the dying seconds of Game 7 as Pittsburgh holds on to win 2-1 in Detroit. At 21, Sidney Crosby becomes the youngest captain ever to hoist the Stanley Cup. Four seasons into his career, 'Sid the Kid' already has a Cup, scoring title, Hart Trophy and Ted Lindsay Award to his name.

HOCKEY FAN A CUP PARTY CRASHER

SEPT. 7, 2009 BY JOHN GRIGG

When the Pittsburgh Penguins bested the Detroit Red Wings in June to win the franchise's third Stanley Cup, an on-ice scene the likes of which has rarely been seen erupted. As usual, players celebrated with family, friends and team officials, but the ice was flooded with media members as well, making it an especially hectic setting.

"I'll tell you, it was an unbelievable night," said Ryan Kraft, a 32-year-old diehard Penguins fan.

Unbelievable, but not only because Kraft was there to watch his favorite team win the Cup in dramatic, seven-game fashion, but because he managed to fake his way onto the ice and into the post-game dressing room party. That's right. A regular Joe — he's a water-treatment company salesman — wearing a "Kraft" jersey and a Penguins hat joined in all the fun.

It took a little ingenuity and some courage, both the usual and the liquid kind, Kraft admitted. But it was quite simple. "I got lucky," he said. "I was lucky to be in the right place at the right time."

The right place was near ice level where the Zamboni doors are located, the right time was when non-credentialed friends and family were being escorted onto the ice by arena security staff.

"After I saw the first player skate over and tell security to let someone on the ice, it popped into my head that maybe I can get lucky," Kraft said.

He positioned himself where he thought other friends and family might be. Then he waited. About 10 minutes later, Penguins defenseman Phillipe Boucher skated over, talked to security and pointed right at Kraft, or rather the person right in front of him. And when that guy raised his hand, so did Kraft.

"I thought 'Holy s---, this is my opportunity,'" he said.

The two made their way to ice level where the security guard let them on. Boucher's guest walked straight for the blueliner and gave him a hug, while Kraft just went right around them and waded into the throng.

There are photos of Kraft with Marc-Andre Fleury, Ruslan Fedotenko, Brooks Orpik, and others, like laying prone to kiss center ice and within hooking distance of Sidney Crosby as he skated with the Cup.

But Kraft's biggest thrill came when he joined in the dressing room delirium.

Neil Diamond's *Sweet Caroline* was playing when he entered and a packed house was singing along — Good times never seemed so good/SO GOOD!/SO GOOD!

"Tyler Kennedy picked me up and spun me and I was slapping him on the back," Kraft said. "People were just drenched in champagne. It was amazing."

Kraft's amazing night came full circle when he again ran into Boucher, this time in the Penguins dressing room. Just before his camera died, Kraft got a picture of himself with the Cup, then he was able to hand it off to the player who

↑ **HANGING WITH MARIO, STANLEY AND FRIENDS**
Hockey fan Ryan Kraft says Mario Lemieux was the only one who gave an inkling he knew the fan was hanging out in an area he shouldn't be.

had inadvertently made his dreams come true. "Boucher is now my hero," Kraft said.

From the time he made it on to the ice until he left the dressing room, Kraft's dream Cup party lasted about 90 minutes. And all that time, he never really felt like anyone knew he wasn't supposed to be there — except, fittingly, the 'Magnificent One' himself.

"One was definitely Mario Lemieux," Kraft said of his childhood hero and current Pens owner, when asked if anyone did a double-take. "He just gave me a sly look, like, 'You're not supposed to be down here, are you?'"

Kraft knows not everyone is happy for him. When his story broke, he took a lot of heat from detractors who felt he was nothing more than an interloper — a criminal, even. But he doesn't see it as such and insists he didn't mean any harm.

"I think what I did was wonderful, even though it's not necessarily allowed," he said. "It kind of gives it an old-school, authentic feel, where fan

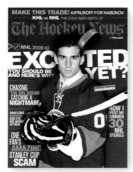

and player interaction used to be a daily part of the sport. You could meet your heroes, but now…it's impossible to talk to your idols. And I think that's a shame.

"I hope I didn't get anyone in trouble. The security was perfect. I just got lucky."

Lucky? He should buy a lottery ticket.

(Editor's Note: THN editor Brian Costello noticed a player wearing the 'Kraft' Penguins jersey on the ice during the post-game celebration. Assuming it was long-forgotten Penguin center Milan Kraft — who last played with Pittsburgh in the 2003-04 season — Costello went over to talk with him, but was interrupted when an interview with Boucher presented itself instead.) **THN**

>2009-10

THE GOLDEN GOAL

↑ CANADA'S MODERN-DAY SUMMIT

When Sidney Crosby fires this puck past Team USA's Ryan Miller to win Canada gold at the 2010 Olympics, he gives a new hockey generation a Paul Henderson moment to call its own.

Newsmakers & Top Headlines

1 Crosby goal clinches Olympic gold for Canada
Following a terrible showing at the 2006 Olympics, Canada reclaims hockey's international crown on its own soil in Vancouver. The star-studded roster faces off against Team USA in the gold-medal game. Canada stakes a 2-0 lead before Ryan Kesler makes it 2-1 late in the second and Zach Parise ties the game with 24 seconds left in the third, forcing overtime. Then, Sidney Crosby adds another career highlight when he beats Ryan Miller to win the game and clinch gold for Canada seven-and-a-half minutes into overtime.

2 Chicago ends 49-year Stanley Cup drought
The sport's longest championship drought ends as the Chicago Blackhawks capture their first Stanley Cup since 1961 and just their fourth since entering the league in 1926. Patrick Kane clinches the final over the Philadelphia Flyers in overtime of Game 6 when his bad-angle shot eludes Michael Leighton.

3 Coyotes file for bankruptcy
The financially fledgling Phoenix Coyotes file for Chapter 11 bankruptcy in May 2009. The NHL reveals it assumed ownership of the team in February 2009 and relieves owner Jerry Moyes of all his control of the club. Canadian businessman Jim Balsillie, co-CEO of Research in Motion, tables a $212.5-million bid for the team with hopes of moving it to Hamilton or Kitchener, Ont., but Moyes sells to the NHL for $140 million, ensuring the team stays in Glendale, Ariz.

Cup Winner
Chicago Blackhawks

Leading Scorers
1. Henrik Sedin, Van, 112 pts
2. Sidney Crosby, Pit, 109 pts
3. Alex Ovechkin, Wsh, 109 pts
4. N. Backstrom, Wsh, 101 pts
5. Steven Stamkos, TB, 95 pts
6. Martin St-Louis, TB, 94 pts
7. Brad Richards, Dal, 91 points
8. Joe Thornton, SJ, 89 points
9. Patrick Kane, Chi, 88 points
10. Marian Gaborik, NYR, 86 pts

Significant Records
Most shootout shots against, one season: Ilya Bryzgalov, Phoenix (62).

First Draft Pick, 2010
Taylor Hall, LW, Edmonton

HHOF Inductees
Dino Ciccarelli
Angela James
↓ Cammi Granato

Nickname of the Year
Jonathan 'Captain Serious' Toews

Worth Noting
Boston's Tuukka Rask leads the NHL in GAA (1.97) and SP (.931) as a rookie, yet finishes fourth in Calder Trophy voting. Buffalo defenseman Tyler Myers takes the award...Boston becomes the third team ever to lose a playoff series after winning the first three games, falling to Philadelphia in seven.

THE WORST TEAM EVER

JAN. 25, 2010 BY BRIAN COSTELLO

↑ **GLUTTON FOR PUNISHMENT**
John Torchetti was a skater on the 1984-85 Plattsburgh Pioneers,
a Quebec League team outscored 185-56 in 17 merciless games.

They were quite literally the worst team in the history of organized hockey. They were disorganized, they were dysfunctional. Before they even won a single game in the Quebec League in 1984-85, they were taken out behind the barn and shot.

It's the 25-year anniversary of the miserable Plattsburgh Pioneers, but you won't find anyone raising a glass to make a toast. Not the fans, not the New York state community, not the players, not the team founder.

"That was a bad situation, I'd rather not talk about it," said team coach-GM-owner Denis Methot, now 65, when asked to reminisce. "I've got nothing to say."

The trailblazing Plattsburgh Pioneers were the QMJHL's first foray into the United States. Dr. Methot, a former university sports science teacher from Trois-Rivieres, Que., saw potential in the city of 35,000, a one-hour drive south of Montreal. He helped finance $500,000 in the project and was sure it would be a hit.

"The problem was, major junior wasn't as big in the States," said Chicago Blackhawks assistant John Torchetti, who played eight games with that miserable Plattsburgh team. "Hockey fans in that area followed the Plattsburgh Cardinals (Div. III NCAA). There wasn't much interest in the Pioneers."

The biggest flaw with the Pioneers was their mandate to ice a team made up exclusively of U.S.-born players. Methot recruited prep schools in the eight Northeastern states and jury-rigged a roster of 17 willing young Americans. It was a disaster waiting to happen.

The high point was Game 1 at home. A 7-6 overtime loss to Hull was witnessed by 1,500 fans. It was the only point in the standings the Pioneers would earn when the plug was pulled after 17 games. Before the team was two weeks old, it had lost 13-0 to Laval, 15-2 to St-Jean and 15-2 to Verdun.

"Things were completely dysfunctional," Torchetti said. "It was a horrible environment to be a part of."

Methot was coach-GM-owner, also handled the recruiting and did much of the marketing and administrative duties as well. Plagued with financial troubles and owing money to the city for rental agreements, he hoped solid attendance figures would allow the team to grow organically.

After seven games, the QMJHL's board gave Methot a list of things to shore up and a one-week deadline. "The problem is the structure of his organization," QMJHL president Gus Morissette told The Hockey News in 1984. "He's doing too much himself. He's a one-man show. You can't run practice and look for players at the same time. (We) gave him a week to get a secretary, a coach and some more players."

Methot complained the league wasn't being helpful by offering guidance. "The league could have given us direction on how to operate," Methot told THN in October of 1984. "It's hard to find a secretary (in Plattsburgh) who speaks and reads French. All communications from the league are in French."

Things continued to spiral downward. Losses of 17-1 to Granby, 11-1 to Hull. Five games were lost by a margin of 73-9.

Average attendance slipped to just 500 after nine home games. Methot was ejected from one game when he sent out the team's backup goalie to serve a penalty given to the starting goaltender.

"I had to leave the team," Torchetti said. "It was a bad situation getting worse. Going there was the first big decision I made in life and my parents let me make it on my own. It was Plattsburgh or go to West Point (U.S. Military Academy) and become a pilot. I gave up my college (playing) eligibility to go there."

The Pioneers soon crashed and burned. An Oct. 27 home game versus St-Jean was postponed when a compressor broke at Plattsburgh's Crete Center. A 9-3 loss in Drummondville the next day was the 17th straight and mercifully final loss when the QMJHL disbanded the team due to financial considerations. The Pioneers were outscored 185-56 in those 17 games. Goalie Frank Currie had a 13.86 GAA and .718 save percentage.

So disgusted was the league, it stripped every Plattsburgh game from the record book and standings. No records realized in games against the Pioneers were recorded. Scoring stats in games against the Pioneers were purged as well. It was as though the team never existed. (The scores and stats you see in this story came from the archives of The Hockey News.)

"I felt so sorry for Mr. Methot, " Torchetti said. "It wasn't his fault. He did everything he could to make it work. He was such a nice person. This whole thing just drained him."

Methot went back to Trois-Rivieres, 12 players went to other teams in major junior, four turned pro in the low minors and six others never played again at this level or higher. Torchetti had the most notable career, playing seven seasons in the low minors.

"I wouldn't say it was all bad," Torchetti said. "I learned about extremes and dealing with the emotional swings of extremes. Being in that situation actually got me thinking like a coach. It got me thinking in a detail-oriented way.

"And I still keep in touch with some guys from that team, like Louis Finocchiaro, Scott Rettew and Ed Considine. We don't talk about Plattsburgh, but we talk. THN

HEAD GAMES

FACTS & STATS
from 2010-11

Cup Winner
Boston Bruins

Leading Scorers
1. Daniel Sedin, Van, 104 points
2. Martin St-Louis, TB, 99 pts
3. Corey Perry, Ana, 98 points
4. Henrik Sedin, Van, 94 points
5. Steven Stamkos, TB, 91 pts
6. Jarome Iginla, Cgy, 86 points
7. Alex Ovechkin, Wsh, 85 pts
8. Teemu Selanne, Ana, 80 pts
9. H. Zetterberg, Det, 80 pts
10. Brad Richards, Dal, 77 points

First Draft Pick, 2011
Ryan Nugent-Hopkins, C, Edmonton

HHOF Inductees
Doug Gilmour
Mark Howe
Joe Nieuwendyk
↓ Ed Belfour

Nickname of the Year
Teemu 'The Finnish Flash' Selanne

Worth Noting
Boston's Mark Recchi becomes the oldest player to score a Stanley Cup final goal at 43…. Carolina's Jeff Skinner, 18, is the youngest All-Star Game participant in league history. He also becomes the youngest to win the Calder Trophy. The league changes its All-Star Game format to a fantasy draft in which selected captains choose players. The first pick is hometown favorite Cam Ward. The last is Toronto sniper Phil Kessel.

← FIT FOR A GIANT
These boots take behemoth, Zdeno Chara, to ultimate hockey glory. Down three games to two to the Canucks, his B's come back to take the Stanley Cup final in seven. Chara is big factor in the Bruins post-season, logging nearly 28 minutes per game against the opposition's top guns while posting a plus-16.

Newsmakers & Top Headlines

1 Crosby's injuries bring concussion debate to fore
Head injuries are already a prominent discussion topic, but they come to the forefront when the game's pre-eminent player loses his season to post-concussion syndrome. During the Jan. 1 Winter Classic, Sidney Crosby sustains a concussion on a hit by Washington's David Steckel. Four days later, he returns to action only to sustain a second concussion on a blow from Tampa's Victor Hedman. With 32 goals and 66 points in 41 games, Crosby is on track for his best year yet, but the second hit results in second-impact syndrome and sidelines No. 87 the rest of the season.

2 Cup final defeat sparks Vancouver riot
A year after hosting the 2010 Winter Olympics, Vancouver soils its reputation following the Canucks' heartbreaking home loss to Boston in Game 7 of the Stanley Cup final. The city erupts into violence as angry fans storm the streets. Hundreds of people are injured, including nine police officers. Fans burn police cars and hundreds are arrested.

3 James, Granato become first female HHOFers
In November 2010, Canada's Angela James and Team USA's Cammi Granato become the Hall of Fame's first female inductees. James was known as "the Wayne Gretzky of women's hockey" and was late in her career by the time women's hockey became an Olympic sport. Granato captained the gold medal-winning American team at the '98 Nagano Games.

PERILOUS FATE OF JAKE DOWELL

MAY 2, 2011 BY KEN CAMPBELL

↑ **THE SPECTER OF UNCERTAINTY**
NHLer Jake Dowell is living with a 50 percent chance he's carrying a gene for the debilitating and deadly Huntington's disease.

MONTREAL, QUE. –

The nasty scar over Jake Dowell's left eye was, like almost all the road maps NHL players wear on their faces, well-earned. It required 40 stitches to close, including the ones under the skin. The gash itself went right down to the skull. He missed three shifts while the medical staff worked to stem the blood flow and reattach the flap of skin.

As the Chicago Blackhawks were chasing a playoff spot in March, Dowell found himself caught up in a battle along the boards with Jarkko Ruutu of Anaheim. Ruutu grabbed Dowell from behind in a bear hug and, as the two players fell forward, Dowell recalls the feeling of powerlessness in the split second prior to him slamming his head against the ice. Ruutu had been holding both his opponent's arms, preventing Dowell from breaking his fall.

For that brief moment in time, Jake Dowell experienced the kind uncertainty, fear and sheer helplessness his father, John, and older brother, Lucas, face almost every day. There are some nights when all 270 pounds of John Dowell falls out of his lift chair and he's as helpless as his son was when he was tackled by Ruutu.

There are just as many days when the voices in Lucas Dowell's head simply won't go away no matter how many doses of medication he takes.

And there are the days when Jake Dowell has what he describes as "pity parties." Sometimes he'll walk around the suburbs of Chicago for two hours with his dog, resenting the fact he was cheated out of normal relationships with his father and brother. Then there are the days when Dowell worries about his own mortality and the fate of his children, should he have any.

As an elite athlete, Dowell often experiences muscle twitches. For Dowell, an uncontrollable and involuntary twitch of the finger or a quadriceps muscle while sitting on the couch could be nothing more than the product of an overworked body. Or it could represent the presence of a rare genetic disease that will rob him of his body and mind before it slowly kills him.

"It used to scare the heck out of me because it would happen all the time," Dowell said. "I would just think to myself, 'I'm doomed.'"

It's an awful lot of weight to carry around for a 26-year-old NHL rookie, one who is finally finding his way in the best league in the world. After graduating from the University of Wisconsin, Dowell slugged it out for three years in the minors. The combination of his perseverance and the Blackhawks' cap constraints finally gave him the chance to fill a role on the fourth line and kill penalties, both of which he has embraced with evangelical zeal.

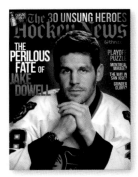

But for the better part of the past decade, Dowell has lived with the specter of Huntington's disease, a genetic disorder in which nerve cells in the brain are irreparably damaged, causing various parts of the brain to deteriorate. Once the disease sets in, a person's abilities to walk, think and reason are slowly stripped away as the body and mind continue to decline. Finally, it gets to the point where the patient is effectively paralyzed and must be fed through a tube. It can last 10 to 20 years before the patient eventually dies, usually of an infection or starvation or sometimes suicide. Some describe it as the worst of Lou Gehrig's, Alzheimer's and Parkinson's.

"No disease is better than the next," Dowell said, "but this one is as bad as it gets."

It has already taken hold of his 55-year-old father, who can no longer speak clearly and relies on 24-hour care, most of it from his wife and Jake's mother, Vicki. The disease almost always begins to manifest itself somewhere between the ages of 35 and 55, but there can also be juvenile-onset Huntington's, which brought on bipolar schizophrenia in his 28-year-old brother and confined the young man to a group home near his parents in Eau Claire, Wisc.

On top of all that, Jake Dowell could be carrying the Huntington's gene around with him right now.

Those whose parents have the disease have a 50 percent chance of developing it themselves, but Dowell has yet to be tested. With a marriage to fiancee Carly Sturges on the horizon in the summer of 2012 and children sometime after that, Dowell is well aware the time is nigh when he must find out the reality one way or the other. If a person is carrying the gene, there is a 100 percent chance he or she will ultimately get the disease.

Vicki Dowell says she knows in her heart Jake isn't carrying the Huntington's gene, which actually doesn't provide a whole lot of comfort to her son, even when he's feeling optimistic.

"She can be as sure as she wants," Dowell said, "but that doesn't make any difference. I always kind of expect the worst and hope for the best."

The way Dowell sees it, had the disease been juvenile-onset, he would have been suffering with it by now. And if it surfaces at the stage of life it does for the vast majority of those who carry the gene, that still leaves him at least 10 years in which to enjoy life and carve out a lucrative and rewarding NHL career. And even though there is no cure, nor is there one on the horizon, modern medicine can move very quickly.

On one hand, many people in Dowell's shoes would want to know their fate. But others who are at risk of carrying the gene don't want to know, arguing there would be little motivation to even get out of bed in the morning knowing they would ultimately be rendered an invalid.

"I'm pretty humble, anyway," Dowell said. "But this has all been a pretty humbling experience." **THN**

HEAVY HEARTS

FACTS & STATS
from 2011-12

Cup Winner

Los Angeles Kings

Leading Scorers

1. Evgeni Malkin, Pit, 109 points
2. Steven Stamkos, TB, 97 pts
3. Claude Giroux, Phi, 93 points
4. Jason Spezza, Ott, 84 points
5. Ilya Kovalchuk, NJ, 83 points
6. Phil Kessel, Tor, 82 points
7. James Neal, Pit, 81 points
8. Henrik Sedin, Van, 81 points
9. John Tavares, NYI, 81 points
10. Patrik Elias, NJ, 78 points

Rule Changes

Rules and penalties are modified to address contact with the head.

Franchise News

Atlanta Thrashers transfer to Winnipeg to become Jets.

First Draft Pick, 2012

Nail Yakupov, RW, Edmonton

HHOF Inductees

Pavel Bure
Joe Sakic
Mats Sundin
↓Adam Oates

Nickname of the Year

Paul 'BizNasty' Bissonnette

Worth Noting

Rangers netminder and Vezina Trophy winner Henrik Lundqvist wins a career-high 39 games, becoming the first NHL goaltender to start his career with seven consecutive 30-win seasons.

↑ WORK HARD, PARTY HARDER

The Los Angeles Kings earn the right to wipe off their sweat with this championship towel after becoming the first eighth seed to win the Cup.

← PUCK LUCK

After taking the first three games of the final, L.A. gets a scare from New Jersey, who win the next two. But the Game 6 puck goes to the Kings as they earn their first-ever crown.

Newsmakers & Top Headlines

1 Devastating plane crash wipes out KHL's Lokomotiv
The game endures perhaps its darkest day ever Sept. 7, 2011. A plane carrying Kontinental League team Yaroslavl Lokomotiv crashes, killing 44 of the 45 passengers on board. Many former NHLers perish in the crash, including Brad McCrimmon, Pavol Demitra, Alexander Karpovtsev, Igor Korolev, Ruslan Salei, Karlis Skrastins and Josef Vasicek. Lokomotiv takes a one-year hiatus from the KHL, but begins a rebuild the following summer and returns to duty in 2012-13.

2 Three NHL enforcers die
When New York Rangers tough guy Derek Boogaard dies of an accidental drug and alcohol overdose in May, his death is mourned as an isolated incident. But when enforcers Rick Rypien of Winnipeg and recently retired Wade Belak take their own lives in August within 16 days of each other, debate rages over the link between fighting, brain trauma and depression in NHL players.

3 Jets land back in Winnipeg
The wait is over. After 15 years without an NHL franchise, Winnipeg gets its beloved Jets back. The original Jets remain in Phoenix; the new incarnation migrates from Atlanta. Armed with a new logo inspired by the Royal Canadian Air Force, the Jets become an instant smash hit, selling out every home game. Unfortunately for Winnipeg's raucous fans, the team scuffles to an 11th-place finish, missing the playoffs.

↑ **BACK TO THE ORIGINAL SIX**
The Chicago Blackhawks show off the
hardware won in the 2012-2013 season.

Newsmakers & Top Headlines

1 Spectacular start sets pace
After a spectacular start to the season, going 24
games without losing a single one in regulation time,
the Chicago Blackhawks defeated the Boston Bruins
in 2013 to win the Stanley Cup for the second time
in four years.

2 Dynasty dreams
Dave Boland scores the winning goal giving Blackhawk fans a foretaste of a possible dynasty in the mold
of the Edmonton Oilers, New York Islanders and the
Montreal Canadiens.

3 Dave Boland joins Leafs
Chicago fans were disappointed to see Boland
sign with the Toronto Maple Leafs off season, but
fans of all stripes were pleased to see an Original Six
final.

BY BOB HILDERLEY

—1927 TO 2013—

THE STANLEY CUP

HOCKEY'S HOLY GRAIL WAS DONATED BY THE GOVERNOR GENERAL OF CANADA TO THE AMATEUR HOCKEY ASSOCIATION IN 1892 AND ADOPTED BY THE NHL IN 1927

"The Stanley Cup is the only trophy I ever wanted," Bobby Orr once declared. "I never even thought about all these individual awards." Ask any NHL player why he plays the game and he will most likely say that he plays, not for the money or the adulation, but to win the Stanley Cup and enjoy the simple spoils of victory — kissing this silver icon of professional hockey supremacy at center ice, hoisting the oldest trophy in North American professional sports history above his head while skating a victory lap, and taking the Cup back to his hometown for a day to bask in the glory with his family and friends. The Stanley Cup has become the universal icon of professional hockey, the inspiration for players of all stripes looking to make their mark on the game. It is hockey's greatest challenge, incredibly difficult, but amazingly rewarding, to win.

Challenge Years

The Stanley Cup has a most curious history with an inauspicious beginning. Donated by Lord Stanley of Preston in 1892, the trophy started out as an award for Canada's top-ranked amateur ice hockey club competing in the Amateur Hockey Association of Canada (AHAC). This league had been operating since 1887, more than a decade after the founding of organized hockey by the father of the game, James G. Creighton, in Montreal. The AHAC league did not stage a playoff series within its own league. Instead, the team to finish in first place was challenged by teams from other leagues, both locally and nationally. In turn, the winning team welcomed a challenge to its title the following year sometimes from more than one team.

This is where it becomes confusing. The Montreal AAA club was the leading team from the AHAC the first year the Cup was awarded, but no team issued a challenge. By default the Montreal AAA club became the first winner of the Stanley Cup in 1893-94 and went unchallenged until the

Montreal Victorias and a team from Queen's University in Kingston, Ont., both threw down the gauntlet in 1895 and vied for hockey supremacy. The Victorias defeated the Montreal AAA club and the Queen's squad, but couldn't handle a challenge from the Winnipeg Victorias in 1896, who were able to wrest the Cup away from the Montrealers and take it west. For the next decade challenges proliferated and the game prospered as a spectator sport, with teams like the Renfrew Millionaires taking to the ice. Fans idolized players. Russell Bowie, Frank McGee, Marty Walsh, Art Ross, Frank Nighbor, Newsy Lalonde, Harvey Pulford, Georges Vezina, Fred 'Cyclone' Taylor, and 'Bad' Joe Hall are a few of the players who became all-stars. Some would go on to play in the NHL and become members of the Hockey Hall of Fame.

League Play

As the popularity of the game grew, more and more leagues were created and equally as many collapsed, it seemed. In 1915, two professional hockey organizations, the National Hockey Association (NHA) and the Pacific Coast Hockey Association (PCHA), laid claim to the Stanley Cup for the annual battle between leaders of their leagues. With the collapse of the NHA in 1917 and the founding of the NHL that same year, the Stanley Cup contestants became the champions of the NHL and the PCHA, renamed the Western Canada Hockey League (WCHL). When the Western league failed to ice a team in the 1927 season, the challenge format came to an end.

During the decade from 1917 to 1927, NHL teams had competed for the O'Brien Cup, with the winner advancing to the Stanley Cup challenge. The O'Brien Cup was assigned to the Canadian division of the NHL, displaced by the more prestigious Stanley Cup. Since 1927, the league's playoff format has changed many times, but today the final is played between the league's conference playoff champions.

↑ WINNERS BY DEFAULT
The Montreal AAA club was the first winner of the Stanley Cup in 1893-94.

→ ACADEMIC CHALLENGE
Jersey and sticks for the Queen's University challengers.

O'Brien Trophy

Donated by Senator J. O'Brien in honor of his son, Ambrose, the O'Brien Trophy has served many purposes. This elegant trophy was first awarded to the NHA champions and then to the NHL champions until 1927. Replaced by the Stanley Cup, the O'Brien Trophy was then awarded to the winner of the Canadian Division of the NHL until 1938 and then to the playoff runner-up until the trophy was retired from use in 1950. The Prince of Wales Trophy was initially awarded to the winner of the American Division.

Multiplying Cups

For good reason, there is more than one Stanley Cup. The original Challenge Cup donated by Lord Stanley remained in action from 1893 until it was replaced in 1963 by the Presentation Cup after being damaged and repaired several times. Now displayed in the Vault Room at the Hockey Hall of Fame, the Presentation Cup is given on ice to the playoff winners. In 1993, the Replica Cup was built to serve as a stand-in for the Presentation Cup whenever the Presentation Cup is not available for display or on the road with players from the winning team.

Post 1927

There you have a brief history of the Stanley Cup to 1927. What follows is a chronicle of the Cup since then, providing a selection of facts and stats, feats and features, as well as a few tall tales. The Stanley Cup seems to have an ability to spin stories from its own magic bowl. These tales grow taller year by year like urban legends. There is little hard evidence to give them credence, but who cares? They all add patina to this silver shrine.

↑ THE LESSER CUP
The O'Brien Trophy was replaced by the Stanley Cup as the award for winning the NHL championship.

>1926 to 1929 Hockey Royalty

1926-27

Winner
Ottawa Senators

Coach
Dave Gill

Team Captain
George Boucher

Contender
Boston Bruins

Winning Goal
Cy Denneny

1927-28

Winner
New York Rangers

Coach
Lester Patrick

Team Captain
Bill Cook

Contender
Montreal Maroons

Winning Goal
Frank Boucher

1928-29

Winner
Boston Bruins

Playing Coach
Cy Denneny

Team Captain
Lionel Hitchman

Contender
New York Rangers

Winning Goal
Bill Carson

Cy Denneny

Feats & Features

Geneology of a Stanley Cup Winner
The surname "Patrick" became synonymous with the Stanley Cup in this era, led by Frank and Lester Patrick, nicknamed the 'Silver Fox', who won two Stanley Cups in 1905-06 and 1906-07 playing for the Montreal Wanderers. He won it again as the coach of the Vancouver Cougars in 1924-25 before leading the New York Rangers to three Stanley Cups in 1927-28, 1932-33 and 1939-40. Lester's sons, Lynn and Muzz (Murray), followed in his footsteps as Stanley Cup winners with the Rangers. Craig Patrick, Lynn's son, has been inducted into the Hockey Hall of Fame, while

Muzz's son, Dick Patrick, has served as President of the Washington Capitals. During the 1927-28 playoffs, Lester was pressed into action as a goalie when Lorne Chabot was seriously injured by a Nels Stewart shot to the eye. He allowed one goal but won the game.

→ Cy 'Cyril' Denneny won four Stanley Cups in the 1920s with the Ottawa Senators, scoring the winning goal in the 1926-27 playoffs, and winning again in 1928-29 as player-coach of the Boston Bruins.

FACTS & STATS

1929-30

Winner
Montreal Canadiens

Coach
Cecil Hart

Team Captain
Sylvio Mantha

Contender
Boston Bruins

Winning Goal
Howie Morenz

1930-31

Winner
Montreal Canadiens

Coach
Cecil Hart

Team Captain
Sylvio Mantha

Contender
Chicago Black Hawks

Winning Goal
Johnny Gagnon

1931-32

Winner
Toronto Maple Leafs

Coach
Dick Irvin

Playing Coach
Cy Denneny

Team Captain
Hap Day

Contender
New York Rangers

Winning Goal
Ace Bailey

Ace Bailey

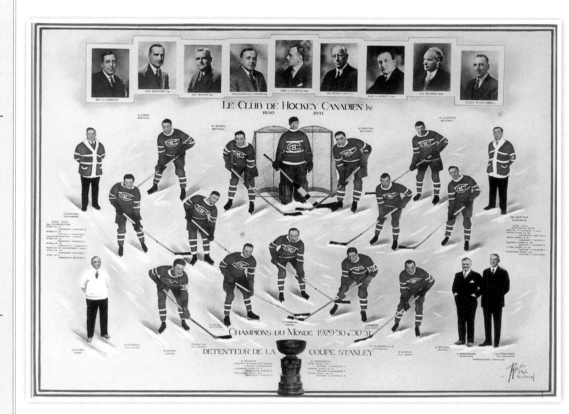

Feats & Features

The Montreal Canadiens, led by the stellar goaltending of George Hainsworth, defeated the heavily favored Boston Bruins in 1929-30. Hainsworth was not scored on for 270 minutes and eight seconds, a feat that has not been surpassed in Stanley Cup history.

← Ace Bailey won the NHL scoring title in 1928-29 and scored the Cup-winning goal for the Toronto Maple Leafs in 1932-33, but his career came to an end when he was hit by Eddie Shore and suffered a fractured skull when his head hit the ice.

The team may have been bolstered by a touch of the occult. Coach Cecil Hart patted a black cat during an overtime semifinal victory over the Rangers at the Montreal Forum. When the series resumed at Madison Square Garden, he found another black cat to pat. The Canadiens won again. With the team almost intact, the Canadiens won the Cup again in 1930-31, with Howie Morenz showing his uncanny scoring genius.

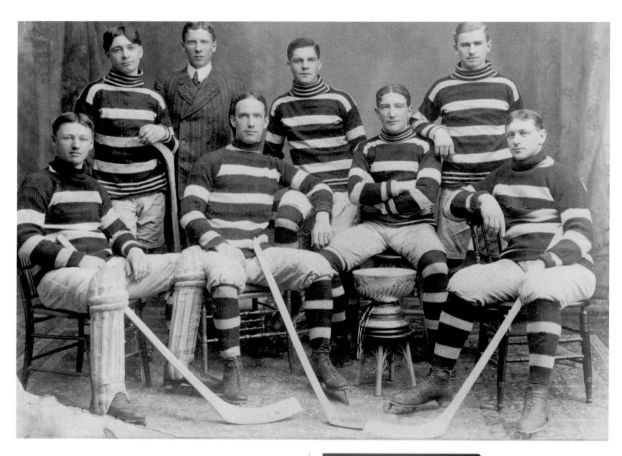

Since 1893-94, the Stanley Cup has gathered little moss. The Cup has been rolled, kicked, sunken, stolen, broken and lost on three continents. It has been spotted in the company of movie stars and presidents, flying by helicopter to Rankin Inlet and playing ball hockey with troops in Afghanistan. During the past century or so more, the Cup has gathered a host of tales. It seems able to spin its own yarns for our amusement. What the players have done to the Cup at times is stranger than fiction.

CUP TOSS

In 1895-96, the Winnipeg Victorias created a ritual by serving champagne in Lord Stanley's silver bowl to celebrate their victory over the Montreal Victorias. The Cup was passed from player to player at a party held at the Manitoba Hotel. At times, the players may have imbibed a bit too much of the bubbly. After defeating the Dawson City challengers for the Stanley Cup in 1905, the Ottawa "Silver Seven" club headed out on the town for their ritual champagne celebration and following a few libations, started an impromptu game of tossing the silver bowl back and forth across the Rideau Canal. The game went along swimmingly until a toss came up short. The Cup landed in the canal, which, fortunately, had frozen over earlier that evening. Rather than risk falling through the ice, the Silver Seven and their entourage called it a day. The bubble-brained players retrieved the dented Cup the next day.

CUP PRIORITIES

The Montreal Canadiens were on their way to a celebration party at Leo Dandurand's home after their NHL championship game against the Boston Bruins in 1929-30. They packed the Cup in the trunk for safe keeping. All was going as planned until they had a flat tire. The driver pulled over to the side of the road for repairs. To get at the spare tire, they had to move the Cup out of the trunk and set Lord Stanley's bowl at the side of the road. With the tire repaired, they carried on to the party. When it was time to begin the ritual of drinking champagne out of the Cup, they realized something was missing. They had brought the champagne, but had left the Cup behind.

MESSING AROUND

Mark Messier won the Stanley Cup six times. Besides being the model of intensity on the ice, he may be the foremost prankster among NHL players off the ice. The night after the Edmonton Oilers won the Cup in 1986-87, Messier and his teammates introduced the chalice to the patrons and staff of their favorite strip club, the Forum Inn. Messier invited everyone to drink their fill of champagne from the Cup and then placed it on stage beside the pole while he urged the dancers to work the Cup into their choreographic routines. Somehow it got dinged and needed repair. The next morning, Mark took the Cup to an autobody shop to have Lord Stanley's pride and joy restored.

← **PEACHY KEEN FEET**
Nicknamed the 'Pembroke Peach,'
Frank Nighbor won the Stanley
Cup four times while playing for
the Ottawa Senators from 1919 to
1930. He was the first winner of the
Hart Trophy (most valuable player)
and the Lady Byng Trophy (most
gentlemanly player).

>1932 to 1935 — Lionel Train Time

FACTS & STATS

1932-33
Winner
New York Rangers

Coach
Lester Patrick

Captain
Bill Cook

Contenders
Toronto Maple Leafs

Winning Goal
Bill Cook

1933-34
Winner
Chicago Black Hawks

Coach
Tommy Gorman

Captain
Charlie Gardiner

Contenders
Detroit Red Wings

Winning Goal
Mush March

1934-35
Winner
Montreal Maroons

Coach
Tommy Gorman

Captain
Hooley Smith

Contender
Toronto Maple Leafs

Winning Goal
Baldy Northcott

↑ BANNER YEAR

The 1932-33 season was a great year for New York Ranger Bill Cook. He was reappointed captain of the team, captured the league scoring crown, and then scored the winning goal in the Stanley Cup final against Toronto. On behalf of his team, he accepted the Stanley Cup awarded by league President Frank Calder at center ice.

→ Jim Connacher (no relation), Charlie Connacher and Roy Connacher.

Lionel 'Big Train' Conacher

Feats & Features

Three Conacher brothers — Lionel, Roy and Charlie — dominated the Stanley Cup playoffs in the 1930s, winning five out of 10 championships between 1931 and 1941, but did not play together on a Cup-winning team. Charlie led the Toronto Maple Leafs to a Stanley Cup victory in 1931-32. Lionel 'Big Train' Conacher won two Cups, in 1933-34 with the Black Hawks and 1934-35 with the Maroons. Roy Conacher won two Cups with the Boston Bruins.

Lionel was named Athlete of the Half Century before pursuing a career in politics. His son Brian played for the Cup-winning Maple Leafs in 1966-67. Charley's son Pete played for the Black Hawks in the 1950s, while Jim Conacher, who played in the NHL at this time, was not related. Charley, however, was ready to adopt him after he scored three goals in one game against the Maple Leafs.

← **TRAINING MITTS**
Gloves worn by Lionel Conacher during part of his 12-year NHL career.

>1935 to 1938 Made in America

FACTS & STATS

1935-36

Winner
Detroit Red Wings

Coach
Jack Adams

Captain
Doug Young

Contenders
Toronto Maple Leafs

Winning Goal
Pete Kelly

1936-37

Winner
Detroit Red Wings

Coach
Jack Adams

Captain
Doug Young

Contender
New York Rangers

Winning Goal
Marty Berry

1937-38

Winner
Chicago Black Hawks

Coach
Bill Stewart

Captain
Johnny Gotselig

Contender
Toronto Maple Leafs

Winning Goal
Carl Voss

Feats & Features

Smoking a stogie, Herbie Lewis celebrates the first Stanley Cup victory for the Detroit Red Wings with owners James D. Norris (L) and James Norris, Sr. (R). The Red Wings went on to win the Cup again in 1936-37. They are third on the list of all-time Stanley Cup winners, behind the Toronto Maple Leafs and the Montreal Canadiens.

↑ Bill Stewart of the Chicago Black Hawks was the first American-born coach in the NHL. He started eight other Americans on his Cup-winning team in 1937-38. This record was not matched until the New Jersey Devils started 12 Americans in the 1994-95 playoffs.

1938 to 1941 ‹

FACTS & STATS

1938-39

Winner
Boston Bruins

Coach
Art Ross

Captain
Cooney Weiland

Contender
Toronto Maple Leafs

Winning Goal
Roy Conacher

1939-40

Winner
New York Rangers

Coach
Frank Boucher

Captain
Art Coulter

Contenders
Toronto Maple Leafs

Winning Goal
Bryan Hextall

1940-41

Winner
Boston Bruins

Coach
Cooney Wieland

Manager
Art Ross

Captain
Dit Clapper

Contender
Detroit Red Wings

Winning Goal
Bobby Bauer

Bryan Hextall

↑ **LINE 'EM UP**
The New York Rangers defense-corp:
(L-R) Muzz Patrick, captain Art Coulter,
Ott Heller, Babe Pratt.

Feats & Features

In 1940 the Rangers won their third Stanley Cup, beating the Maple Leafs, but it would be many years before they drank from the Cup again. The story goes that the mortgage on Madison Square Garden was paid off in 1940 and the papers were burned ceremoniously in the Cup. The ghost of Lord Stanley apparently didn't take kindly to this sacrilege. The Rangers wouldn't win the Cup again until 1994. And they may not again for

another half of a century given the dishonor they bestowed upon Lord Stanley's bequest. The Cup was invited to appear on the *Late Show with David Letterman,* where the host and his Ranger guests played a game called "stupid cup tricks." The Cup also appeared on MTV, where it was filled with raw clams and oysters, for reasons no one can fathom.

← Bryan Hextall, who led the league in 1939-40 with 24 goals in 48 games, scored the overtime Cup-winning goal for the New York Rangers against the Maple Leafs to win the series.

>1941 to 1944 Come from Behind

→ Syl Apps with Ontario Premier George Drew at the Stanley Cup reception for the victorious Toronto Maple Leafs.

FACTS & STATS

1941-42
Winner
Toronto Maple Leafs

Coach
Hap Day

Captain
Syl Apps

Contender
Detroit Red Wings

Winning Goal
Pete Langelle

1942-43
Winner
Detroit Red Wings

Player Coach
Ebbie Goodfellow

Captain
Sid Abel

Contender
Boston Bruins

Winning Goal
Joe Carveth

1943-44
Winner
Montreal Canadiens

Coach
Dick Irvin

Captain
Toe Blake

Contender
Chicago Black Hawks

Winning Goal
Toe Blake

Toe Blake

Feats & Features

Never before and never after has an NHL team won a final series after falling behind three games to none. The 1941-42 Toronto Maple Leafs, captained by Syl Apps and backstopped by Turk Broda, achieved this feat in their series with the Detroit Red Wings. Game 7 drew a crowd of more than 16,000 fans, the largest gate on record to that date for a hockey game played at Maple Leaf Gardens.

→ Toe Blake scored 18 points in nine games during the 1943-44 playoffs to set a new record and scored the Stanley Cup-clinching goal in overtime. He would score the Cup-winner again in 1945-46.

FACTS & STATS

1944-45

Winner
Toronto Maple Leafs

Coach
Hap Day

Captain
Bob Davidson

Contender
Detroit Red Wings

Winning Goal
Babe Pratt

1945-46

Winner
Montreal Canadiens

Coach
Dick Irvin

Captain
Toe Blake

Contender
Boston Bruins

Winning Goal
Toe Blake

1946-47

Winner
Toronto Maple Leafs

Coach
Hap Day

Captain
Syl Apps

Contender
Montreal Canadiens

Winning Goal
Ted Kennedy

Ted Kennedy

↓ **DON'T SWEAT IT**
Turk Broda accepts challenge from
Conn Smythe to lose weight.

Feats & Features

Fan favorite Turk Broda cradles the "stove-pipe cup," which by 1944-45 could barely stand on its own as a new band of engravings was added each year to list team members and executives. NHL President Clarence Campbell began work on a new Cup design, which he unveiled in 1958. This became known as the President's Cup.

← During 1944-45, Ted 'Teeder' Kennedy led the Maple Leafs with 29 goals and 25 assists and then led all players in the Stanley Cup playoffs, scoring seven goals in 13 games.

>1947 to 1950

Hoisting the Cup

1947-48

Winner
Toronto Maple Leafs

Coach
Hap Day

Captain
Syl Apps

Contender
Detroit Red Wings

Winning Goal
Harry Watson

1948-49

Winner
Toronto Maple Leafs

Coach
Hap Day

Captain
Ted Kennedy

Contender
Detroit Red Wings

Winning Goal
Cal Gardner

1949-50

Winner
Detroit Red Wings

Coach
Tommy Ivan

Captain
Sid Abel

Contender
New York Rangers

Winning Goal
Pete Babando

Pete Babando

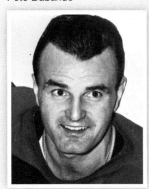

Feats & Features

Ted Lindsay of the 1950 champion Detroit Red Wings was the first captain to hoist the Cup overhead and skate a victory lap around the rink after the NHL president presented it to him. According to Lindsay, he did so to allow the fans a better view of the Cup. Since then, it has been a tradition for each member of the winning team, beginning with the captain, to take a lap around the rink with the trophy hoisted above his head.

→ In the 1949-50 playoffs, Pete Babando of the Red Wings scored in overtime to defeat the New York Rangers. Teammate Leo Reise had scored two overtime goals in their semifinal series against Toronto.

FACTS & STATS

1950-51

Winner
Toronto Maple Leafs

Coach
Joe Primeau

Captain
Ted Kennedy

Contender
Montreal Canadiens

Winning Goal
Bill Barilko

1951-52

Winner
Detroit Red Wings

Coach
Tommy Ivan

Captain
Sid Abel

Contender
Montreal Canadiens

Winning Goal
Metro Prystai

1952-53

Winner
Montreal Canadiens

Coach
Dick Irvin

Captain
Butch Bouchard

Contender
Boston Bruins

Winning Goal
Elmer Lach

Doug Harvey

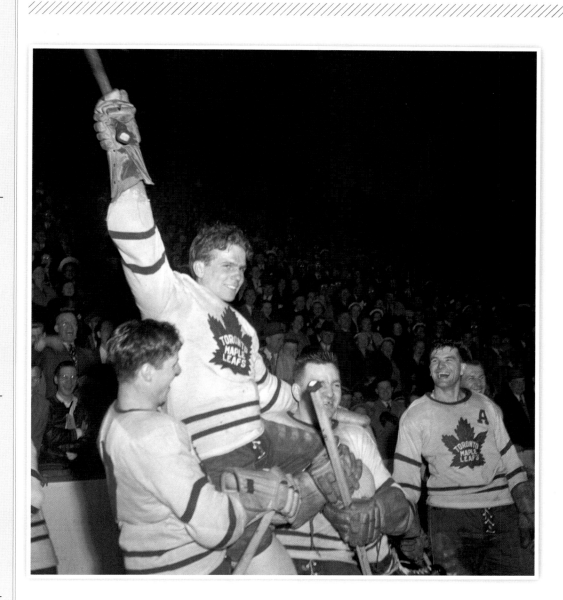

Feats & Features

After scoring the 1950-51 Cup-winning goal in overtime, 'Bashing' Bill Barilko was taken for a victory lap on the shoulders of his teammates: (L-R) coach Joe Primeau, Howie Meeker, Cal Gardner, Bill Juzda, Harry Watson and Joe Klukay. That August, Barilko set off with a friend in a bush plane to go fishing near Cochrane, Ont. The plane crashed, and despite the most extensive search in Canadian history, Barilko was not found for 11 years, until 1962, the same year the Leafs won the Cup again.

← During the battles between Montreal and Detroit in the 1950s, Doug Harvey anchored the Canadien's defence, winning his first Stanley Cup in 1952-53.

↑ Barilko's "flying" overtime Cup-winning goal presaged Bobby Orr's famous Cup-winning goal 20 years later.

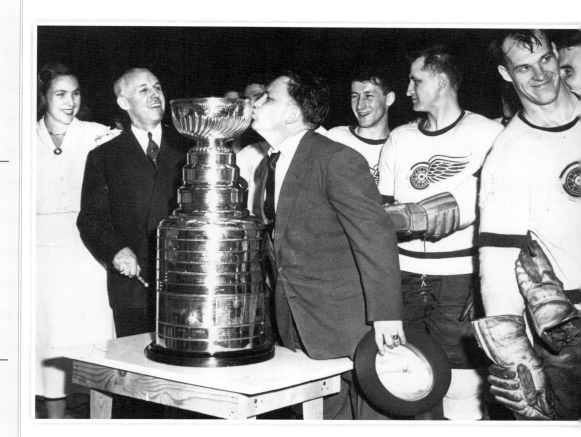

Feats & Features

LOOK, HE'S KISSING THE CUP

Gordie Howe looks positively bewildered as coach Jimmy Skinner kisses the Cup while executives and other players share the fun: (L-R) president Margueritte Norris, NHL president Clarence Campbell, Bill Dineen and Benny Woit. During the 1950s, fans endlessly debated whether 'The Rocket' or 'Mr Hockey' was the greatest player. Both could score and both could fight.

→ Maurice Richard scored four goals in the first game of the 1955-56 finals matching a record set by Newsy Lalonde in 1919, Babe Dye in 1922 and Ted Lindsay the previous season in 1954-55.

HOISTING THE CUP

Prior to the 1950s, the Cup was presented to the captain of the winning team at a civic celebration or banquet. Since then, it has been a tradition to have each member of the winning team take a lap with the trophy hoisted above his head. This "captain's first" custom has been broken a few times, for good reason.

CARBONNEAU & SAVARD

Denis Savard played most of his career with the Chicago Blackhawks without winning the Cup. He was traded to the Montreal Canadiens in 1990, but did not dress for the playoffs. The Canadiens won the Cup again in 1993, and captain Guy Carbonneau caught Denis by surprise when he passed him the Stanley Cup to hoist in honor of his sportsmanship.

YZERMAN & KONSTANTINOV

In 1997-98, NHL commissioner Gary Bettman went to hand the Cup to Detroit Red Wings captain Steve Yzerman, but 'Stevie Y' passed the Cup on to his teammate, Vladimir Konstantinov, who had suffered a crippling, career-ending automobile accident the season prior.

SAKIC & BOURQUE

Ray Bourque played with the Boston Bruins for 22 years without winning the Stanley Cup. He asked to be traded to a Cup contender and won Lord Stanley's hardware in 2001 playing for the Colorado Avalanche. When the Cup was passed to captain Joe Sakic, he did not hoist it, but handed it to Bourque to take the victory lap.

ISLANDERS FANS

To show their appreciation for their fans, the New York Islanders, led by captain Bryan Trottier, carried the Cup into the stands for everyone to touch. (L-R: Mike Bossy, Duane Sutter, Wayne Merrick, coach Al Arbour and Stephan Persson). Their games against the Edmonton Oilers in the 1982-83 and 1983-84 playoffs rank as some of the most exciting hockey ever played.

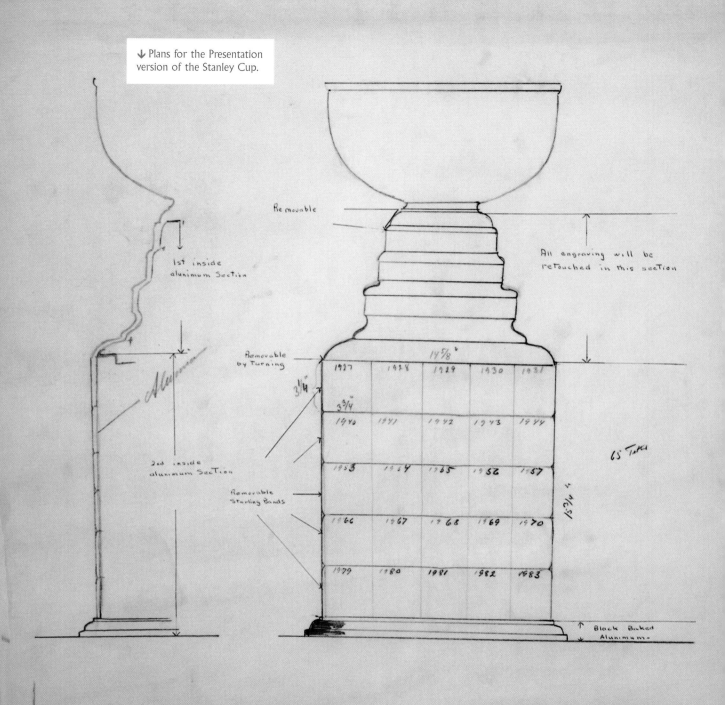

Removable

All engraving will be retouched in this section

1st inside aluminum Section

Removable by Turning

14 5/8"

2nd inside aluminum Section

Removable Sterling Bands

3 1/4"

3 3/4"

1927	1928	1929	1930	1931
1940	1941	1942	1943	1944
1953	1954	1955	1956	1957
1966	1967	1968	1969	1970
1979	1980	1981	1982	1983

65 Total

13 1/2"

Black Baked Aluminum.

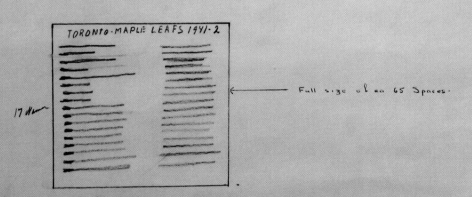

TORONTO-MAPLE LEAFS 1941-2

Full size of an 65 Spaces.

17 High

>1956 to 1959

First Montreal Dynasty

↑ Marcel Bonin

FACTS & STATS

1956-57

Winner
Montreal Canadiens

Coach
Toe Blake

Captain
Maurice Richard

Contenders
Boston Bruins

Winning Goal
Dickie Moore

1957-58

Winner
Montreal Canadiens

Coach
Toe Blake

Captain
Maurice Richard

Contender
Boston Bruins

Winning Goal
Bernie Geoffrion

1958-59

Winner
Montreal Canadiens

Coach
Toe Blake

Captain
Maurice Richard

Contender
Toronto Maple Leafs

Winning Goal
Marcel Bonin

'Boom Boom' Geoffrion

Feats & Features

Bernie 'Boom Boom' Geoffrion was among the great players who starred with the Canadiens under Toe Blake's leadership during their five-year dynasty in the late 1950s. Two decades later, from 1976 to 1979, the Canadiens won four Cups in a row and six Cups total in the 1970s, led by Ken Dryden, Guy LaFleur and Serge Savard. Although Detroit, Toronto and Edmonton have also shown dynastic tendencies, only the New York Islanders have come close to matching the Canadiens feat of winning five Cups in a row, notching four straight from 1979-80 to 1982-83.

→ If not for a scoring feat in the 1958-59 playoffs, Marcel Bonin would be forgotten among his illustrious Canadiens teammates. He led the likes of Maurice Richard and Dickie Moore by scoring 10 goals in 11 games. For good luck, Bonin wore one of the Rocket's gloves.

1959 to 1962 ‹

1959-60

Winner
Montreal Canadiens

Coach
Toe Blake

Captain
Maurice Richard

Contender
Toronto Maple leafs

Winning Goal
Jean Beliveau

1960-61

Winner
Chicago Black Hawks

Coach
Rudy Pilous

Captain
Ed Litzenberger

Contender
Detroit Red Wings

Winning Goal
Ab McDonald

1961-62

Winner
Toronto Maple Leafs

Coach
Punch Imlach

Captain
George Armstrong

Contender
Chicago Black Hawks

Winning Goal
Dick Duff

Ab McDonald

Feats & Features

Bob Nevin and Dick Duff celebrate in the dressing room after defeating the Chicago Black Hawks in the 1962 Stanley Cup final. Duff had scored the winning goal. In the first game of the series, Duff and Nevin both scored two goals. Duff scored in the first minute, at the 49 second mark, and then nine seconds later. This feat remains a Stanley Cup record. Later in his career while playing for the Montreal Canadiens, Duff gained a well-earned reputation as a "money" player who excelled in Stanley Cup competition.

← After winning three Cups while playing for the Montreal Canadiens, Ab McDonald was traded to the Chicago Black Hawks at the start of the 1960-61 season and won the Cup again that year. Other NHL players who have enjoyed this good fortune include Al Arbour and Ed Litzenberger, both traded from Chicago to Toronto the following year in 1961-62. What goes around, comes around.

FACTS & STATS

1962-63

Winner
Toronto Maple Leafs

Coach
Punch Imlach

Captain
George Armstrong

Contender
Detroit Red Wings

Winning Goal
Eddie Shack

1963-64

Winner
Toronto Maple Leafs

Coach
Punch Imlach

Captain
George Armstrong

Contender
Detroit Red Wings

Winning Goal
Bobby Baun

1964-65

Winner
Montreal Canadiens

Coach
Toe Blake

Captain
Jean Beliveau

Contender
Chicago Black Hawks

Winning Goal
Jean Beliveau

Jean Beliveau

Feats & Features

There are many tales of physical courage attached to Stanley Cup play, none as heroic as the case of Bobby Baun during the sixth game of a series against Detroit in 1963-64. Late in the third period with the game tied, Baun took a faceoff against Gordie Howe, and in the ensuing scuffle, he felt his ankle crack. At Baun's request, his ankle was taped and frozen. He returned to the bench in time for the overtime period to begin. At 1:43 Baun intercepted a pass at the blueline and fired a shot at the net that Detroit defenseman Bill Gadsby deflected past his own goalie, Terry Sawchuk.

Some things are simply meant to be. Baun hobbled around for four days on a fractured fibula before they confirmed the diagnosis with an x-ray.

→ In 1964-65, Jean Beliveau won the Hart Trophy, awarded by Gordie Howe. In the seventh game of the 1964-65 Cup final, Beliveau took things into his own hands, scoring what proved to be the winning goal 14 seconds into the game. Five minutes later he set up Dick Duff to score the clinching goal. As a player and executive, Beliveau has won more Stanley Cups than anyone in history.

FACTS & STATS

1965-66

Winner
Montreal Canadiens

Coach
Toe Blake

Captain
Jean Beliveau

Contender
Detroit Red Wings

Winning Goal
Henri Richard

1966-67

Winner
Toronto Maple Leafs

Coach
Punch Imlach

Captain
George Armstrong

Contender
Montreal Canadiens

Winning Goal
Jim Pappin

1967-68

Winner
Montreal Canadiens

Coach
Toe Blake

Captain
Jean Beliveau

Contender
St Louis Blues

Winning Goal
J.C. Tremblay

Henri Richard

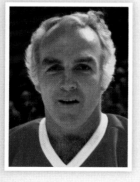

Feats & Features

Terry Sawchuk and Johnny Bower were platooned during the 1966-67 playoffs, with the hot goalie getting the nod from coach Punch Imlach to start the game. The strategy worked, but for the last time — the Leafs have not won the Stanley Cup since beating their archrival, Montreal, that year. Sawchuk's fate was much darker. For the next few years, he bounced around the league until he landed with the New York Rangers. In a "domestic" fight with his roommate, Ron Stewart, Sawchuk was seriously injured and died suddenly. His shutout record of 103 lasted until surpassed by Martin Brodeur.

← Henri Richard scored the Cup-winning goal in overtime against the Detroit Red Wings in the 1965–66 season and again in 1970-71 against the Black Hawks. 'The Pocket Rocket' played in 65 Stanley Cup final games and won 11 championships during his career.

>1968 to 1971 Gold Orr

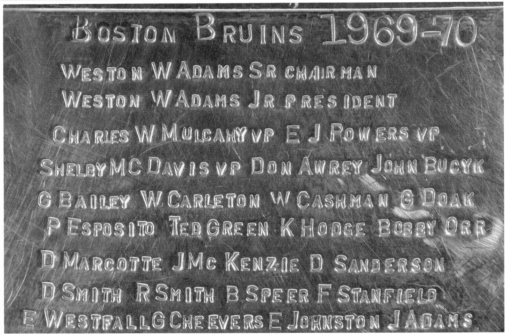

BOSTON BRUINS 1969-70
WESTON W ADAMS SR CHAIRMAN
WESTON W ADAMS JR PRESIDENT
CHARLES W MULCAHY VP E J POWERS VP
SHELBY MC DAVIS VP DON AWREY JOHN BUCYK
G BAILEY W CARLETON W CASHMAN G DOAK
P ESPOSITO TED GREEN K HODGE BOBBY ORR
D MARCOTTE J MC KENZIE D SANDERSON
D SMITH R SMITH B SPEER F STANFIELD
E WESTFALL G CHEEVERS E JOHNSTON J ADAMS

Feats & Features

After missing the playoffs eight years in a row from 1960 to 1967, the Boston Bruins, inspired by Phil Esposito and Bobby Orr, won the Stanley Cup in 1969-70. Esposito became the first player to score more than 100 points in a season in 1968-69 and then led the Boston Bruins to a Stanley Cup in 1969-70, setting several records by scoring 27 points in 14 games. He surpassed Stan Makita's 21 points, and his 13 goals surpassed the 12-goal record held by Jean Beliveau and Maurice Richard.

→ Bobby Orr became the first defenseman to win a scoring title, finishing the year with 120 points and scoring the Cup-winning goal in overtime.

1968-69

Winner
Montreal Canadiens

Coach
Claude Ruel

Captain
Jean Beliveau

Contender
St Louis Blues

Winning Goal
John Ferguson

1969-70

Winner
Boston Bruins

Coach
Harry Sinden

Captain
John Bucyk (ceremonial)

Contender
St Louis Blues

Winning Goal
Bobby Orr

1970-71

Winner
Montreal Canadiens

Coach
Claude Ruel

Captain
Jean Beliveau

Contender
Chicago Black Hawks

Winning Goal
Henri Richard

Bobby Orr

↑ FLYING GOAL
Bobby Orr's overtime Cup-winning goal against the St. Louis Blues in 1969-70 is the most famous goal in NHL history.

>1971 to 1974

Five and Counting

FACTS & STATS

1971-72

Winner
Boston Bruins

Coach
Tom Johnson

Captain
John Bucyk

Contender
New York Rangers

Winning Goal
Bobby Orr

1972-73

Winner
Montreal Canadiens

Coach
Scotty Bowman

Captain
Henri Richard

Contender
Chicago Black Hawks

Winning Goal
Yvan Cournoyer

1973-74

Winner
Philadelphia Flyers

Coach
Fred Shero

Captain
Bobby Clarke

Contender
Boston Bruins

Winning Goal

Rick MacLeish

Ken Dryden

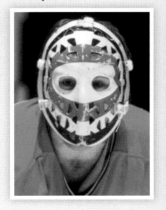

Feats & Features

Scotty Bowman joined the Montreal Canadiens as their coach in the 1972-73 season and won five Cups with the Canadiens during the 1970s. His winning days were not over as he later won Cups with the Pittsburgh Penguins and Detroit Red Wings. He has also helped his son Stan, who was named after Lord Stanley, manage the Chicago Blackhawks in their Cup runs in 2010 and 2013.

→ After playing only six regular season games, Ken Dryden stymied the high-powered Boston Bruins in the first round of the 1970-71 playoffs and back-stopped his team to a Stanley Cup victory, receiving the Conn Smythe Trophy.

FACTS & STATS

1974-75

Winner
Philadelphia Flyers

Coach
Fred Shero

Captain
Bobby Clarke

Contender
Buffalo Sabres

Winning Goal
Bob Kelly

1975-76

Winner
Montreal Canadians

Coach
Scotty Bowman

Captain
Yvan Cournoyer

Contender
Philadelphia Flyers

Winning Goal
Guy Lafleur

1976-77

Winner
Montreal Canadiens

Coach
Scotty Bowman

Captain
Yvan Cournoyer

Contender
Boston Bruins

Winning Goal
Jacques Lemaire

Bernie Parent

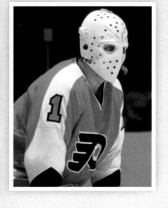

Feats & Features

Cheered on by Kate Smith's singing of *God Bless America* before each home game and inspired by the hard-nosed play of Bobby Clarke and Bill Barber, the Philadelphia Flyers were the first expansion team to win the Stanley Cup in 1973-74 and again the next year. They also won a reputation for pugnacious play and were nicknamed the Broad Street Bullies by the local media. Broad Street is a main street in Philadelphia.

← If not for the goaltending heroics of Bernie Parent, the Philadelphia Flyers would have been hard-pressed to win the Stanley Cup regardless of how many goons they deployed. Parent recorded shutouts in the final series games in 1974 and 1975, and won the Conn Smythe Trophy back-to-back, still a record for goalies.

HEISTING THE CUP

Hockey players were not the only people who have found the Stanley Cup appealing. During the early years of the NHL, the Montreal Wanderers hired a photographer to take their picture with the Cup, but the photographer absconded with the silverware to pawn it or fence it, the Wanderers presumed. When they tracked him down, they discovered that he had given the Cup to his mother as a birthday gift. She was using it as a flower vase. The team chose not to press charges.

1960-61 STOP THIEF!

During the 1960-61 playoffs between Montreal and Chicago, with the Canadiens about to lose and thus end their five-year dynasty, a fan took action to prevent this from happening. He broke into the glass case in the lobby displaying the Cup, hoisted it over his shoulders and made a victory run for the exit, where he was promptly arrested. In court the next day he pleaded his case to the judge: "Your Honor, I was simply taking the Stanley Cup back to Montreal where it belongs."

1978-79 CUP PLANTING

The Montreal Canadiens won the NHL championship again in 1978-79, with Guy Lafleur leading the team against the pesky New York Rangers. Following the civic celebrations and parade through the streets of Montreal, Lafleur stole the Cup and drove to his home town of Thurso, Que. In the middle of the night, he "planted" the Cup in his parents' front lawn. When his father looked out in the morning and saw the Cup, he called all of their friends, neighbors and relatives to come by and pay homage. Of course, a champagne party ensued. Lafleur returned the Cup the next day without repercussions. As Lafleur reflected years later, "Old people were crying and kissing the Cup. The Cup means a lot to them, especially when they could see it and touch it. ... My sister had had a baby and she put the baby in the Cup and took pictures. It was something special."

↓ **ALL CHOKED UP**
Statue in honour of Guy Lafleur
erected in Thurso, Que., his hometown.

↓ Helmet worn by New York Islanders defenseman Denis Potvin during the late 1970s and early 1980s.

>1977 to 1980

On Parade

→ Guy Lafleur and Steve Shutt

1977-78

Winner
Montreal Canadiens

Coach
Scotty Bowman

Captain
Yvan Cournoyer

Contender
Boston Bruins

Winning Goal
Mario Tremblay

1978-79

Winner
Montreal Canadiens

Coach
Scotty Bowman

Captain
Yvan Cournoyer

Contender
New York Rangers

Winning Goal
Jacques Lemaire

1979-80

Winner
New York Islanders

Coach
Al Arbour

Captain
Denis Potvin

Contender
Philadelphia Flyers

Winning Goal
Bob Nystrom

Jacques Lemaire

Feats & Features

For four years in a row, the Montreal Canadiens won the Stanley Cup, from 1975-76 to 1978-79, and their fans showed their appreciation at parades hosted by the city. Despite their effort, the team was not able to match the five consecutive Cup victories the franchise had won in the late 1950s, when the team was coached by Toe Blake. Before 1979-80, Stanley Cup star Ken Dryden retired and Scotty Bowman shuffled off to manage the Buffalo Sabres.

→ Although his linemates, Steve Shutt and Guy Lafleur, received most of the accolades from Habs fans, Jacques Lemaire went about his business, scoring Cup-winning goals in 1976-77 in overtime and again in 1978-79. He also won the Cup as coach of the New Jersey Devils in 1994-95.

Ken Morrow

Feats & Features

As one dynasty ended in Montreal, a new one had begun on Long Island. The Islanders set a host of Stanley Cup playoff scoring records during their four-year reign. In 18 games, Mike Bossy notched 35 points and Brian Trottier picked up 29. Close behind was Denis Potvin setting a record for a defenseman with nine points in one four-game series. As the Islanders dynasty ended, the Edmonton one began.

← Ken Morrow won an Olympic gold medal with the Miracle on Ice American team and the Stanley Cup, all in the 1979-80 season. He continued to anchor the Islanders defense for three more back-to-back Cup victories.

ENGRAVING THE CUP

Each year, the names of the players in the winning teams are stamped on the Cup. There have been a number of peculiar misprints and omissions over the years, such as "Bqstqn" Bruins in 1971-72, and a few legends have grown tall.

MAKE BELIEVE

Following the 1924-25 Stanley Cup playoff won by the Victoria Cougars, coach and manager Lester Patrick took the Cup home for safekeeping until the next challenge, as was the custom. One day while playing in their basement, Lester's sons, Lynn and Muzz (Murray), found the Cup stored away in a closet and set out to make themselves immortal by scratching their names on the Cup with a nail. The inscription was a bit premature, though, as both boys eventually had their names professionally engraved on the Cup in 1939-40 when they played for their father's team, the Cup-winning New York Rangers.

BUBBA BOURQUE

Following the victory of the Pittsburg Penguins over the Minesota North Stars in 1990-91, Phil Bourque took the Cup home and discovered a rattle in the works. A DIY (do it yourself) kind of guy, Phil set about to fix things by taking the Cup apart. Inside he discovered that previous repairmen had etched the Cup with their names. Bourque added this message for posterity: "Enjoy it, Phil Bubba Bourque, '91 Penguins." He may be the only player to have his name on the outside and the inside of the Cup.

STAMPED OUT

When the Edmonton Oilers first won the Stanley Cup in 1983-84, the name of each player was stamped on to the Cup, along with name of Basil Pocklington, son of owner Peter Pocklington. The NHL was not pleased with this crude act of nepotism and demanded that Basil's name be removed. The only way to do so was to stamp out the letters with a row of x's: XXXXXX.

↑ (L-R) Lynn and Muzz Patrick.

↓ Stacked pads (top to bottom): Mike D'Alessandro, University of Western (2001-02), Jocelyn Thibault, Pittsburgh Penguins (2006-07), Mike Dunham, Nashville Predators (1998-99), and the Stanley Cup winning pads worn by Marc-Andre Fleury, Pittsburgh Penguins (2006-07).

>1983 to 1986

The Great One

1983-84

Winner
Edmonton Oilers

Coach
Glen Sather

Captain
Wayne Gretzky

Contender
New York Islanders

Winning Goal
Ken Linseman

1984-85

Winner
Edmonton Oilers

Coach
Glen Sather

Captain
Wayne Gretzky

Contender
Philadelphia Flyers

Winning Goal
Paul Coffey

1985-86

Winner
Montreal Canadiens

Coach
Jean Perron

Captain
Bob Gainey

Contender
Calgary Flames

Winning Goal
Bobby Smith

Feats & Features

Records fell as Wayne Gretzky led his team to victories in 1983-84 and 1984-85, when he scored 17 goals and 30 assists in the playoffs, for a total of 37 points, surpassing Mike Bossy's record.

The Oilers almost matched the five consecutive Cups the Montreal Canadiens notched in the late 1950s — if not for the Canadiens themselves, who spoiled the run by winning the cup in 1985-86. Igniting an Alberta rivalry, the Calgary Flames stunned the Oilers in the first round, while rookie goalie Patrick Roy carried the Habs past the Flames in the Cup final.

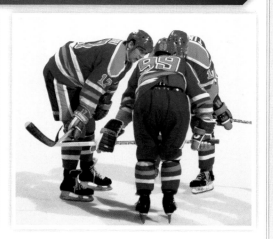

← Wayne Gretzky, Jari Kurri and Essa Tikonen plan their attack. Kurri proved to be as lethal a playoff goal scorer as his line-mate Gretzky, scoring 19 goals in 18 games in the 1984-85 playoffs, which included an amazing four hat tricks.

FACTS & STATS

1986-87

Winner
Edmonton Oilers

Coach
Glen Sather

Captain
Wayne Gretsky

Contender
Philadelphia Flyers

Winning Goal
Jari Kurri

1987-88

Winner
Edmonton Oilers

Coach
Glen Sather

Captain
Wayne Gretsky

Contender
Boston Bruins

Winning Goal
Wayne Gretzsky

1988-89

Winner
Calgary Flames

Coach
Terry Crisp

Captain
Lanny McDonald/Jim Peplinski

Contender
Montreal Canadiens

Winning Goal
Doug Gilmour

Doug Gilmour

↑ Lanny McDonald.

Feats & Features

After pushing the Edmonton Oilers to their limit the Flames persisted to win the Cup in 1988-89. Veteran Lanny McDonald led the charge of the victorious Flames. A fan favorite, McDonald retired at the end of the year. The team fell to their archrivals, the Edmonton Oilers in the 1989-90 playoffs.

← Doug Gilmour played his signature hustle game and scored the Cup-winning goal for Calgary in 1988-89.

>1989 to 1992 Mario and Company

↑ Mario Lemieux

1989-90

Winner
Edmonton Oilers

Coach
John Muckler

Captain
Mark Messier

Contender
Boston Bruins

Winning Goal
Craig Simpson

1990-91

Winner
Pittsburgh Penguins

Coach
Bob Johnson

Captain
Mario Lemieux

Contender
Minnesota Stars

Winning Goal
Ulf Samuelsson

1991-92

Winner
Pittsburgh Penguins

Coach
Scotty Bowman/Bob Johnson

General Manager
Craig Patrick

Contender
Chicago Blackhawks

Winning Goal
Ron Francis

Craig Patrick

Feats & Features

More Cup records fell as 'Super Mario' scored 16 goals and 28 assists in 23 playoff games to lead the Penguins past the North Stars in the 1990-91 Cup final. He led the Penguins to another Cup victory against Chicago the following year. Lemieux's supporting cast included two Stanley Cup winning veterans, Bryan Trottier from the New York Islanders and Paul Coffey from the Edmonton Oilers, and rookie Jaromir Jagr.

→ Craig Patrick, grandson of Lester Patrick and son of Lynn Patrick, was the GM of the Cup-winning Pittsburgh Penguins in 1991 and '92.

1992 to 1995 ‹

Brian Leetch

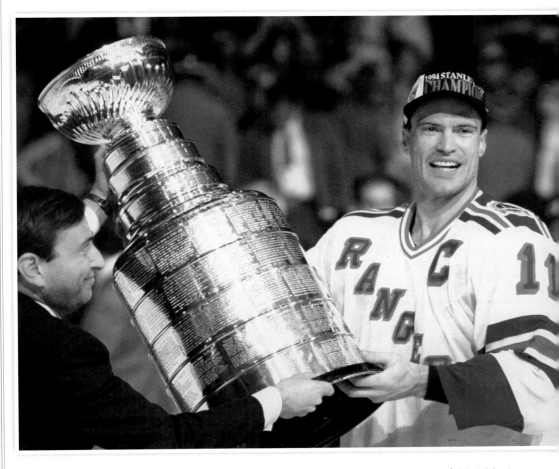

↑ Mark Messier

Feats & Features

Mark Messier promised the New York Rangers fans that the team would win the sixth game of their series with the Vancouver Canucks. Down 2-0 near the end of the second period, Messier set up Alexei Kovalev for a goal, and in the third period, he scored a hat trick to win the game 4-2.

← As the first American-born winner of the Conn Smythe Trophy, Brian Leetch helped to dispel the 54-year Curse of the Ranger by scoring 34 points in 23 games and directing the power play to 19 goals in 23 chances.

SWIMMING WITH THE CUP

The Cup seems to have an affinity for water, from the time the Silver Seven tossed the silver bowl across the Rideau Canal to celebrations in 2012-13 when Cup-winner Jonathan Toews of the Chicago Blackhawks took the Cup wakeboarding.

1990-91 POOL PARTY

On several occasions the Cup has gone swimming with the winning team. The Pittsburg Penguins won the Cup for the first time in 1990-91, and to celebrate, captain Mario Lemieux held a pool party in his backyard. His teammates tested to see if the Cup was buoyant. It floated like an inflatable toy to start, but eventually sank, breaking in two as it hit the bottom. They fixed the Cup with duct tape.

1993-94 SOLDERED

Legendary NHL tough guy Joey Kocur won the Cup with the Rangers in 1993-94. When his day arrived to visit with the Cup, it came to him in two pieces. Kocur took it to a local machine shop and had them solder it back together. The fix proved strong enough while he hugged the Cup riding in a water tube pulled behind his speed boat.

2009-10 MADE OF THE MIST

Patrick Kane grew up with the roar of Niagara Falls in his ears. Following the Blackhawks' victory in 2009-10, he took the Cup for a trip under the Falls in the *Maid of the Mist* tour boat, holding on tightly as he hoisted the Cup into the spray.

→ Every year the diligent Cup Keepers set the ground rules for the winning team on appropriate behaviour with the Stanley Cup. This includes not allowing the Cup to be dunked in pool water. Chicago Blackhawk Michael Frolik at his home in Kladno, Czech Republic, is hoisting the Cup in the right direction, unlike other players who have used the Cup for buoyancy experiments in the past.

↓ Blocker and trapper worn by netminder Nikolai Khabibulin of the Tampa Bay Lightning during the team's run to the 2004 Stanley Cup.

>1995 to 1998

Foreign Affairs

FACTS & STATS

1995-96

Winner
Colorado Avalanche

Coach
Marc Crawford

Captain
Joe Sakic

Contender
Florida Panthers

Winning Goal
Uwe Krupp

1996-97

Winner
Detroit Red Wings

Coach
Scotty Bowman

Captain
Steve Yzerman

Contender
Philadelphia Flyers

Winning Goal
Darren Carty

1997-98

Winner
Detroit Red Wings

Coach
Scotty Bowman

Captain
Steve Yzerman

Contender
Washington Capitals

Winning Goal
Larry Murphy

Nicklas Lidstrom

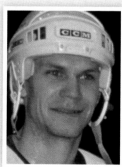

Feats & Features

The Detroit Red Wings had not won the Stanley Cup since 1955, but reversed this trend with back-to-back victories over the Philadelphia Flyers in 1996-97 and the Washington Capitals 1997-98, guided by coach Scotty Bowman and captain Steve Yzerman. Yzerman was the captain of the Red Wings for 19 years, which is still a record, and led the team to four Stanley Cups during that time.

→ The Motor City became known as Hockey Town. The team featured several Swedes, including Nicklas Lidstrom, who would win the Norris Trophy seven times, as well as Russians, including Igor Larionov and Sergei Fedorov, who would lead the team in scoring.

FACTS & STATS

1998-99

Winner
Dallas Stars

Coach
Ken Hitchcock

Captain
Derian Hatcher

Contender
Buffalo Sabres

Winning Goal
Brett Hull

1999-00

Winner
New Jersey Devils

Coach
Larry Robinson

Captain
Scott Stevens

Contender
Dallas Stars

Winning Goal
Jason Arnott

2000-01

Winner
Colorado Avalanche

Coach
Bob Hartley

Captain
Joe Sakic

Contender
New Jersey Devils

Winning Goal
Alex Tanguay

Joe Sakic

↑ Martin Brodeur and Bruce Driver of the New Jersey Devils hoist the Cup.

Feats & Features

← Joe Sakic came to life in the playoffs, setting and matching records as he led the Avalanche to two Stanley Cups, in 1995-96 and in 2000-01. He scored six overtime goals to match Maurice Richard's record, and 18 goals in total, leaving him short of the record of 19 goals shared by Reggie Leach of the Flyers and Jari Karri of the Oilers. To top if off, Sakic was awarded the Conn Smythe Trophy in 1995-96.

The New Jersey Devils mastered the trap defence, which carried them to the Stanley Cup in 1999-00, with the help of stellar goaltending by rookie Martin Brodeur. Brodeur starred for the New Jersey Devils in their Cup victories in 1994-95, 1999-00, and 2002-03, posting a record-setting 11 shutouts.

>2002 to 2003

Goalies Reign

↑ Goalie pads worn by Martin Brodeur of the New Jersey Devils during his rookie NHL season in 1993-94.

Feats & Features

P atrick Roy won the Conn Smythe Trophy for a record-setting third time, each in a different decade (Montreal Canadiens in 1985-86 and 1992-93 and the Colorado Avalanche in 2000-01).

→ Pat Burns coached the New Jersey Devils to the Stanley Cup in 2002-03. He also won the Jack Adams Award as coach of the year for the third time, an NHL record.

2000-01

Winner
Colorado Avalanche

Coach
Bob Hartley

Captain
Joe Sakic

Contender
New Jersey Devils

Winning Goal
Alex Tanguay

2001-02

Winner
Detroit Red Wings

Coach
Scotty Bowman

Captain
Steve Yzerman

Contender
Carolina Hurricanes

Winning Goal
Brendan Shanahan

2002-03

Winner
New Jersey Devils

Coach
Pat Burns

Captain
Scott Stevens

Contender
Mighty Ducks of Anaheim

Winning Goal
Michael Rupp

Pat Burns

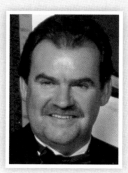

FACTS & STATS

2003-04

Winner
Tampa Bay Lightning

Coach
John Tortorella

Captain
Dave Andreychuk

Contender
Calgary Flames

Winning Goal
Ruslan Fedotenko

2004-05
Locked Out

2005-06

Winner
Carolina Hurricanes

Coach
Peter Laviolette

Captain
Rod Brind'Amour

Contender
Edmonton Oilers

Winning Goal
Frantisek Kaberle

Cam Ward

Feats & Features

During the 2004-04 Tampa Bay Lightning's run to the Stanley Cup, Brad Richards scored 12 playoff goals, including seven game winners, which surpassed the record of six game winners shared by Joe Sakic and Joe Niewendyk. He also won a half dozen individual awards.

The Carolina Hurricanes bucked the trend in recent years for the Stanley Cup winners to be a young team by starting a set of veteran players — Glen Wesley, Rod Brind'Amour, Doug Weight, Brett

← Cam Ward joined Ken Dryden, Patrick Roy and Ron Hextall as a rookie goalie who was awarded the Conn Smythe Trophy. He won the first seven games he started to tie a record set by Tiny Thompson in 1929-30.

Hedican and Ray Whitney. Collectively, these five players had more than 75 years of experience in the NHL. The Cup was now firmly ensconced in the American South, with back-to-back victories by the Lightning and Hurricanes. The Cup would soon find an equally hot home in Anaheim and Los Angeles.

Ray Bourque had played his entire 22-year NHL career with the Boston Bruins until requesting a trade to the Colorado Avalanche, who were vying for the Cup. The final series against New Jersey went to seven games, with an overtime goal by Alex Tanguay winning the day. When captain Joe Sakic received the trophy, he did not hoist it, as is the custom. Instead, he handed it to Bourque for him to hoist with Patrick Roy's help.

>2006 to 2009 Age Advantage

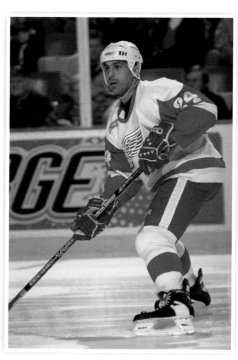

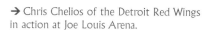
→ Chris Chelios of the Detroit Red Wings in action at Joe Louis Arena.

↓ After being dropped off via helicopter near the peak of Bull Mountain, brothers Rob (left) and Scott (right) Niedermayer prepare for their dream photo with the Stanley Cup atop a glacier.

2006-07

Winner
Anaheim Ducks

Coach
Randy Carlyle

Captain
Scott Niedermayer

Contender
Ottawa Senators

Winning Goal
Travis Moen

2007-08

Winner
Detroit Red Wings

Coach
Mike Babcock

Captain
Nicklas Lidstrom

Contender
Pittsburgh Penguins

Winning Goal
Henrik Zetterberg

2008-09

Winner
Pittsburgh Penguins

Coach
Dan Bylsma

Contender
Detroit Red Wings

Winning Goal
Maxime Talbot

Jean Sebastien-Giguere

Feats & Features

Despite losing to the Anaheim Mighty Ducks in five games, three Ottawa Senators led the Stanley Cup playoffs in scoring. Daniel Alfredson, Dany Heatley and Jason Spezza each had 22 points in 20 games, to no avail. The Niedermayer brothers, Robb and Scott, joined the ranks of other brother Cup winners, including most recently the Sutter brothers, Brent and Duane, with the Islanders in 1982-93, not to mention Maurice and Henri Richard.

Chris Chelios became the oldest player ever to win the Stanley Cup when the Red Wings defeated the Penguins in the 2007-08 Stanley Cup playoffs. Chelios also set the record for most years in the playoffs at 23 and the record for most games played at 2009.

→ Jean Sebastien-Giguere, goaltender for the Anaheim Ducks in their Cup final loss to the New Jersey Devils in 2002-03, was awarded the Conn Smythe Trophy for his outstanding play, posting three shutouts in a row against the Minnesota Wild and a playoff goals against average of 1.62, lower than Martin Brodeur's Cup winning average of 1.73. The Ducks would have to wait until the 2006-07 season to win the Cup, even though Giguere's goals against average in that series against the Ottawa Senators was only 2.21.

FACTS & STATS

2009-10

Winner
Chicago Blackhawks

Coach
Joel Quenneville

Captain
Jonathan Toews

Contender
Philadelphia Flyers

Winning Goal
Patrick Kane

2010-11

Winner
Boston Bruins

Coach
Claude Julien

Captain
Zedono Chara

Contender
Vancouver Canucks

Winning Goal
Patrice Bergeron

Evgeni Malkin

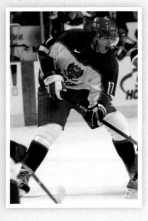

Youth Movement # 2009 to 2011 〈

↑ Marc-Andre Fleury   ↑ Sidney Crosby

Feats & Features

In 2005-06, Sidney Crosby became the youngest player in NHL history to score more than 100 points as a rookie and the youngest team captain to win the Stanley Cup in 2008-09. Marc-Andre Fleury backstopped the offensive-minded Penguins.

← Following in the footsteps of Mario Lemieux, Evgeni Malkin won the scoring championship in the regular season and in the playoffs, counting 23 points in 24 games. Just as Lemieux was awarded the Conn Smythe Trophy when he first won the Cup in 1990-91, so did Malkin walk away with this most valuable player award.

With the Pittsburgh's victory over Detroit in the 2008-09 playoffs, Lemieux joined the Royal Family of Frank and Lester Patrick as the only individuals to have their names etched on the Stanley Cup as players and as owners.

→ Marc-Andre Fleury's chest protector.

FACTS & STATS

2011-12

Winner
Los Angeles Kings

Coach
Darryl Sutter

Captain
Dustin Brown

Contender
New Jersey Devils

Winning Goal
Jeff Carter

2012-13

Winner
Chicago Blackhawks

Coach
Joel Quenneville

Captain
Jonathan Toews

Contender
Boston Bruins

Winning Goal
Dave Bolland

Patrick Kane

↑ Jonathan Quick poses with the Stanley Cup, Clarence Campbell Bowl and Conn Smythe Trophy.

Feats & Features

The Los Angeles Kings set a string of records on their way to winning the Stanley Cup in 2011-12 for the first time in franchise history. They won 10 road games in a row and all four overtime games they played, including two overtime games in the final. Jonathan Quick starred in goal, posting one shutout and a goals against average of 1.10. In Game 6, the Kings scored three power play goals in less than four minutes.

← Patrick Kane was awarded the Conn Smythe Trophy again in 2012-13 as the Chicago Blackhawks defeated the Boston Bruins in dramatic fashion, scoring two goals in the final minutes of Game 6 to win the game 2-1, and the Stanley Cup.

After a spectacular start to the season, winning the first 10 games they played, the Chicago Blackhawks defeated the Boston Bruins in six games to win the Stanley Cup for the second time in four years, giving fans a foretaste of a possible dynasty in the mold of the Edmonton Oilers, New York Islanders, and the venerated Montreal Canadiens. Fans of all stripes were pleased to see an Original Six final.

CUP SPOTTING

Following championships by the Anaheim Ducks and Los Angeles Kings, the Cup has become a celebrity in Hollywood, appearing on tv late night talk shows and primetime dramas — even on soap operas.

HOLLYWOOD HEROES

The Cup has been seen taking a ride on the roller coaster at Universal Studios, accompanied by Luc Robitaille, who photographed the Cup in front of the Hollywood sign in Hollywood Hills. The Cup joined the 2008 Rose Bowl Parade, riding on the float for the City of Anaheim. It has been seen on talk shows and news shows, including *The Late Show with David Letterman, Meet the Press with Tim Russert, Late Night with Conan O'Brien* and *The Tonight Show with Jay Leno.*

PRESIDENTIAL CUP

The Stanley Cup has also been seen hanging out at the White House under the administration of seven presidents including: Ronald Reagan, George H. W. Bush, Bill Clinton, George W. Bush and Barack Obama. It is customary for the President to invite the NHL champion if the team is from an American city.

DROPPED AGAIN

The Cup has also appeared in soap operas (*Guiding Light*) and prime-time dramas, including *30 Rock, Chicago Fire, Heroes* and, most notably, *Boston Legal,* produced after the Boston Bruins refreshed enthusiasm for hockey in Beantown by winning the Stanley Cup in 2010-11. The story goes like this. Denny Crane (a.k.a. Canadian actor William Shatner) manages to get his hands on the Cup for a day, just like the Boston players, and takes the silver bowl to work. In the privacy of his law office, he engraves his name on the Cup. During the final act, Crane sits out on his penthouse patio with Alan Shore to drink their ritual shot of scotch — out of the Stanley Cup. As Crane stretches out his legs, he kicks the Cup over the railing. The Cup can't get no respect off the ice.

↑ Comedian Martin Short shares a moment with the Los Angeles Kings and the Stanley Cup prior to appearing on the *Jimmy Kimmel Live Show.*

VISITATIONS

Since 1994, the NHL and Hockey Hall of Fame have let the Cup-winning players take the icon of professional hockey home for a day or so in summer. Most visitations have gone without a hitch. Others have not. In fact, so many have gone awry that the Hockey Hall of Fame typically sends along a "guardian" of the Cup for most visits.

GOOD OLD HOCKEY SONG

Southwestern Ontario, along the shores of Lake Erie, has been a hot spot for Cup visitations. Port Dover, in particular, has become a favorite destination. When Jassen Culimore won the Cup playing for the Tampa Bay Lightning in 2004, he was the fourth NHLer to bring the silver chalice home to this hockey-crazed town. Just up the road in Simcoe, the city celebrated hometown-boy Rob Blake, winner of the Cup with the Colorado Avalanche in 2001, with a parade. Twenty miles away, New York Rangers assistant coach Colin Campbell brought the Cup home to Tillsonburg, Ont. after the Rangers won in 1993-94. Stompin' Tom Connors had already put Tillsonburg on the map when he sang a tribute to this tobacco and hockey town in "The Hockey Song."

NEWFIE CUP LORE

The first Newfoundlander to win the Cup, Detroit Red Wing Daniel Cleary, carried the prize across land and sea, to his hometown of Harbour Grace, where a crowd of 27,000 assembled in this town of 3,000 people. Brad Richards from Murray Harbour, PEI took the Stanley Cup out to sea on a fishing boat after the Tampa Bay Lightning won it in '04. The Cup has been flown to Rankin Inlet to deliver an engagement ring for André Roy. The helicopter was flown by Guy Lafleur.

AIR MILES

The Stanley Cup may be the most visible trophy in professional sports, logging more than 400,000 miles in visits to players in their hometowns in Canada and abroad during the past decade. Hosted by Cup-winning players, it has traversed Europe, from Sweden (Peter Forsberg) to the Ukraine (Ruslan Fedotenko), from Finland (Teemu Selanne) to Slovenia (Anze Kopitar), and from Slovakia (Zdeno Chara) to Russia (Evgeni Malkin), the Czech Republic (Dominik Hasek) and beyond.

TO SERVE AND PROTECT

As an inspiration to troups at home and abroad, the Cup has visited wounded soldiers from the United States Marine Corp at Camp Lejeune, N.C., accompanied by Glen Wesley after his Carolina Hurricanes won the Cup in 2006. The next year, the Cup arrived at the Canadian Forces Base in Kandahar, Afghanistan, along with 17 former players. They challenged the soldiers to a ball hockey game, with the Stanley Cup and bragging rights as the prize.

KEEPERS OF THE CUP

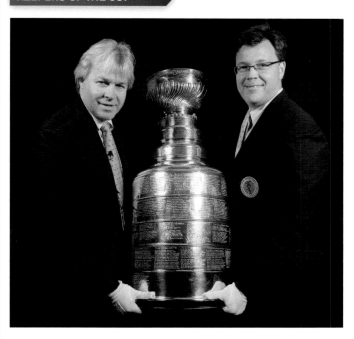

↑ Phil Pritchard (L) and Craig Campbell (R) of the Hockey Hall of Fame pose with the Stanley Cup during Game 6 of the 2012 final at the Staples Center on June 11, 2012 in Los Angeles, Calif.

→ **LIFE SAVER**
Captain Mike Richards of the Los Angeles Kings takes no risks of the Cup drowning.

← WAKE'S UP!
Chicago Blackhawk captain Jonathan Toews takes the Cup wake boarding in Kenora, Ont.

PHOTOGRAPHY AND EXHIBIT CREDITS

The following abbreviations are used in this list of credits.
- Hockey Hall of Fame: HHOF
- Getty Images: Getty
- Original Hockey Hall of Fame (Kingston): OHHOF
- Imperial Oil: IO

PAGE	PLAYER/ARTIFACT	AGENCY/COLLECTION	PHOTOGRAPHER/EXHIBIT DESIGNER
1	W. MITCHELL	GETTY	JEFF VINNICK
2	STANLEY CUP	HHOF	DAVE SANDFORD
3	MASKS	HHOF	DOUG MACLELLAN
4	S. CROSBY/A. OVECHKIN	GETTY	BRIAN BABINEAU
6	STITCH IN PADS	HHOF	MATTHEW MANOR
6	J. KAY	THN	THE HOCKEY NEWS
7	HANDS UP	HHOF	MECCA
8	MASKS	HHOF	DOUG MACLELLAN
9	STICKS	HHOF	MATTHEW MANOR
11	SHORE-BAILEY	HHOF	UNKNOWN
11	ACE BAILEY	HHOF	IO-TUROFSKY
12	H. MORENZ	GETTY	BRUCE BENNETT STUDIOS
12	A. JOLIAT	HHOF	UNKNOWN
13	A. JOLIAT	HHOF	UNKNOWN
14	BREAD LINE	OHHOF	UNKNOWN
16	TOUQUE AND PENNANT	HHOF	DOUG MACLELLAN
17	CONTRACT	HHOF	DAVE SANDFORD
17	JOE HALL	HHOF	HOCKEY HALL OF FAME
18	G. VEZINA	HHOF	DAVE SANDFORD
19	CLIPPING	HHOF	SEATTLE TIMES
20	BELL	HHOF	HOCKEY HALL OF FAME
20	SENATORS	GETTY	B. BENNETT
21	PROGRAM	HHOF	DAVE SANDFORD
21	CLANCY	HHOF	IO-TUROFSKY
22	HART TROPHY	HHOF	DAVE SANDFORD
22	CLEGHORN	HHOF	HOCKEY HALL OF FAME
22	A. JOLIAT	HHOF	UNKNOWN
22	B. BOUCHER	HTTP://WWW.STARSOFTHEDIAMOND.COM	UNKNOWN
23	BRICK		DOUG MACLELLAN
23	MONTREAL FORUM	MCCORD MUSEUM	UNKNOWN
24	JERSEY	HHOF	MATTHEW MANOR
24	FC HEADLEY	HHOF	DAVE SANDFORD
25	BOOK	HHOF	DAVE SANDFORD
25	N. STEWART	HHOF	JAMES RICE
26	PROGRAM	HHOF	DAVE SANDFORD
26	TICKET	HHOF	DAVE SANDFORD
27	PUCK	HHOF	DAVE SANDFORD
28	CONTRACT	HHOF	STEVE POIRIER
28	BABE SIEBERT	HHOF	JAMES RICE
29	JERSEY	HHOF	MATTHEW MANOR
29	TEAPOT	HHOF	DAVE SANDFORD
30	PUCK & PROGRAM	HHOF	DAVE SANDFORD
30	BUSHER JACKSON	HHOF	IO-TUROFSKY
31	HELMET	HHOF	CRAIG CAMPBELL
31	D. CLAPPER	GETTY	BRUCE BENNETT STUDIOS
31	C. CONACHER	HHOF	IO-TUROFSKY
32	RECORD BOOK	HHOF	DAVE SANDFORD
32	REG NOBLE	HHOF	JAMES RICE
33	J. ADAMS	THN	UNKNOWN
34	PAINTING	HHOF	DAVE SANDFORD
34	PLATE	HHOF	DAVE SANDFORD
34	C. GARDINER	HHOF	HOCKEY HALL OF FAME
35	RED HORNET	HHOF	HOCKEY HALL OF FAME
36	CARVING & CAP	HHOF	DAVE SANDFORD
36	L. AURIE	THN	UNKNOWN
36	S. APPS	HHOF	IO-TAROFSKY
37	CRUTCHES	GETTY	BRUCE BENNETT STUDIOS
37	HOWIE MORENZ	HHOF	JAMES RICE
38	SWEATER	HHOF	UNKNOWN
39	SKATES	HHOF	CRAIG CAMPBELL
40	MAGAZINE	HHOF	STEVE POIRIER
40	MILT SCHMIDT	HHOF	IO-TUROFSKY
41	PANTS	HHOF	GRAIG ABEL
41	BOBBY BAUER	HHOF	IO-TUROFSKY
41	STICK	HHOF	GRAIG ABEL
41	PANTS	HHOF	CRAIG CAMPBELL
42	SWEATER	HHOF	UNKNOWN
43	KID LINE (TOP)	HHOF	IO-TUROFSKY
43	KID LINE (BOTTOM)	HHOF	IO-TUROFSKY
45	TURK BRODA	HHOF	UNKNOWN
46	BOBBY HULL	HHOF	PORTNOY
47	PUNCH LINE	HHOF	IO-TUROFSKY
47	MAURICE RICHARD	HHOF	FRANK PRAZAK
48	PROGRAM	HHOF	HOCKEY HALL OF FAME
48	D. BENTLEY	HHOF	IO-TUROFSKY
49	PROGRAM	HHOF	HOCKEY HALL OF FAME
51	JACKET	HHOF	DOUG MACLELLAN
52	KRAUT LINE	HHOF	IO-TUROFSKY
52	M. BENTLEY	HHOF	IO-TUROFSKY
52	STICK	HHOF	DAVE SANDFORD
53	PADS	HHOF	MATTHEW MANOR
54	COVER LETTER	HHOF	UNKNOWN
55	BODY CHECK	GETTY	BERT HARDY/PICTURE POST
56	JACKET	HHOF	CRAIG CAMPBELL
56	D. RALEIGH	GETTY	UNKNOWN
56	ELMER LACH	HHOF	IO-TUROFSKY
57	H. CARNEGIE	THN	UNKNOWN
58	LIGHTER	HHOF	HOCKEY HALL OF FAME
59	CONACHER	HHOF	IO-TUROFSKY
59	THE HOCKEY NEWS	THN	THE HOCKEY NEWS
60	GLOVES	HHOF	MATTHEW MANOR
60	PUCK	HHOF	CRAIG CAMPBELL
60	SAWCHUK	HHOF	IO-TUROFSKY
61	PRODUCTION LINE	GETTY	HOWARD SOCHUREK/TIME LIFE
61	THE HOCKEY NEWS	THN	THE HOCKEY NEWS
62	PAINTING	HHOF	STEVE POIRIER
62	CARD	HHOF	DAVE SANDFORD
63	JACK GELINEAU	HHOF	IO-TUROFSKY
63	THE HOCKEY NEWS	THN	THE HOCKEY NEWS
64	PIN BALL	HHOF	CRAIG CAMPBELL
64	T. LINDSAY	GETTY	BRUCE BENNETT STUDIOS
64	G. HOWE	HHOF	FRANK PRAZAK
65	HOWE GLOVES	HHOF	MATTHEW MANOR
66	POUCH	HHOF	DAVE SANDFORD
66	L. KELLY	HHOF	FRANK PRAZAK
67	THE HOCKEY NEWS	THN	THE HOCKEY NEWS
67	F. SASKAMOOSE	HHOF	HOCKEY HALL OF FAME
68	RIOTS	THN	UNKNOWN
68	RIOT LETTER	HHOF	HOCKEY HALL OF FAME
69	FORUM	GETTY	WILLIAM TETLOW
69	THE HOCKEY NEWS	THN	THE HOCKEY NEWS
70	MINI VEZINA TROPHY	HHOF	DAVE SANDFORD
70	MASK	HHOF	MATTHEW MANOR
70	TOE BLAKE	OHHF	UNKNOWN
71	PADS	OHHF	STEVE POIRIER
71	ELBOW PADS	HHOF	HOCKEY HALL OF FAME
72	PUCK	HHOF	DAVE SANDFORD
72	ROCKET	GETTY	PICTORIAL PARADE
73	THE HOCKEY NEWS	THN	THE HOCKEY NEWS
73	W. O'REE	THN	UNKNOWN
74	J. BOWER	HHOF	UNKNOWN
74	CHEST PROTECTOR	HHOF	MATTHEW MANOR
75	THE HOCKEY NEWS	THN	THE HOCKEY NEWS
75	G. HOWE	THN	UNKNOWN
76	J. PLANTE	VIU.CA	DAILY NEWS
77	E. LITZENBERGER	HHOF	IO-TUROFSKY
77	THE HOCKEY NEWS	THN	THE HOCKEY NEWS
78	G. WORSLEY	HHOF	DAVE SANDFORD
78	P. PILOTE	HHOF	FRANK PRAZAK
79	D. SIMMONS	HHOF	IO-TUROFSKY
79	THE HOCKEY NEWS	THN	THE HOCKEY NEWS

↑ Hockey Hall of Fame Vault, where the Stanley Cup is on display.

↑ The Hockey Hall of Fame, located in Toronto, Ont.

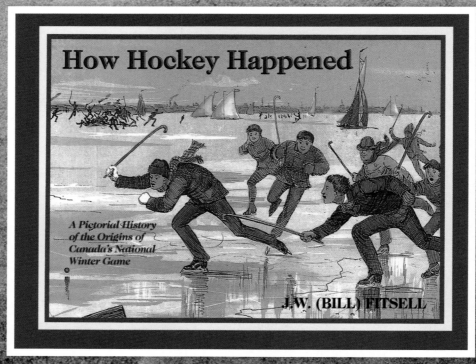

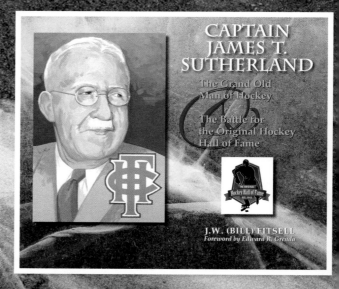

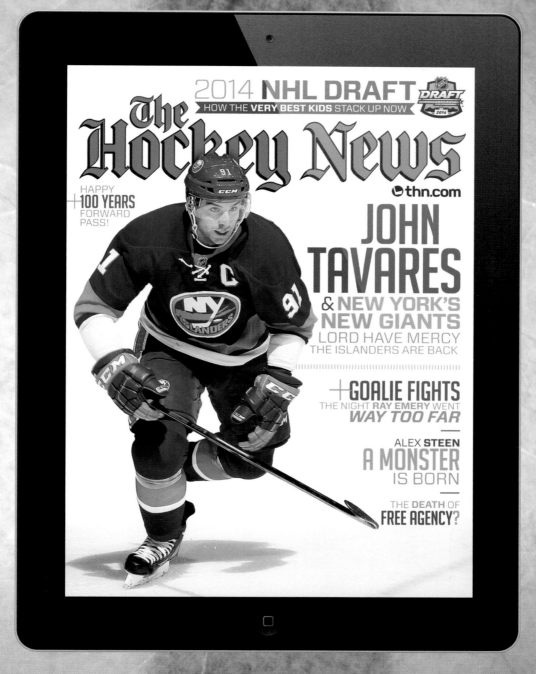

GO DEEP INTO THE CREASE
WITH THE IPAD EDITION OF THE HOCKEY NEWS